MAHATMA JOTIRAO PHOOLEY

AF652419

BY THE SAME AUTHOR

English Edition

- Dr. Babasaheb Ambedkar: Life and Mission (1954) (Fifth Edition)
- Lokamanya Tilak: Father of the Indian Freedom Struggle (1959) (Third Edition)
- Veer Savarkar (1966) (Fourth Edition)
- Mahatma Gandhi: Political Saint & Unarmed Prophet (1973) (Second Edition)
- Shahu Chhatrapati: A Royal Revolutionary (1976)
- Dr. Ambedkar: A Memorial Album (1982)

Marathi Edition

- Dr. Babasaheb Ambedkar (1966) (Fifth Edition)
- Mahatma Jotirao Phooley: Amachya Samaj Krantiche Janak (1968) (Fifth Edition)
- Swatantryaveer Savarkar (1972) (Third Edition)
- Rajarshi Shahu Chhatrapati (1979) (Third Edition)
- Krutagya Mi, Krutartha Mi (1987) (Second Edition)
- Lokamanya Tilak (2015)

Hindi Edition

- Dr. Babasaheb Ambedkar: Jeevan-Charit (1996) (Third Edition)

Other Publishers

- Tilak aani Rajarshi Shahu Maharaj: Ek Mulyamapan (1971)
- Teen Mahan Saraswat (1979)
- Vishvabhushan Dr. Babasaheb Ambedkar: Manas Ani Tatwa Vichar Yani Itihas Ghadvila (1980)
- Mahatma Phooley Samagra Wangmaya, edited in collaboration with Dr. S. G. Malshe (1969)
- Shetakaryacha Asud by Mahatma Jotirao Phooley (Marathi), edited in collaboration with Dr. S. G. Malshe
- Guruvarya Krushnrav Arjun Keluskar: Atma Charitra ani Charitra, edited by Dhananjay Keer

Mahatma Jotirao Phooley
(Birth: 1827; Death: November 28, 1890)

NIRMALA SADANAND SERIES

MAHATMA JOTIRAO PHOOLEY

Father of the Indian Social Revolution

DHANANJAY KEER

Popular Prakashan
www.popularprakashan.com

Published by
Asmita Mohite for
POPULAR PRAKASHAN PVT. LTD.
301, Mahalaxmi Chambers
22, Bhulabhai Desai Road
Mumbai - 400 026
info@popularprakashan.com

© Dr. Suneet Keer
First Published October 1964
Second Edition 1973
Third Edition 2013
Fourth Edition October 2021

(3082)
ISBN: 978-81-7154-066-2

WORLD RIGHTS RESERVED. The contents are original and copyrighted. No portion of this book shall be reproduced, stored in a retrieval system or transmitted by any means, electronic, mechanical, photocopying, recording or otherwise, without the written permission of the author and the publisher.

Disclaimer: The views and opinions expressed in this work are the author's own and the facts are as reported by him, and the publisher is in no way liable for the same.

PRINTED IN INDIA
by Rama Printer
4743/23, Ansari Road, Daryaganj
New Delhi - 110002

TO
MY WIFE
SUDHA

Publisher's Note

'NIRMALA SADANAND SERIES' is being introduced under Popular Prakashan imprint to commemorate Nirmala (1924-2011) and Sadanand Bhatkal (1922-2011), who along with G.R. Bhatkal (1896-1972) laid the foundation of Popular Book Depot (established in 1924) and its publishing division Popular Prakashan. Apart from their sterling contribution to the book world, particularly as editors of the *Journal Indian Publisher & Bookseller* (1950-1985), they played a leading role in community and cultural work. Before 1947, they had both participated in India's freedom movement. Sadanand was the president of the Federation of Publishers and Booksellers Associations in India and put Indian publishing on the world map. He edited a three-volume Marathi 'Encyclopaedia of Marathi Literature', the first of its kind.

Keer's biography of Mahatma Jotirao Phooley is being brought out with important additions. Jotirao Phooley was born in Maharashtra, a little after the fall of the Peshwas in Maharashtra. He died in 1890 a little after the formation of the Indian National Congress. He lived through the period of transition from feudal period to the modern era. His attitude towards the Rising in 1857 was unconventional. He pioneered social revolution through education for the under privileged. He started schools for the so-called lower castes and also for girls. His wife Savitribai was taught by him and she joined in these efforts. Their extraordinary work was a source of inspiration to those who followed them in this uphill task.

Dhananjay Keer (b.1913), the foremost biographer in India, had the privilege of personal dialogue with the protagonists when he wrote on Vinayak Damodar Savarkar (1883-1966) and Bhimrao Ambedkar (1888-1956). When Dr. Ambedkar expressed regret at his not being able to write a biography of Mahatma Phooley, whom he considered his Guru, Keer promised to complete this task. He had to look through archives, old newspapers and reports and Phooley's own writings in

Marathi to collect hitherto little known facts. Later he, along with Prof. S.G. Malashe, edited the collected works of Mahatma Jotirao Phooley.

Keer's biography *'Mahatma Phooley: Father of the Indian Social Revolution'* made Phooley's monumental work known outside Maharashtra. Scholars from different parts of India, not familiar with Marathi, began exploring this path-breaking chapter in India's history. Keer's biographies of Phooley, Shahu Maharaj and Dr. Ambedkar have played an important role in rewriting social history of India, just as his works on Bal Gangadhar Tilak, Mahatma Gandhi and Veer Savarkar have provided a different perspective on the political history of modem India. All these biographies are being reissued to mark the birth centenary of Dhananjay Keer.

In this new edition we have added a chronology of important events and bibliography that will enable the reader in persuing further this important topic.

Mumbai
20 February 2013

Preface to Second Edition

I AM extremely happy to present this new edition of Mahatma Jotirao Phooley's biography which was first published in October 1964 and had been out of print for the last four years. The biography was accorded a favourable reception by reviewers and scholars.

The sub-title of the original book was 'Father of our Social Revolution' but now it is changed to 'Father of the Indian Social Revolution.' I am glad to note that almost all the critics and scholars have accepted Mahatma Phooley as one of the greatest social reformers or 'Father of our Social Revolution.' Moreover it was held by many that Jotirao was the first leader of modern India to denounce Brahminism as the curse of India. He struggled hard to liberate the lower classes and Indian women from the thraldom of its scriptures, priestcraft and caste system and to reconstruct Indian society on the basis of equality, justice and reason. In fact, his was a demand for a new India.

A study of Jotirao's life and work is, therefore, very useful for the scholars and historians who are interested in the history of modern India. It will also stimulate social and political workers and leaders to renewed effort in eradicating inequality, injustice and poverty.

After the publication of the original book, some material shedding light on Jotirao's activities and speeches was found and is placed at proper places in historical sequence.

I express my sincere gratitude to all the readers and admirers for their appreciation and encouragement.

DHANANJAY KEER

Bombay
30 December 1973

Preface

CHIEF ARCHITECT of the Constitution of India, Dr. B. R. Ambedkar had planned a biography of Mahatma Jotirao Phooley. When he gave me interviews in 1954, he said on one occasion that he intended writing a life of Mahatma Phooley, whom he hailed as one of India's greatest social reformers and regarded as one of his masters along with the Buddha and Kabir. But as his health was deteriorating, he expressed his doubts as to the work being ever completed. I then felt inspired to tell him that if he was not able to fulfil the task, I would try to do so.

I am now really very happy that I have been able to fulfil the task and to present to a waiting public this biography of Jotirao Phooley, the first Indian to proclaim in modern India the dawn of a new age for the common man. the downtrodden, the underdog and the Indian woman.

Jotirao was the first Indian to start a school for the Untouchables and a girls' school in Maharashtra. He wanted to remove the ignorance and superstition of the Shudras, Atishudra's and Indian women and to break the shackles of their slavery. So he heroically threw open the gates of knowledge to the lower classes and to Indian women. It was his aim to reconstruct the social order on the basis of social equality, justice and reason.

Jotirao naturally had to face opposition and also indifference at the hands of the Maharashtrian writers and authors of his day who were mainly Brahmins. The prejudices of his adversaries who came from the Brahmin caste were so intense and the boycott of his name by them so complete that even those who carried on his battle for social justice, for educational opportunities and for removal of ignorance and superstition, could not come forward to work on a biography of Jotirao.

Of course, Pandharinath Patil attempted in his own way a life of Jotirao in Marathi, in 1927, and a host of small books followed. Yet no life of Jotirao has been written with the kind of effort, methods and research that go to make modern biography. I sincerely acknowledge my debt to Patil for whatever data his book supplied to me. I can however mention that during my talks with him and with some research scholars I got some clues and I searched for the material which no biographer of Jotirao before me had reached or verified. I thus dug out valuable material which had lain unexplored.

I am very sorry to mention here that an endorsement made in December 1927 by the then Records Officer of the Bombay Secretariat states that compilation No. 413 of 1852 containing the correspondence on the subject of the presentation of a pair of shawls to Jotirao Phooley has been destroyed.

I have done my utmost to vitalize the material I have put together, have added flesh and blood to it and understanding the motivations of Jotirao, breathed life into it. Most of the material is in Marathi and I have done a free rendering of it.

Jotirao's attack on Brahminism was unmistakable. The Hinduism of his day had decayed and deteriorated into Brahminism which, according to him, bred social inequality and resulted into privileges and power for and deification of the Brahmins as a class. He realized that the seeds of their power, supremacy and privileges lay in their scriptures and puranas; and these works and the caste system were created to exploit the lower classes.

It is not Jotirao alone who said that Brahmanical scriptures were written to exploit the lower classes. A few years after Jotirao's death, Swami Vivekanand, giving his verdict on them, expressed. the same view. The Swami said that whenever the Brahmins wrote anything they would deny all rights to others and he added that Vyasa tried to put meanings upon the Vedas to cheat the poor Shudras.[1]

So Jotirao attacked the Brahmanical scriptures and puranas, revolted against priestcraft and the caste sysem and set on foot a social movement for the liberation of the Shudras, Atishudras (Untouchables) and women. He was above caste. He agitated for the welfare of the Indian peasants and labour and it should be noted that the Indian Labour Movement is an offshoot of his social movement. His sympathies were broader and were not confined to the labour classes. He started girls'

1. The complete works of Swami Vivekananda, Mayvati Memorial Edition, Vol IV (1948), p. 305.

schools for the benefit of all classes, championed the cause of widow remarriage, conducted an orphanage and praised the work of those Brahmins who stood for social justice and reason.

In short, Jotirao stood for the dignity of man, religious toleration and human rights. He regarded all Indians as equal and free and declared that one law should be applicable to man and woman.

Since Pandit Jawaharlal Nehru's *Discovery Of India*, attempts have been made by scholars to re-discover India, her past, her ideals and her soul. So in that spirit of inquiry it would be proper to study Mahatma Phooley, the prophet of the common man, whom Mahatma Gandhi called a real Mahatma and whom Veer Savarkar described as a social revolutionary.

If the makers and rulers of the present-day India do not study the life of Mahatma Phooley, they will not be able to make the progress they desire; for, unless social equality is enthroned it is well-nigh impossible for them to establish economic equality. The politicians who did not understand the life of Jotirao and his movement have miserably failed in Maharashtra. Had they paid heed to the social philosophy of Lokahitavadi Deshmukh, M. G. Ranade and Veer Savarkar, they would have understood the work and mission of Jotirao.

The Indian Socialist leaders who mostly come from privileged castes place an emphasis on political and economic equality either sidetracking or without understanding the social revolution. Once a year the Socialists and the upholders of the socialistic pattern of society denounce casteism, but in private and during elections most of them selfishly cling to it.

The President of the Indian Republic once publicly bathed the feet of Brahmin pandits on the banks of the Ganga, not because these men were the symbols of erudition, virtues and humanity and were selected for honour irrespective of caste and creed, but because they belonged to the Brahmin caste. This is nothing but the sanctification of the Brahmin caste when the Republic aims at abolishing casteism. Who would say that the puranic story cited by Jotirao in which Bhrugu, a Brahmin sage, gives a kick on the chest of the god Vishnu, is not significant?

Jotirao attacked mercilessly Brahminism which is the keystone of casteism. Casteism is more dangerous than communalism, because the storm centres of the latter can be easily watched and its mischief ruthlessly rooted out, but the former creeps slyly with leaders, ministers, administrators and businessmen and where it finds it honourable to do so, it goes under the cloak of merit. Caste is decaying; but casteism may live under the cloak of 'merit'. When the question of admission of students into Engineering, Medical and Technical Institutions arises, merit shrewdly demands that a Brahmin boy whose ancestors have been trained in intellectual pursuits be compared with a boy belonging to a class kept away from education for scores of generations. Merit should certainly prevail in the Army, Navy and Air Forces. But if in other fields the lower classes are not given preferential treatment, they will not rise in the scale of life, and the strength and solidarity of the nation will suffer.

Fuss should not be made about Jotirao's attack on the Congress of his day. The earlier leaders of the Indian National Congress openly said that they wished to make British rule permanent in India. On the contrary, Jotirao, who had opposed the Poona Municipality spending money on the decoration of the city and on the Address to be given to a British Governor-General on the occasion of his visit, believed that British rule would some day end. He had nothing to do with the Congress leaders of his day who did not care to associate themselves with the peasants, labour and Untouchables. A patriot of humanity, he was not prepared to regard those leaders as patriots who did not respect human dignity and the human rights of their countrymen, So high was the level of his patriotism.

Jotirao's life is thus an inspiration to those who really aim at achieving emotional integration and at giving a human, social and economic content to the Swaraj of India.

DHANANJAY KEER

September 1964
Bombay

Acknowledgements

Three friends have gone through the manuscript and it has benefited from their suggestions. They are Prof. Nissim Ezekiel, A. S. Bhide (Guruji) and Vishwasrao Patil. Bhide Guruji also performed the hard task of reading the proofs. I owe these friends a deep debt of gratitude.

In the course of my research I received some material or some help to secure it, from the Hon'ble Mr. Balasaheb Desai, Home Minister of Maharashtra State, Pandharinath Patil, Acharya P. K. Atre, Bhai Madhavrao Bagal, Prabodhankar K. S. Thakare, Vithalrao Ghate, Prof. A. K. Priolkar, G. D. Khanolkar, Prof. G. B. Sardar, H. M. Joshi, P. B. Kulkarni, Dr. M. P. Mangudkar, N. D. Patil, Principal Airan of the Wilson College, Bombay, The Rev. J. Reid Graham, Dr. M. S. Rege, P. V. Navale, Vasantrao Chitre, Miss Vatsala Pinge and R. N. Chavan. I am indebted to Dr. S. G. Malshe for transcribing the microfilm of Jotirao's *Cultivator's Whipcord* and to Dr. R. D. Nayak for copying the old photographs.

I sincerely thank the librarians and the members of the staff of Mumbai Marathi Grantha Sangrahalaya, Marathi Grantha Sangrahalaya, Thana, the Prarthana Samaj, Bombay, National Library, Calcutta, Maharashtra Granthalaya, Poona, Kesari Office Library, Bombay University Library, Cama Library, The Asiatic Society of Bombay and above all the office of the Director ot Archives and Historical Monuments, Government of Maharashtra.

I acknowledge my greatest debt to those authors and publishers from whose journals and publications I have derived help.

My sincere thanks go to my brother Vinayak Keer who, dutifully and laboriously, did the work of typing long and illegible manuscripts of all the biographies written by me.

I express my deep debt of gratitude to Mr. Ramdas Bhatkal who readily and generously responded to the idea of this biography and brought out the publication swiftly.

DHANANJAY KEER

15 September 1964

77, Bhageshwar Bhuvan,
Lady Hardinge Road,
Bombay 400 016.

Contents

Jotirao in his youth

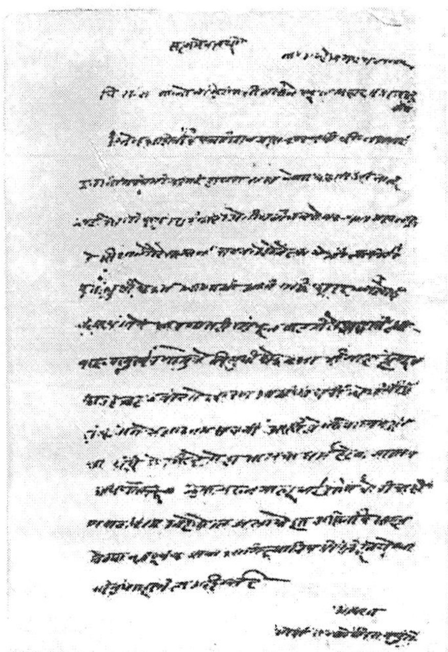

Jotirao's handwritten letter

Pune residence of Mahatma Phooley
(a national monument now)

The well near Mahatma Phooley's home that he made accessible to the untouchables

Mahatma Jotirao Phooley with his son Yashwant

Hari Ravaji Chiplunkar (Shinde)
Jotirao's assistant and friend

Bhau Kondaji Patil Dumbre, Otu
Satya Shodhak Samaj leader

Ramchandrapant Dhamnaskar
Disciple, later became Diwan of Baroda

Ramaiya Venkaiya Aiyyaru
One of the pillars of the Satya Shodhak Movement

Narayanrao Lokhande
Right hand of Jotirao and founder of Bhartiya Kamgar movement

Dr. Santuji Lad
Trustworthy leader of Satya Shodhak Samaj leader

Krishnarao Bhalerao
Orator, author, upholder of the lower caste rights

Dr. Vishram Ramji Gholay
Renowned physician and Satyashodhak Movement's well-wisher

Tukaram Tatya Padwal
Author of 'Jaatibhed Viveksara' and supporter of social equality

Maharaja Sayajirao Gaikwad
People's raja

Wasudeo Babaji Nowrange
'Practice as you preach'

'Mama' Parmanand
Maharashtra politics, 'sage'

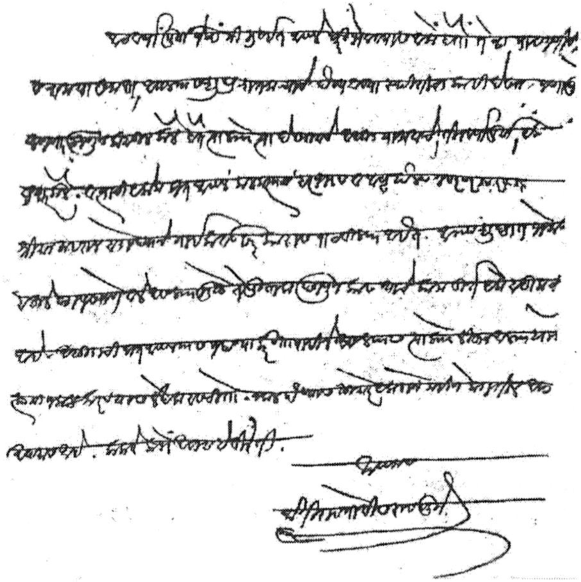

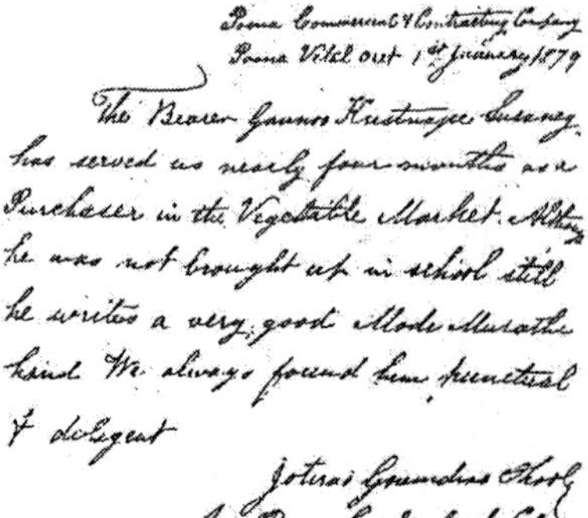

Poona Commercial & Contracting Company
Poona Vithal out 1st January 1879

The Bearer Ganoo Rustmajee Susaney has served us nearly four months as a Purchaser in the Vegetable Market. Although he was not brought up in school still he writes a very good Mode Marathi hand. We always found him punctual & diligent

Jotirai Govindrao Phooly
for Poona Coml & Contg Co.

Mahatma Phooley's hand-written documents
in Modi, Marathi and English

CHAPTER I

Birth and Background

JOTIRAO PHOOLEY'S great grandfather was a chaugula, an inferior village servant, at Katgun, which is twenty-five miles from Satara. Various kinds of duties were assigned to such inferior servants. They served the village officers. The chaugulas carried their records, assisted them in recovering land revenue, and accompanied them at the time of crop inspection.

The family of this great grandfather of Jotirao belonged to the Kshatriya Mali caste and subsisted on the meagre produce its petty farm yielded. His family name was Gorhe. One day he had a clash with the Brahmin Kulkarni who used to be one of the two main village officers in the village. Truth, justice and liberty got drowned when a Kulkarni came to the surface with his guiles and wiles. The village den thrilled and throbbed with his commanding voice. The Brahmin Kulkarni harassed the chaugula and made it impossible for him to live in the village peacefully. Driven to despair, the chaugula one night slew him and fled for his life.

Then the chaugula shifted his family to Khanwadi, a village in the Purandar Taluka of Poona District. There, a son was born to him. He was named Shetiba. This only son of the chaugula was a simpleton, but a darling of his father who had gradually become prosperous. Having passed his day in easy circumstances, Shetiba acquired the habits of a spendthrift. After some time, he was, as are all reckless men who run through their fortunes, reduced to poverty and was obliged to find some means of livelihood. He, therefore, removed his family to Poona.

Shetiba had three sons, Ranoji, Krishna and Govind. They were forced by their father's straitened circumstances to earn their daily bread from early boyhood. At first they tended goats; they got each a pie a day for their work. As these boys grew up, they were engaged in his trade by their kind master who was a florist. He taught them this trade and the art. The boys did their work conscientiously and became proficient in it.

The boys made a name for themselves in their trade so much so that they attracted the attention of the Peshwa, and he utilized their services in his private capacity. They made flower mattresses, pillows and some garments for the use of the Peshwa. He conferred on these brothers thirty-five acres of land in appreciation of their useful, sweet and scented services. They were now known as florists. So the family assumed the name Phooley, and the original surname Gorhe gave place to the new one.

The Phooley family belonged to the agriculturist class of the lower strata of Hindu society: They reared flower and fruit trees, grew vegetables and dealt in flowers. They were found in the Deccan. The community had not made any history; nor was it considered a caste of importance.

It had, however, to its credit the name of a great saint who flourished about the year 1250 in Maharashtra. His name was Savata Mali. He was a contemporary of Namdeo who stands very high in the galaxy of the great saint-poets of Maharashtra. Savata Mali resided at a village near Pandharpur which is aptly called the southern Kashi. He was a great devotee of the god Vithoba. While he worked in his fields growing vegetables, sugarcane and onions, he sang the glory of Vithoba, and it was believed that he could talk and walk with this god.

Shetiba Phooley had not a little satisfaction when he saw that his sons had now settled in their trade. After some days, he died peacefully, leaving his three sons Ranoji, Krishnaji and Govindrao to look after .his trade. The first son Ranoji was much older than his brothers and seems to have been a very shrewd and selfish man. He managed somehow to get his name recorded as the sole owner of the *inam* land which the Peshwa had so benevolently made over to the brothers as a gift for their meritorious services.

After Shetiba's death the three brothers lived with one Zagade who was the maternal uncle of their father. Ranoji wanted Zagade to drive his two brothers out of his grandfather's house. He had an eye on Zagade's landed property, and it was through his machinations that the two boys were compelled to leave Zagade's house. They, then, clung together, worked assiduously, and earned their living.

II

In the meanwhile the worthless profligate Peshwa Bajirao II lost his gadi. With this great change, which upset the fates of thousands of families dependent upon Peshwa rule in the Deccan, Phooley family also had to pass through a crisis. Being left in the lurch by their elder brother Ranoji, Krishnaji and Govind had to struggle. Naturally Govind worked hard on the farm in neighbouring village, set up a greengrocery at Poona to the produce of that soil, and improved his position. Sure of his stability now, he continued his flower shop in Poona and was content to lead a peaceful life. He married a Mali girl named Chimnabai, who was a daughter of one Zagade Patil of Kavadi village near Poona.

Chimnabai gave birth to two sons. The elder was Rajaram. younger was Joti, who was born in 1827. He was named Joti, which means a flame.

Joti's father Govindrao had seen the declining glory of Maratha rule. Poona had lost its prestige and power, and the were reduced to utter degradation. The Maratha Empire long worn out by the disease of deep-rooted caste jealousies and dissensions, and overpowered by the superiority of power, ultimately collapsed under the pressure of wily diplomacy and the conquering spirit of the empire-builders of England.

Bajirao II, chief of the Brahmin raj, was a worthless profligate. He was surrounded by weak female characters who were representatives of a decrepit society that bred spies, produced greed, depraved wine-bibbers. That society also conducted gambling houses, fostered corruption and connived at debachery The scene of these vices was so obnoxious that Robertson, the British Collector of Poona, was terribly shocked to see that the people had lost all notions of morality. Both Bajirao II in the south and Daulatrao Shinde in the north became traitors to the nation and lost the independence of the Marathas[2].

Almost all the Maratha leaders were rotten to the core and ignorant of the stream of world progress and world thought. The principle of heredity in military, diplomatic and governmental

1. Chokshi, R. D., *The Last Phase*, pp. 220-21.
2. Sardesai, G. S. *New History of the Marathas*, pp. 613-22.

services even at village level and in occupation, which regulated the life of both the state and the individual in society, led to degradation and degeneration. Elevation of the Brahmins, and that too mainly of the Chitpavan Brahmins, to eminent positions, political and social, and elimination of the men of other communities, however able and strong, from these offices, was the rule of the day.

The Brahmins adulated Bajirao II as an incarnation of Krishna or Shiva. During Peshwa rule the Brahmins came to regard themselves as the governing class with special privileges and exemptions which did not exist under the system founded by Shivaji.[3] The Brahmins under the last Peshwa had their lands assessed at half or lower rates than were levied on the lands of other classes. Brahmin culprits were exempted from the extreme penalty of the law. All advantages, monopolies and charities were reserved for and bestowed on Brahmins. Bajirao II lavishly fed about forty thousand pauperised and worthless Brahmins who flattered him as their Lord.

In times of famine the Government of Bajirao II helped only the Brahmins.[4] The noise created by the serving of meals to countless Brahmin beggars and the chant of their mantras filled the Poona skies. A Brahmin who devoured, so went a popular aphorism in those days, four seers of rice, milk and sugar at a sitting would have the honour of a palanquin!

The farmers and the toiling masses on the farms were inhumanly harassed by the officers of the Peshwa and by his adopted brother Amritrao. If the farmers failed to pay him the desired amount even during a severe draught or famine, he poured[5] over their children boiling oil from the frying-pan. Heavy stones were mercilessly placed on their backs. Flogging was performed on their stooping backs, and their heads were bent over suffocating smoke. Gunpowder was blown on their navels and ears.

The rulers thought that the lower classes of the society were

3. *The Miscellaneous Writings of the Late Hon'ble Mr. Justice Ranade*, pp. 350-52.
4. Acworth, H. R. and Shaligram, T. S., *Powadas or Historic Ballads of the Marathas*, p. 186.
5. *Lokahitavadinchi Shatapatre* (Marathi), edited by Tikekar, S. R., pp. 9-10.

born to slave for them, for their community and their families, to produce corn, to weave cloth and to labour in the hot sun. The money-lenders were chiefly Brahmins, and the Government was in their keeping; so they thrashed their tenants and debtors as much as they desired.

These money-lenders got under regular documents[6] daughters and sons of farmers to slave for them till the payment of the endless interest on ornament or land pawned to them, was made. This slavery, enforced by an eternal interest, haunted their lives for generations. They seized the goods of the peasants, sold their cattle, and harassed their children and women. For failure to pay a cess of Rs. 7 their farms were seized; cattle were sold. They were deprived of their well and fields. Driven to desperation, several of them pined away or perished in utter penury.

III

At the hands of the ruling hierarchy women fared no better. Women at Wai committed suicide on the eve of an impending visit of Bajirao, the profligate. The atmosphere of his capital was as immoral as that of any capital of a decaying empire of the past. Evil blossomed in it like wild plants in a field. As a result, men of prowess, integrity and reputation abandoned Poona, leaving the debased diplomats and shameless sirdars to earn basely Bajirao's favour and to get their position elevated in a crumbling empire. In those days Poona had also been infested with the Shakta cult whose members were naked worshippers of God. It was period of moral stagnation, cultural demoralization, and religious petrification; a period of decline and decay caused by intellectual and physical fatigue. There was no new blood in politics, nor was there any influx of new ideas. And when the Maratha Empire collapsed in 1818, not a tear was shed, the virtuous and valiant passing their days help lessly in the country. Women rejoiced and were quoted as saying: "We are happy that there is now no more the rule of Bajirao II. The scoundrel has met the fate he deserved."[7]

God's mills grind to powder those who grind the poor. The reign of terror and torture had ended. Life and property had

6. Joshi, N. V., *Poona, Ancient and Modern*, pp. 10-11.
7. *Lokahitavadinchi Shatapatre*, edited by Tikekar, S. R., p. 10.

no security in it. Repeated raids and internal revolts had caused unending suffering to the people.

The farmers heaved a sigh of relief. They were glad that they could reap the fruits of their labour in peace, the turmoil of generations having ceased. Their feeling of patriotism was stiffled by the doings of the ruling class and by the wine-bibbers who styled themselves the terrestrial gods and suffered terribly from pollution phobia. Only the lackeys of the ruling class must have been sorry for the downfall of the Peshwa. The Brahmins felt the change even more deeply than the chieftains. Their lofty claims were ignored. They had to obey the law like ordinary men; and if a Brahmin committed murder he was now to be put to death. Such a thing had been, for many generations, unheard of in Maharashtra.

The Maratha Empire, founded by Shivaji and transformed into Brahmin raj by the last Peshwas, collapsed after the death of Shahu under the Brahmin leadership. The Brahmins, who were not noted so much as founders of any empire, had here in Maharashtra their turn for about a century to govern an empire founded by Shivaji and expanded and consolidated by Bajirao I. The conquering spirit of the Marathas under the leadership of the first four Brahmin Peshwas liberated the Hindus, destroyed the Mogul Empire and valiantly expanded the empire in forty years; but under the decrepit and depraved leadership of the last Peshwas in no less than another forty years it collapsed.

The Village Panchayats, fondly described as village republics, did not realise what had happened. They remained unconcerned, for it was their age-long belief that he who ruled over them must be an incarnation of the god Vishnu! The shrewd British rulers were cautious enough not to disturb their normal life and to interfere in the affairs of the village dens.

Historians of repute offer in their own way various interpretations of the downfall of the Maratha Empire. A majority of them have attributed the failure to the internal strifes for which the leadership of the last Peshwas was mainly responsible. The Brahmins ruined the country: this was the verdict passed by the Lokahitavadi. Poona, the capital of the Maratha Empire, fell and lost its lustre; it fretted and chafed under the yoke of an impure foreign empire. Its palatial but unimposing buildings fell in ruin; its military gentry lay gasping; its glory faded. On the fall of Poona, India became for the first time a part of an empire ruled from without for the benefit of foreigners.

In those days Poona constituted the universe of the learned Brahmins. It was their honest belief that the god Indra asked the clouds, which were believed to be his elephants, to shower rain on the earth, and rain fell. Poona had become a den of ignorance and immorality, vice and disease. It had no proper roads; camel, horse, and palanquin were the modes of transport. Custom compelled women to walk barefoot; rich women wore shoes.

CHAPTER II

Dawn of a New Era

When Joti was about a year old his mother Chimnabai died. She was a pious and devout lady. Govindrao was greatly grieved at the loss of his wife. Instead of marrying a second time, he engaged a wet-nurse to look after the infant boy. The nurse turned to be a happy choice and a god-send. She did her duty sincerely by Joti and caused no worry to Govindrao who tended his garden and conducted his flower shop. A respectable man of his caste, he was by nature religious, quiet and straightforward and observed traditional norms and ways of life. When Joti became five years old, Govindrao was happy to see that the motherless boy was quite strong, healthy and handsome. Although men of his generation had no education, as it was not a thing to be aspired to by men of castes other than the Brahmin, he gave his thought to this question and decided to put his loving son to school.

Education in India, in the modern sense of the word, did not exist before the birth of Joti. Schools were run by private individuals at centres containing a considerable high caste population where Pundits gave instruction in Sanskrit, Grammar, Logic, Philosophy and Law. The lower classes were not supposed to receive education; nor did they feel the necessity of it either. Village schools were scattered over the country where rudimentary education was given to the children of traders and rich cultivators. Qualification for business was the sole end in view. Hardly anyone but a Brahmin learned to read the Nagari script. Others wrote and read the *Modi*. Arithmetic was taught sometimes fairly well. History or Geography was not thought of. All books were in manuscript. They generally contained legends of gods or goddesses.

Each pupil formed a class by himself. In preparing their lessons, all shouted simultaneously at the top of their voices. The senior pupils looked after the beginners. Finally the wretched school master, in nearly every case self-appointed, made desperate efforts to find a more lucrative and honourable occupation. Recruits for the profession came from disabled members of society. The classes met often at the house of the teacher, or at a temple. Rich landlords often employed teachers to teach their children, and poor children of the neighbourhood joined them.

The village schools were started in 1836 as an experimental measure to impart knowledge of the three R's at a minimum cost to Government. Later, in 1862, the scheme was given up. As late as 1953 it was said that the reports on the work of these schools could be of immense use to the present educational administrators in successfully tackling the problem of rural education. This is considered a unique experiment in the history of education in India.[1]

Before the advent of British rule in India, education was not one of the responsibilities of the State. In Maharashtra, where the power of both the priest and the prince vested in Brahmins, they alone were entitled to recite and read the holy books. And those of the lower castes who recited the holy scriptures were severely dealt with.

But with the new Lords came the new Laws! It was the Charter Act of 1813 that laid down that "out of the surplus revenues of India a sum of not less than one lakh of rupees in each year shall be set apart and applied to the revival and improvement of literature and the encouragement of the learned natives of India, and for the introduction and promotion of a knowledge of sciences among the inhabitants of the British territories in India". Thus under the Act of 1813 education was set free in India! A new dawn broke, bringing education for a new society and for a changing civilization. The grant was at first used for encouragement of oriental methods of instruction by paying stipends to students although grant-in-aid to schools in England also was not paid until 1833.[2]

The history of the nineteenth century is the history of westernization of the world. The presence of the British in India brought about profound changes in the social and

1. Parulekar, R. V., *Selections from the Records of the Government of Bombay—Education*—Part I, Preface.
2. Hampton, H. V., *Biographical Studies in Modern Indian Eduacation*, p. 25.

administrative conditions of the country, and these in their turn reacted on the educational policy of Government. The impulse towards reform came from two sources: the need for public servants with a knowledge of English and the influence in favour of both English and vernacular education which was exercised by the missionaries in the early years of the nineteenth century. In 1824 the missionaries had started Marathi schools in Poona.

There was some controversy between those who favoured Western education through the medium of the English language and those who supported oriental learning through the medium of the vernaculars. However, when Thomas Babington Macaulay, who was the first Legal Member of the Governor-General's Council and Chairman of the Committee of Public Instruction, wrote on February 2, 1835, his famous Minute in favour of Western education, the Government of Lord William Bentick decided on March 7, 1835, that the great object of the British Government ought to be the promotion of European literature and science among the natives of India.

During this period of transition, when the doors of education were ajar for low-caste students, some wise and far-seeing men sent their children to school. Govindrao, too, thought it wise to send his son to school, and at the age of seven Joti began his rudimentary studies at a Marathi school. In those days indigenous schools were sometimes found at great distance from one another. They were conducted by teachers who were called Pantojis. In Konkan they were called Shenavis,[3] since the teachers belonged to the Shenavi caste.

The Government established in 1821 a Hindu college at Poona known as Sanskrit College, but it was open only to Brahmin students. The Bombay Native Education Society, which was the first organized attempt in India to spread education, started schools in 1820, and by 1833 there were two or three American schools at Poona. As early as 1825, the Government of Bombay had begun to establish primary schools at its own expense in district towns and had placed them under the control of the Collectors. In order to co-ordinate the activities of these two

3. Priolkar, A. K., *Dadoba Pandurang* (Marathi), p.17.

bodies, Government later formed a Board of Education in 1840.

Leather-binding of the books, some said, caused pollution. Ink was a matter of pollution; learning by heart the word owl in a house was an ill-omen. Children had to keep their satchel in a nook and had to take a bath on their return home to wipe out the pollution contacted outside by pronouncing ominous words like owl, handling defiling articles such as books, and by touching pupils of other castes. Learning the English language, according to the orthodox, not only caused pollution but also deprived the learner of his Brahminhood. Joti's Brahmin contemporary Gopalrao Hari Deshmukh had to keep his books in the corner of a well just to avoid polluting things in his house!

In 1830 an attempt was made to educate girls. Some energetic and bold men had undertaken this risk in consultation with the British officers at Poona and started a school at the old residence of the Peshwa, but their attempt came to naught. For some time children studied clandestinely there and dispersed secretly.

There were other notions that hampered the growth of education. It was the sincere belief of the Brahmins that Shudras and Atishudras had no right to education, only Brahmins had it. Sanskrit scriptures contained all the knowledge then existing in the world. Rich men had only to roll in ease at home. There was no need for them to exert themselves in any way or to study.

Education was not a subject that had attracted so far the attention and respect of the upper classes who had not come out of the rut of their old social conditions. Inured to social and religious injunctions, some thought it below their dignity to receive education, much less to attend a school conducted by missionaries.

II

It redounds to his credit that in these circumstances Govindrao Phooley should have thought it wise to have his son educated. The young, intelligent and ardent student made remarkable progress in his studies. While everything was going well with the boy and his studies, something happened, and somebody poisoned his father's ears against the idea of education. His mind was then filled with doubts as to its utility for his son.

It is not impossible, seeing the hostility and opposition of the Brahmins to the education of the lower classes, as late as the days of Hunter Commission, that a Brahmin who was working as a clerk at Govindrao's shop should mislead him into withdrawing his son from the school. The boy had almost completed his Marathi course and was able to read, write and do mental arithmetic. "What earthly use is the education to your son? Education will make him unfit for the work in the field. Besides present education makes one an irreligious man and he becomes a rebel."

Such must have been the arguments employed and advice tendered by the Brahmin clerk to his master Govindrao Phooley. Even in the early decades of this century cunning Brahmin teachers slyly discouraged the non-Brahmin boys in devious ways. The higher classes thought that the lower classes, if educated, would be partners in employment, and a fairly large portion of the jobs would go to them. Once it so happened that boys from lower classes were summarily dismissed from the school of the Bombay Native Education Society at the instance of Dhakji Dadaji Prabhu, an orthodox leader in Bombay, who was a notable member of the Bombay Native Education Society.[4]

Govindrao withdrew Joti from the school. Having bid farewell to school, Joti took up axe, spade and pickaxe and began rearing the garden of his father and cultivating the fields. He was preparing himself for his future role of gardener by weeding out the plants, watering the flower-beds in the early hours of the morning and plucking the best flowers. Trimming the hedge and mowing grass and hoeing the soil, he must have enjoyed heartily. His father felt much relief to see that the able-bodied boy was sincere and enthusiastic and worked untiringly.

Govindrao now thought of settling Joti's marriage in accordance with the prevailing customs. So his marriage was celebrated when he was about thirteen. The girl-wife was about eight years old and came of a family called Zagade Patil from the village Kavadi near Poona. Joti did not have to bother about the maintenance of his girl-wife. The husband and the girl-wife did not know what marriage was meant for. So young were the children when they married in those days that one of Joti's would-be colleagues, Keshav Bhawalkar, asked his mother in his boyhood, when he was told that his marriage ceremony

4. Priolkar, Prof. A. K., *Dadoba Pandurang*, pp. 45-46.

was to be celebrated, whether she would take him to it.[5]

Nature, however, repaid Joti's devout services with a great reward. It strengthened his love for an industrious life. Though there was a break in his schooling, he had not given up his love of books. After his day's work in field and garden, he used to read by the light of the metal-lamp at night. Such an intelligent, active and energetic boy naturally attracted the attention of some well-intentioned neighbours and sympathetic acquaintances.

Among such neighbours were two learned men. One was Gaffvhar Baig Munshi, who was a teacher of Urdu and Persian. The other was Legit. He was either an official or a missionary. Both were men of letters. They both impressed upon Govindrao Phooley the necessity of education for his son and urged him to give him a chance for the betterment of his mind and future. Govindrao was thoroughly convinced of the mishandling of the education of his son and agreed to send him back to school. He must have been sorry that he had wasted over three precious years of the best part of his son's life.

Govindrao, therefore, again sent Joti in 1841 to a mission school. He was now about fourteen. A boy with resolute will and eager to grasp the lessons, he showed a keen interest in his studies. He scored high marks in his examinations and won the approbation of his teachers and classmates. During his school days he formed a lasting friendship with Sadashiv Ballal Govande. This Brahmin friend of Joti was born in 1824 at Poona. He came of a poor Brahmin family. By dint of unflagging industry and iron will, he was making progress in his life. He was a classmate of Joti at the school kept by the Scottish Mission and also at the Government school at Budhwar Wada, Poona. This school was handed over to Government by Stevenson, who had established it in September 1832, in Poona.

At home Joti's playmates were Muslim boys from the neighbouring houses. Through his association with them, he came to know about the craftiness practised in the name of Hinduism; and the false beliefs connected with it, such as caste prejudices began to trouble his mind. He obtained much of his knowledge at the Scottish Mission, which taught him the duties and rights of Man.

5. Bhawalkar, K. S., *Autobiography* (Marathi), p. 47.

Joti and Govande were full of energy, spirit and ambition. They read the lives of Shivaji and George Washington. Their heroism, love of country and noble ambition inspired them to attempt similar deeds for the emancipation of their motherland.

The two boys decided to devote their lives to uplifting their ignorant countrymen and arousing them from lethargy and the thraldom of outdated beliefs. There was another great book that made its impact on these two boys. It was Thomas Paine's *Rights of Man*. So, influenced deeply by the ideals of service, and having drunk freely at the fountain of the *Rights of Man*, they decided to build up their bodies and to prepare themselves for their future work. They took various manly exercises and also played the sword and *dandpatta** under one Lahuji Buva Mang, an Untouchable, who was an expert at these military exercises. Joti had attained such a mastery over this art that when he performed crowds gathered to witness his performance, and his name spread in every part of the city as a youth of first-rate gymnastic gifts. Joti was the personification of a healthy mind in a sound, muscular body; a quite impressive figure.

It seems this Lahuji Buva was a well-known guide to young men who were spirited, energetic and patriotic. It was under him that twenty years later Wasudeo Balwant, who rose in revolt against British rule in Maharashtra in 1879, too, learnt military exercises. Govande became a teacher at the Poona Sanskrit College in 1843, and Joti continued his education at the English school till he completed the course.

In those days there was no college, or any kind of academy in Poona. It was during this time that Govande made friends with Moro Vithal Walvekar and the latter's Brahmin friend Sakharam Yeshwant Paranjpye. Walvekar was also a poor Brahmin lad. He had received his education at a mission school in Poona.

III

Western education and missionary teaching had their effect upon the minds of these four friends. To a Hindu who could read

* An exercise with a fencing stick in one hand and the weapon called the Patta in the other.

an English book with any measure of intelligence, an entire world of new thought had been now opened up. Walvekar writes in his autobiographic sketch that there were moments when he lost his faith in Hinduism and thought seriously of embracing Christianity. But then it was decided by the four friends after a comparative study, that in every religion there were some dogmas that were to be accepted as mere matters of faith. So they agreed that the common principles which prevailed in all religions should be followed in daily life.[6]

What were these principles? That religion consisted in believing in one God; He alone should be worshipped. Principles of morality that were common and acceptable should be observed. The main tenet was: To do good to others was virtue; to do evil to others was sin. These young students no doubt derived inspiration from the work of missionaries. Their example of service to people and their mission to spread education were worth emulating.

In 1847 Joti completed his studies in the English school. The inspiration he had derived from the American freedom struggle was deep-rooted, profound and pulsating in his veins. While he was thus engrossed in these thoughts of the equality of man, the rights of man, and the freedom of man, one day he happened to meet two British soldiers. Their feeling of superiority and arrogance made them bluster out something which Joti could not tolerate, and the matter ended in a fight. Stout, sturdy and valiant, Joti thrashed them both, giving pursuit with a strong sugarcane when they ran away.

Joti says in his work *Slavery* that at that time he was possessed with the ideas of driving out the British from India. During his student days, a series of revolts broke out in Maharashtra against British rule. These revolts must have deeply impressed the young minds of Joti and his friends. Ramoshis led by Umaji Naik in 1826 fought and fell. Umaji became a legendary figure:. The Kolis in the north-western part of Poona District rose in revolt in 1830. Over a generation they continued their sporadic disturbances. Pratapsingh of Satara, who had been installed in the gadi in 1822, was deported to Benaras on September 4, 1839. His deposition had created no less dissatisfaction.

6. *Parag*, February and March 1949, edited by C. G. Karve.

Between 1839 and 1846, Bhau Khare, Chimnaji Jadhav and Nana Darbare rose in revolt in the name of the deposed Peshwa. The revolt was put down. Ramchandra Gore and a koli were hanged. The revolt raised by Bapu and Raghoji Bhangre was suppressed in 1848. Raghoji Bhangre was hanged on May 2, 1848. They were daring and fanatical patriots, but their stray attempts were foredoomed to failure. Although Joti saw those patriots perish in the struggle, he had planned in collaboration with his friends to throw the British out and make his country free and great.

These seeds of the thoughts of freedom, Joti observes, had been sown into his mind by his Brahmin student friends and Brahmin teachers. The Brahmins were terribly upset and affected by the fall of Peshwa rule. Being the leaders and priests of society, they, true to their ambitious and patriotic spirit, never wished well of British rule, even though they were in its service. The British rulers, too, knew this well. Sir Richard Temple, Governor of Bombay, in his report of July 1879 to Lord Lytton, Governor-General of India, observed: "But nothing that we do now by way of education, emolument, or advancement in the public service at all satisfies the Chitpawans. They will never be satisfied till they regain their ascendancy in the country." "But never have I known," Sir Richard Temple continued, "a national and political ambition, so continuous, so enduring, so far-reaching, so utterly impossible for us to satisfy, as that of the Brahmins of western India."[7]

7. Sir Richard Temple's letter, *The Hindustan Times Weekly*, 8 July 1962

CHAPTER III

The Banner of Revolt Unfurled

SCHOOLING OVER, Joti, a gardener's son, was marked for the trade of florist, just as a carpenter's son was expected in those days to be a carpenter. But Joti was not a path-follower; he was a path-finder. While the thoughts of service and welfare of the people were revolving in his mind, an incident took place which gave a turn to his life.

Joti was invited to attend the marriage ceremony of a Brahmin friend. Since he loved his Brahmin friends sincerely, he attended the ceremony. The bridegroom was going in a procession to the house of the bride. The procession consisted of Brahmins, men and women and children. There was hardly any person from other communities. Joti was walking along with the processionists.

Some blue-blooded orthodox Brahmin recognised him and was infuriated at the thought of the outrage a Mali, a low caste boy, had committed by walking along with the terrestrial gods, the Brahmins. He bawled out: "How dare you walk along with Brahmins! You Shudra, you have violated all caste rules and inflicted an insult on us. You are not our equal. You should have thought a hundred times before behaving like this. Get behind; otherwise go away. People have nowadays lost all shame. They violate caste rules; they are growing arrogant under this British raj!" Joti was perplexed. He was dazed. In a moment he came to himself. He was now perturbed. He felt the insult deeply. He felt its pricking in every muscle of his body, in every cell in his brain and in every drop of his blood. He abandoned the procession and returned home.

With the burden of these thoughts on his mind, Joti entered his house. He narrated the whole incident to his father with anguish and anger in his eyes. He sobbed, he groaned, he raged. His father, who was a respecter of traditions and customs, said that because they belonged to the Shudra class they could not be the equal of Brahmins who were standing on the top of the ladder of the caste system and were the central figure in the religion and social life of the Hindus. It was very kind of the Brahmins to drive him away instead of punishing him outright. He said that he had seen non-Brahmins humiliated and trampled under an elephant's feet. In the sphere of justice, there was one law for the Brahmins and another for non-Brahmins. The Gultekadi over there was redolent of many ghastly deeds perpetrated by the Brahmin class. Those non-Brahmin classes who considered themselves equals of the Brahmins in society, Govindrao observed, were prevented from wearing certain types of garments.

The poor Untouchables were the worst sufferers in Brahmin-ruled Maharashtra. Every Untouchable was required to walk through the streets of Poona with a branch of leaves tied to his waist and a pot hanging from his neck in which to spit if he wanted to; but he could not enjoy even this liberty of walking in the streets, in the early morning or late evening, lest his long shadow defile the Brahmins. Govindrao concluded.

Joti listened to his father who advised him to preserve the old customs and not to incur the wrath of the Brahmins. It was no use doing a thing that was outside the pale of customs and traditions. But Joti had not derived in vain his faith from the lives of Shivaji, Washington and Luther.

That night Joti did not have sound sleep. He sat far into the night brooding over the revolutionary thought of the equality of human beings. He recalled his father's fresh warning that had he done such a thing during the regime of the Peshwas he would have met the fate of a rebel. Having analysed the causes, he soon realized the genesis of Brahmanical ascendancy and domination in every sphere of life. He felt the full force of mental slavery and poverty which the Shudras had been suffering for centuries. They were born in poverty and they died in poverty and slavery. They suffered their slavery resignedly believing it to be the inevitable heritage of a Shudra birth. The life of a Shudra meant loss of dignity and loss of respectable means of livelihood. A deep-seated craving decided his attitude to the prevailing *milieu.* He abandoned the path of blood and iron which he had decided on for the salvation of his country.

It was not merely a craving for recognition or status. Joti resolved to rebel against the debasement of society, to throw off the shackles and to fight the grossest vices and petrified customs reared in the name of religion which exercised an evil influence on Hindu society. Conscious of the extent and enormity of those customs and dogmas, he resolved to release the lower castes from their debasing thraldom, and to regenerate them. The taint of social inferiority provoked a galling sense of injustice; and revolt was the natural reaction to it.

A force gathered in Joti's stout heart. It strove towards its objectives. All his actions, thoughts, emotions, dreams and desires were directed to it. A style of life developed. The goal makes the man. All great changes precede a vigorous intellectual revaluation and reorganization. This was the inward history of Joti. The taint of social inferiority proved a specific source of several of his later drives. This was a new awakening. With this awakening, the struggle of truth against untruth, of justice against injustice began. Having formulated a philosophy and a programme, Joti put on a rebel's robe. Very often the children of pious parents detest the doctrinal position in which they are trained and revolt against parental orthodoxy. Joti felt convinced that social slavery was worse than political slavery.

Joti said to himself that he was well-educated; he knew what was good and what was evil. He belonged to the religion to which Brahmins belonged. Then what led them to believe that he was inferior to them? Was it religion that made them act like that? But religion was the relation between Man and God. He then came to the conclusion that the Brahmins enjoyed power as a priestly class and as the head of the caste system. So he realized that caste was the bane of corporate life, the enemy of solidarity, of organized and cultural life. And Brahminism was the outer form of its expression. In order to annihilate Brahminism that condemned the non-Brahmins to perpetual subordination and humiliation, he ruminated, heredity as the basis of society must be discarded.

The caste system was solid, unbreakable and enduring. Because the lower classes had no education, they had respected this mental slavery for ages. Joti, therefore, resolved to raise the banner of revolt against the mental slavery and to throw open the gates of knowledge to the lower classes by disseminating education among them. Imbued with the idea of social equality, the lower castes, he thought, would fight for it. There is a piece of fortune, it is said, in every misfortune. Joti gave himself up to turning this insult into the mainspring of his actions. In the ordinary course Joti, like Ram Mohun Roy in the previous generation, would have been appointed a government servant in some capacity and would have slowly climbed the ladder of position. For in those pre-university days there was no criterion to test the merits of a candidate. But Joti was the first brilliant exception among the first-rate Maharashtrian leaders who never entered Government service. Jagannath Shankarsett was a millionaire. Joti's contemporary, the Lokahitwadi, rose from the post of a clerk to judgeship; Balshastri Jambhekar, another brilliant contemporary, entered Government service. Krishnashastri Chiplunkar did the same thing, the brilliant exception being that of Bhau Mahajan who conducted weeklies and other magazines. Later, Lokamanya Tilak, G. G. Agarkar, G. K. Gokhale, N. C. Kelkar, D. K. Karve, Karmaveer V. R. Shinde and Veer Savarkar were the other extraordinary exceptions in Maharashtra. They never entered the service of the British Government.

II

The year 1848 was a year of great change all over the world. In that year Karl Marx released his *Communist Manifesto*. In America an earnest movement was started for the emancipation of women. The first woman's rights convention was held in 1848 at the Wesleyan Church, in Seneca Falls, New York. While the American woman was at the cross-roads, the Hindu woman was in bondage. Hindu scriptures had assigned to her a very low position in the scale of social life. According to that, philosophy, she was regarded as an inferior, a subordinate human being for centuries excluding the period of the ascendancy of the *shrutis*. In India political changes were taking place rapidly. The *gadi* of Satara in Maharashtra was liquidated by the British rulers in 1848.

In Maharashtra the old leadership was giving place to a new type of leadership. Formerly, the leadership of society rested with some families which had won a name for themselves by their military exploits or by their wealth and statesmanship. It had nothing to do with the structural changes in society. Under

British rule the old traditions of statesmen and administrators had come to an end. British administration and Western education had tremendous impact upon both the social and the political ideas of the Marathas. A new generation of scholars, patriots and social reformers with Western knowledge replaced the old leadership.

Maharashtra had begun to react to Western education and thought. Tall trees quickly catch the wind. The really tall men had caught the ideas of progress. Of these, the most prominent was Balshastri Jambhekar. Born in a Karhada Brahmin family at Pomburle in Rajapur Taluka, he was the first leader who by his precocious brain, brilliant academic career, young professorship, research scholarship, fine patriotism and wonderful memory made a profound impression on his generation.

Jambhekar (1812-1846) was the first Hindu professor in Western India and soon rose to be an Educational Inspector. A little later, in 1845, he became Head of the Teachers' Training Institution. It was he who started on January 6, 1832, the *Durpan*, the first Marathi fortnightly magazine whose English section brilliantly written by Balshastri himself represented the people's views and grievances to the British Government. Its Marathi section was written by Govind Vithal alias Bhau Mahajan who had an equally brilliant educational career and was a patriotic, progressive-minded young man. Bhau Mahajan (1815-1890), almost self-taught in his boyhood, outshone many of his classmates in the final year examination of his college career. He started *Prabhakar*, a Marathi weekly in 1841, and also conducted Dig-Durshan, a Marathi magazine, *Dhumketu*, a Marathi Weekly, and *Dnyana-Durshan*, a Marathi quarterly.

Both Balshastri and Bhau Mahajan attacked the die-hard prejudices and ignorance of Hindus, appealed for broader sympathies and social reforms, and were in favour even of widow-remarriage.

The third important leader was Dadoba Pandurang Tarkhadkar (1814-1882). Poor but intelligent, this Vaishya boy studied hard, became an educational inspector and later became an Assistant Collector. He was a religious reformer of note and was regarded by all as a religious thinker of the two generations that followed him. He had just then formed a secret theistic society called Paramahansa Sabha with a view to breaking down all social barriers and the caste system. When Poona Brahmins met this man of learning who was a well-known grammarian, they envied him for his weighty discussions of the Vedas and said that in a theocracy Dadoba Pandurang[1] and his disciples would have been severely dealt with for having studied the Vedas!

These were leaders of new thought. But all of them were helped forward in one way or other by the protecting hand of Nana Shankarshett (1803-1865) who was one of India's eminent men of his time. He was a leading business magnate. His liberalism, his perennial magnanimity, and his noble patriotism actively supported various educational, social and cultural activities in Bombay. These men, Balshastri, Bhau Mahajan, Nana Shankarshett and Dadoba Pandurang, were mostly known as Bombay leaders, Bombay being in those days the centre of progressive ideas and Western thought.

About this time a young man from Poona, the old capital of Maharashtra, gave a trumpet call, awakening people to the new ideas of progress and new knowledge. His name was Gopal Hari Deshmukh. He came of a Sirdar family. He devoted himself boldly to Western education, completed his studies at the English school and took service with the Inam Commission. Better known as the Lokahitavadi (1823-1892), a well-wisher of the people, he had begun in 1848 his historic series of Marathi articles in the *Prabhakar*. His articles, mostly addressed to the Brahmins, advised them to give up their fruitless ancient learning and rigid social conservatism and to take to modern learning and Western thought. He made a very bitter attack on the lazy and debased Brahmins of his day. In those times of darkness it was a bold act to write against the Brahmin orthodoxy. The Brahmins of his day never forgave him for these writings.

The new leaders belonged to the middle class families and rose to eminence by sheer dint of their merit and intelligence. Some of Joti's contemporaries had more learning than he had: but they lacked his courage, candour and sacrifice. With Joti the new age became more conscious of its existence. He felt boundlessly inspired with the freshness and transparence of its

1. Bhavalkar, K. S., *Autobiography* (Marathi), p. 90.

dawn. Sprung from the lower stratum of society, he gave a new kind of leadership to Maharashtra.

Jotiba* resolved to ring the bell of social reform in Maharashtra. He was barely twenty-one. He decided to emancipate Hindu woman from her ancient thraldom. India had kept woman and the Shudra out of the pale of education. Ignorance meant darkness and education meant light. Education is an axe which cuts down slowly but surely the tree of ignorance. It is one of the principal means to a full life. It is a prerequisite of speedy social change. With education comes the critical attitude and a desire for self-respect. Jotiba made a noble resolve to throw open the gates of knowledge to woman and to the Shudra. He had realised the truth of the proverb—the hand that rocks the cradle rules the world. He, therefore, decided to open a school for girls, as he thought that women were the guides of the destinies of their children and if they knew their duty by them well, the nation would improve considerably. Jotiba, a product of the new age, and a personality with romantic self-dedication, could not bear postponement.

In 1848 Jotiba's bosom friend Sadashiv Ballal Govande, who was in service with the Inam Commission, was transferred to judge's office at Ahmednagar, which was a well-known centre of Missionary schools. The strong man and the waterfall, says the proverb, channel their own path. When Jotiba was about to start a girl's school he went to pay a visit to his friend Sadashiv Govande at Ahmednagar.

Jotiba himself tells us what he did on the eve of starting the first girl's school. "The low castes, Mahars, Mangs, Chambhars, etc.," he narrates, "composing a great part of my countrymen, being sunk deep in ignorance and misery, the Lord was pleased to excite in me a desire to better their conditions through means of education." "Female schools," he observes, "first of all attracted my notice, as upon mature consideration, they were found to be even more necessary than male ones, the root of education lying in the proper turn mothers give to the disposition of children between their second and third years. In this state of mind I visited, while at Ahmednagar, in company with

* Joti was called 'Jotiba' by his friends and people. The suffix 'ba' shows respect and endearment.

a particular friend, the female schools belonging to the American Mission conducted by Miss Farrar and was highly pleased with the manner in which the girls in those schools were educated.[2]

Miss Farrar expressed to Jotiba and Govande great sorrow at the neglect of female education in this country. They were impressed by the foreigners' perseverance in improving their country and felt for their countrymen's neglect of it. "Immediately on my return to Poona," Jotiba continues, "I opened a Low Caste Female school, allowing, however, such boys as wished to do so to attend also. In this I commenced to teach reading, arithmetic and the elements of grammar."

Jotiba's school met at the house of one Bhide in Budhwar Peth. His friends, Sadashiv Govind Hate and Sadashiv Ballal Govande, helped him to run the school. A school started by a non-Brahmin, a Shudra, and for the girls of Shudras and Ati-shudras! The stronghold of orthodox Brahmins raised an outcry against this act, which was to them horrible and sacrilegious. They said knowledge and learning was seeking shelter in Shudra homes. It was against the will of God, religion and society to teach the Shudras who had no right to education according to scriptures. And teaching girls was the worst kind of sacrilege, a horrible outlandish attack on Hindu religion. To send a girl to any school at which a man could be present was so entirely at variance with people's feelings.

Women and the Shudras had no right to education. A woman by nature was regarded as a frail, untrustworthy, wicked, thoughtless, lewd person. If a woman was educated she would elope with anybody, would easily be led astray, would destroy happiness at home. For a woman to receive education meant a sacrilegious act against the caste and society. If a girl received an education her husband would die prematurely. Wearing of sandals by women was a profane act. Using an umbrella by a woman was an affront to men. To have a chat with one's husband in the presence of elders was an indecent act. One couple was discovered engaged in conversation in daylight; the father thereupon locked them in for a day or two for this disrespect.

2. The *Dnyanodaya*, 16 December 1853.

To eat one's meals with one's husband was doubly disrespectful. To leave the village or town of one's father-in-law and to accompany one's husband to the place of his service or business was not tolerated. The wife must languish and pine away under the roof of her father-in-law. If educated, the girl would have no regard for her father; she would be at once in the company of girls from other castes. She would be impudent and would read bad books. Instead, if married in early girlhood, she would look after the children of her father-in-law, would slave for them and would keep both religion and virtue! Thus not a grain of independence was granted her. Woman was to lead a pitiable existence. Religion and social traditions had ordained it.

III

Jotiba threw a challenge to the *Manusmriti*. He declared:

> "Follow me, falter not now,
> Down with Manu's injunctions,
> Education imparts you happiness,
> Joti tells you with confidence."

As Jotiba did not conform to social traditions, the tradition-mongers shouted: "Orthodoxy is our doxy! Our religion is in danger. Jotiba is an enemy of society. He is a nobody and a descendant of generations of nobodies!"

The Poona Brahmins hotly discussed this unfamiliar attack on their religion and regarded Jotiba's work as a disgrace to the holy city. Their hatred for Jotiba knew no bounds. Their immediate forefathers had put an end to such innovations and revolts. Had Jotiba performed such a vile deed in their time he would have been trampled under an elephant's feet. But they were powerless. They threatened Jotiba through his caste-men with dire consequences. But their threats were of no avail.

Instead, Jotiba added fuel to the fire. As he could not get a teacher to help him, he took the help of his wife whom he had taught at home. A wave of uncontrollable excitement and anger swept over Poona. A woman going out of step with society and doing the work of a teacher! An unholy, unheard of thing! An affront to national honour! The learned Brahmins and their hirelings hated the very sight of Savitri. They threw mud, dirt, stones at her when she was on her way to the school. Embarrassed by this unholy uproar and upsurge, she would stop in the street and say serenely to her persecutors, "God forgive you. I am doing my duty. May He bless you." It is said that in India women teachers had practically disappeared from the scene by the beginning of the Christian era.[3] It was after Savitribai Phooley had appeared on the scene that Indian woman began to take part in public work.

Jotiba was a rebel. A rebellion was simmering in his blood. People thought he was out of step with the majority, with religion and society. And he was fervently, feverishly, fanatically so. His genius was in rebellion against the prevailing decayed customs and worn-out social traditions. The reign of superstitions had been long and severe; the wicked customs and prejudices were galling, sickening to humanity, and odious to God. He began to debunk them, decry them, denounce them. He did not falter in his work. In entering upon a mission, a great man anticipates misconceptions, misrepresentation and ridicule.

The men at the top are always faithful slaves of the social organization. Brahmins, who were well trained in the technique of social control, stormed at Jotiba's father. They exerted their social pressure on him as they had always done to maintain social order and support established traditions. They said to Govind-rao with rage in their eyes: "Your son has been a disgrace to religion and society. So is his shameless wife. You are incurring the displeasure of God. In the name of religion and God we command you to stop this or drive him out!" The poor Mali, who was taught to preserve his traditions and customs which he styled religion, was frightened out of his wits; and he yielded to wicked pressure. Who was there to support the poor gardener of the lower class against the Brahmins? The orthodox and the reactionaries triumphed!

Govindrao, however, yielded at last, not so much willingly, to social pressure. Although father and son were extremely fond of each other, Govindrao asked his son more in sorrow than in anger to leave either the school or the house.

3. **Altekar, Dr. A. S.,** *The Position of Women in Hindu Civilization,* p. 41.

Jotiba drew a deep breath of sorrow. He tried to convince his father of the nobility and utility of his mission. But the father would not listen to the son's appeal! With a sad heart, he told his genial father frankly: "Even at the risk of life I shall not give up the cause." A quick shudder passed through his father. There was a dreadful silence for a while. "Then go where you like," said the father grimly, "but leave my house together with your wife whom I am unable to keep under the same roof." She, too, was represented as a tradition-breaker and a disgrace to his house. A really typical Indian woman, she preferred to live with her husband facing trouble and torment from the society which they had vowed to liberate! He believed with saint Tukaram: "And once decision as to truth I made, Goodbye to majority opinion I bade."

Jotiba describes the scene himself: "Having, however, by my teaching the low castes, become odious to my castemen, my father at last drove me out of his house and left me to shift for myself in the best way I could. So the school was, as a matter of course closed, and I was compelled to engage in business to gain a livelihood."[4]

Jotiba with his wife bade farewell to his father's house. It was a great grief to his father! Shy, modest, intelligent and graceful, Savitri followed her husband with the spirit of sacrifice. She had her share of sufferings with her husband.

A man of mission sacrifices his whole life to force society to accept his goal. He does not fear to be out of step with society. He is not afraid to be different from society. Not worried about their petitions and protests, he follows his bent. An unfortunate experience will not deter him or disengage him. All progress is made by such men of strange and strong originality. Originality presupposes a deviation from the normal and the traditional. The thought that stems from active thinking is new and original. It is original not in the sense that nobody had come across it before, but in the sense that this man has used thinking as a means to discover something new in the world.

IV

Modern schools were started in India in the second decade of the

4. The *Bombay Guardian*, 16 December 1853.

nineteenth century. The first school for Hindu girls was started in Calcutta in 1819. The American Mission started one in Bombay in 1824 when the teacher had to go every day to the house of his pupils and bring them to the school. Every child was paid for attending the school. The teacher's pay depended on the number of pupils he brought to school. The American Mission started girls' schools in the neighbourhood of Poona in 1840. There was a girls' school in Poona kept by the Scottish Missionaries. It was attended by about ten girls. As it was a Christian girls' school, it could not grow. Jotiba was the first Indian to start a girls' school.

Jotiba's school continued its work for five or six months. Sadashiv Govande sent books from Ahmednagar at his own expense. Jotiba worked in the schoul so untiringly that he could not find time for his meals and often went without food till evening. But he could not conduct the school any longer. As his father drove him and his wife out of his house bag and baggage, he had to earn his living. He therefore had to close the school. Giving an account of this school for the girls of Mahars and Mangs in the *Bombay Guardian*, a certain lover of 'truth' observes: "Five or six months after this, the goddess of misfortune frowned upon the good intentions. Influenced by the foolish prejudices of the people, Jotee Govind Phooley's father went so far as to drive his son out of his house. On this account everything fell into disorder, and the school was closed."[5]

Meanwhile Jotiba and his friends were teaching and preparing their wives, so that they might be able to teach at the girls' schools which they proposed to open. Jotiba's wife was a friend of Saraswatibai Govande. They studied together for some time at her place in Ahmednagar. By this time Keshav Shivram Bhavalkar, who was appointed from 1st November 1848 [6] a teacher at a Government Marathi School, Poona, took upon himself [7] the trouble of teaching Savitribai. Bhavalkar was a member of the Paramahansa Sabha, which had been started in 1848 by Dadoba Pandurang in Bombay. Bhavalkar

5. The Bombay *Guardian*. 28 November 1851.
6. Bhavalkar, K. S., *Autobiography* (Marathi), p. 94.
7. The *Bombay Guardian*, 28 November 1851.

laboured sincerely in preparing a class of women for the posts of teachers in the last quarter of 1848.

Jotiba, finding himself in better circumstances, reopened the school at a place provided by Sadashiv Govande in Peth Joona Ganj, as no one let his, for the school. Jotiba's physical instructor, Lahuji Rangraoot Mang, and Ranba Mahar enrolled a good number of children of both sexes. Govande also provided the school with slates and a subscription of Rs. 2 per mensem. As the number of students increased, a Brahmin teacher Vishnupant Thatte kindly assisted him in teaching the class; but he, too, soon left the school as he was harassed by Brahmins. The children of low castes were not permitted to drink at public cisterns and wells; so drinking water at Joti's cost was supplied to the students. Even clothes were supplied to them to enable them to attend the school. When the number of children increased Jotiba hired a place belonging to a Mohammedan in the same locality. Moro Vithal Walvekar and Deorao Thosar assisted Jotiba in preparing and sending circulars and letters to different people.[8] Major Candy supplied books.

This was a great achievement. The gates of knowledge were opened to the lowest of the low for the first time in India during her history of three thousand years. Jotiba was the first Indian to effect this miraculous change in India. If the Shudra heard the Vedas recited, molten lead should be poured into his ears; that was the injunction of the *Manusmriti*. The question of the education of the Shudras or Atishudras never arose in the past. The Mahars and Mangs were Untouchables. So sagacious and learned a pandit as saint-poet Eknath says in his *Bhagavat*; "The pollution caused by the touch of an Untouchable is removed by having a dip in the river. If however an Untouchable has a dip in the river his pollution will not be removed." Realizing the historic importance of this epoch-making event in the life of Jotiba, Mahatma Gandhi, while he was in Yeravda Jail in May 1933, paid a worthy tribute to this precursor of a great movement, and said that Jotiba was a real Mahatma.[9]

With the experience Jotiba had for more than two years in the field of education, he now made bold to establish another

8. The *Bombay Guardian*, 16 December 1853.
9. The *Din Bandhoo, Matiatma Phooley Special Number*, 25 November 1949.

school for girls on July 3, 1851, at Annasaheb Chiplunkar's house in Budhawar Peth. Annasaheb Wasudeo Chiplunkar was a wealthy man and was a friend of Keshavrao Bhavalkar who took an enthusiastic interest in Jotiba's schools in Poona. There was great opposition to them. In the words of John Warden, President of the Board of Education, it was a small school established by stealth.[10] Jotiba worked gratuitously in this school for four hours a day and trained his wife for the office of school mistress.[11] She was brought to this new school from the Low Caste Female School as he himself was working in it.

Intensely conscious of his mission and full of endless, energetic activity, Jotiba imbued his colleagues and friends with a part of his own passion and spirit and strove untiringly to organise the work and place it on a sounder basis. He must have also thought that many hands make work light. Jotiba, therefore, placed his school under a Managing Committee which consisted of Joti, Jagannath Sadashiv, a surveyor in the Executive Engineer's Office, who became Secretary, and Keshav Shivram Joshi, a teacher in the Government Marathi School. It seems he was Keshav Shivram Bhavalkar. Because he was a Government servant, he might have changed his name. The Committee also included Anna Sahasrabudhe, a teacher in the Mission School, Vishnu Moreshwar Bhide, Assistant Head Teacher in the Poona College, Bapoo Rawjee Mande, clerk in the office of the Commissioner, Krishnashastri Chiplunkar, Assistant Professor of Vernacular literature in Poona College, and Vishnooshastri Pandit, a student in Poona College, who later became famous as a champion of widow-remarriage.

Jotiba's name stood first in the list of members submitted to Government and he is described as 'a benevolent person who has devoted his life to the work of education.'[12]

Describing the aims and objects of the society, its Secretary observes: "A few enlightened individuals who have been educated in Government schools, deeply lamenting the ignorance in which females have been kept for ages in this country often discussed various plans for improving their condition and placing them in the position in which God and Nature have intended."

10. The *Dnyanodaya*, 15 July 1853.
11. Report of the Board of Education for the year 1853-54.
12. G. D. Vol. VII, 1852, p. 205.

"The fruit of these discussions was a determination to establish a school for girls in spite of every difficulty which beset such an undertaking. Accordingly, the consent of a few parents was obtained and a school was opened in Annasaheb Chiplunkar's Wada in Budhwar Peth on the 3rd of July 1851 with Eight girls on rolls which rose to 48 in a short time."

"The state of the school funds has compelled the committee to appoint teachers on small salaries who soon give up the school business when they find a better appointment and thus the constant changes of teachers counteract the advantages that would otherwise accrue."

"Savitribai, the School Mistress, has nobly volunteered to devote herself to improvement of female education without any remuneration. We hope that as the knowledge advances the people of this country will be awakened to the advantages of the female education and they will cordially assist in all such plans as are calculated to improve the condition of those who have hitherto been unaccountably neglected by the tyranny of prejudice which has no foundation in the sacred law of the country and which has no voice of reason for its support nor hand of expediency for its plea."[13]

V

The school started with eight girls on the roll, and soon the number rose to 48. Savitribai was made Head Mistress of the school. The persecution of Savitribai Phooley continued also at this school. A peon was employed to take her to and from her house. Jotiba was the main pillar of the institution, the leader of this movement for female education. He laboured unflaggingly and suffered untold hardships. He himself taught self lessly, without even eating his daily meals in time. He had to overcome all sorts of difficulties and to make some arrangements personally. Girls were brought to school and taken home. They were induced to keep daily attendance by providing eatables for them and allowing them to play in the school. Some of them had to be provided with clothes. Success was thus achieved by Jotiba's constant, untiring efforts. He had to respect the prejudice

13. G. D. Vol. VII, 1852, pp. 207-09.

of the guardians of his pupils in not allowing any stranger to visit the school without permission of any one of the members of the Female Education Society.

On September 17, 1851, Jotiba started another girls' school under the Society at Rasta Peth, and the third school[14] on March 15, 1852, at Vetal Peth. Dadoba Pandurang Tarkhadkar, Superintendent of Government Vernacular Schools, inspected the school at Budhwar Peth on October 16, 1851, and expressed satisfaction at the progress of the pupils. It was creditable, he added, considering the short time the school had conducted its work. The course of tuition comprised reading of the *Neeti Bodh Katha* and writing in *Balbodh*-characters, distinguishing parts of speech, explaining geographical terms, doing subtraction, learning the history of the Marathas and reading the maps of Asia, Europe and Hindustan.

In his report Major Candy, Superintendent of the Poona College, said: "I have been much pleased with the intelligence and progress of the scholars."[15]

Referring to the first two schools, Hon. Mr. Warden, President of the Board of Education, said at an annual distribution of prizes and scholarships in Bombay: "When I first went to Poona jn 1851 as judicial commissioner, I visited the first two girls' schools established in the city; they were lodged in small houses and my visit to them reminded me of the account of the assembly of the early Christians 'in an upper room with the doorsshut for fear of the Jews'. The school mistress, the wife of a gardener who educated her in order that she might be the means of elevating her countrymen from their state of miserable ignorance, was with difficulty persuaded to examine a class in my presence; and a class of young matrons, who had formed them selves into a normal class refused to see me on any terms, though I am told my honourable predecessors, Sir Erskinene Perry and his colleague Mr. Lumsden, were shortly after admitted to the presence of these ladies. Such was the state of matters in 1851."[16]

On February 17, 1852, Jotiba's school was publicly examined.

14.G. D. Vol. VII, 1852, p. 203.

15.*Ibid.*

16.*Report of the Board of Education*, 1853-54, pp. 100-101.

A vast crowd of citizens assembled to witness the function. After the examination was over, Bhausaheb Manday said in a speech that he was sorry that the worthy citizens assembled had not so far realized the importance of female education. Quoting the great English epic-poet Milton, the judge Brown said that happiness and usefulness would bless the home if women were educated. He was glad at least some natives were thinking in the right direction and trying to uplift the country.

VI

Young Jotiba was not only the first saviour of a suppressed people in modern India, but was also a saviour of the reformers. The dauntless courage he showed in ushering in a social revolution had earned him high respect and he was regarded a personaltiy of great consequence. Brahmins of progressive views were, at this time, involved inadvertently in an affair which ended in a tussle with the orthodox section of the Brahmins. It was over the distribution of half the balance of Rs. 3,000 from the Dakshina Fund.

Dakshina means a present or gift to Brahmins. Distributing dakshina was regarded as an act of religious merit. On his coronation in 1674, Shivaji started distributing dakshina in the month of *Shravan* supposed to be most auspicious for religious acts. It consisted of corn or coin in proportion to the attainments of Brahmins who were subjected to a test by Panditrao, Minister for Religion. Shivaji's sons, Sambhaji and Rajaram, continued the practice. Shahu, however, entrusted this distribution to his Senapati Dabhade who spent about four lacs from the revenue due to Shahu. Dabhade's son Trimbakrao continued it. Bajirao I, after his victory over Dabhade, kept up the practice. Peshwa Madhavrao confined donations principally to poor Brahmins who were proficient in learning.

During the reign of Bajirao II, the practice degenerated into indiscriminate donations conforming to the notion that a gift to any Brahmin was an act of merit and piety. Commencing from *Shravan*, the fifth month of the Hindu year, this work of distribution of the dakshina took a considerable number of days. The proficient Brahmins were examined at Shanwar Wada, and those who did not submit themselves to examination were given dakshina in an enclosure called the 'Ramana' at the foot of the Parvati Hill. Bajirao II gave the latter class as much dakshina as he gave to their *Shaligram.** For want of real *Shaligrams* the Brahmins secured the unreal ones ready-made from the stables of the Peshwa. The servants of the Peshwa dried the refuse of the camels and turned it into *Shaligrams*. The Brahmins covered these false *Shaligrams* with tulsi plants and flowers. Bajirao bowed in reverence to them. Dakshina was also given to Brahmins who flocked to Poona from all parts of India, Kanchi, Shrirangpattam, Kumbhakonam, Tanjore, Kashi, Kanoj and Mathura.

The largest number of dakshina recipients in one year was sixty thousand and the amount spent Rs. 10 lakhs. Had these men fought on the side of the Peshwa whom they styled an incarnation of Krishna, his *Gadi* would have been saved. After the fall of Peshwa rule, for some years the British rulers continued this practice partly through a desire to conciliate the Brahmins, the most influential class among the conquered subjects, and partly with the object of encouraging the studies of learned Brahmins. Though Bajirao II sometimes spent lakhs of rupees over dakshina, Elphinstone fixed the amount for it at Rs. 50,000 a year. Shortly after, a sum of Rs. 20,000 was alienated to defray the expenses of Hindu College at Poona which was open to Brahmins only.

In 1840 the British rulers, finding that bogus persons and spates of worthless Brahmins took advantage of the Dakshina Fund, stopped adding new names to the list of dakshina holders. On death or on absence for three years, names of recipients were removed.

Lokahitwadi Gopalrao Deshmukh publicly voiced in June 1849 opposition to this practice as it was useless, he said, to recite by rote books the meaning of which the Brahmins did not know. At that time he was acting as Head Clerk in the Agent's Office. He therefore persuaded his friends to petition the Government to utilize half the sum of Rs. 3,000 from the balance of the Dakshina Fund every year towards giving prizes for books in Marathi, either original or translation of good books. Bapu Manday drafted the petition and Damodarpant Atre copied it.

* A black stone worshipped as the god Vishnu.

Annasaheb Chiplunkar obtained on the petition signatures of Lokahitawadi Gopalrao Deshmukh, Bapurao Manday, Vishnu Moreshwar Bhidc, Vishnu Moreshwar Ranade, and several other persons.

Some teachers from the Government English school at Budhavarwada signed it, and then Annasaheb Chiplunkar took it to the teachers and students at Vishrambagwada. There some signed it at his request. Balaram Kirad, the head teacher, read the petition and refused to sign it as it was against the Hindu religion. At this, those who had signed it pounced upon Annasaheb Chiplunkar to seize the petition. He returned the paper on which they had signed. Immediately he ran to Keshavrao Bhavalkar who was waiting for him at a house nearby. The students from Vishrambagwada pursued him hotly but Annasaheb refused to show them the original petition. They threatened him and then went away.

The application was signed by thirty-nine persons among whom there were some members of the Paramahansa Sabha. It was posted to the Governor of Bombay. The teachers and pupils at Vishrambagwada and other orthodox Brahmins from the city and neighbouring villages gathered together and decided to take the petitioners to task. Seven persons from among the signatories were served with notices and threatened with social boycott if they did not explain their conduct before the committee appointed by the community. There was a stir among the social reformers. Young bold Bhavalkar said that he was prepared to bear the blame himself.

But somehow they met Jotiba on the previous night of the meeting of the committee. Jotiba, whose personality was stamped all over with 'I-dare-to-denounce-your-scriptural authority' and who had acquired sufficient notoriety with the orthodox, at once agreed. He was not a wordy social reformer. He was a practical reformer. A man of amazing energy and an able organizer, he had the courage of his convictions. With Jotiba's appearance on the scene, the affair assumed a wider proportion and turned into a battle royal. The reformers implored Jotiba to give them protection. So he called a batch of two hundred strong men from the Mahar-Mang locality.

The next day at noon these lovers of Marathi marched in a line. Some of Jotiba's men walked in front of them and some in their rear. They escorted this group, when an angry mob lined either side of the street. They were assisted by Taraquand, a British official, who asked the police sub-inspector to give the party protection. The police officer was a Brahmin and was in the opposite camp, but had to obey the Sahib. They reached Tulsibag, where the trial was to take place. The noble gentry had absented themselves as Lokahitwadi Gopalrao Deshmukh was the acting Head clerk at the Agent's office where they had things to settle. One Bandu Nana Ranade, leader of the orthodox, inquired about the petition. Bhavalkar said he had posted the petition, and there was no copy of it. Thereupon he demanded the name of the man who had drafted the petition. Bhavalkar boldly said, "It was Jotiba!"[17]

A wave of helpless rage swept over the orthodox. Jotiba was beyond their power. He was now a force to be reckoned with. Their blue, greedy eyes narrowed scornfully. This incident throws a profound light on Jotiba's leadership. He was then hardly twenty-two. Poona has indeed been the cockpit of modern India, both social and political.

The Government described the petition as a bold and forcible appeal on the subject, although most of its signatories who had turned opponents, asserted that their signatures were obtained on false pretences, and therefore they entreated Government to cancel the petition. Thereupon the reformer's party renewed their petition. The Government agreed to the proposal by sanctioning half the amount for distributing prizes open for competition to all natives of India, for the best original essays in 'Marathi', or for best translations of useful books into 'Marathi' from English, Sanskrit or other *lanuages*.[18] Thus the fight between the lovers of Marathi and the lovers of Sanskrit came to an end. To the great sorrow and shame of the Sanskritists, the Government accorded its consent to spending money on Marathi.

17. Bhavalkar, K. S., *Autobiography* (Marathi), pp. 103-09.
18. Parulekar, R. V., *Selections from the Record of the Goverment of Bombay—Education*—Part I, p. 67.

CHAPTER IV

Laurels for the Liberator

JOTIBA NOW became known all over Maharashtra as the champion of female education and of the low caste people. Major Candy, Head of Poona Sanskrit College, and Sir Erskin Perry, the President of the Board, Commissioner Reeves and his friend Colonel Meadows Taylor from Hyderabad all were admirers of Jotiba. All good-natured Brahmins were all praise for him. A native observer wrote in the *Telegraph and Courier*[1] under the title 'Native progress', that though the Brahmins were the greatest enemies of the lower castes, they were at that time beginning to feel the many injuries done to these people by their forefathers, and were therefore thinking of some redress for it.

"There is a Brahmin," he observed, "named Balla Charya, who is at present a Government servant and who, though drawing a salary of Rs. 12 per mensem, yet on seeing a school opened for the instruction of the children of lower classes, made a present of one month's pay to Joti Govind Phooley for his opening a way for the good of those people, as an encouragement to others that may find out ways for the welfare of those miserable people."

"From the above fact," he continues, "it clearly appears that the Brahmins have commenced to think of doing good to their brethren and I hope God will be pleased to infuse such ideas in the minds of the people of this country that they may try their utmost to assist such benevolent and exemplary deeds as done by Joti Govind Phooley. That benevolent person has, I hear, written to Nana Sunkarshett, the great and liberal Saokar and a lover of educating the lower castes (which appears from the opinion given by him in the Board of Education for the instruction of those wretched people) that he may be pleased to assist the school by giving a place for it, as there is the greatest want of it."

1. 19 February 1852.

"I have no doubt," the native observer concludes, "that this great and liberal man will not fail in doing the favour to his poor and miserable brethren, but he, I think, will support the school in every way. I further hope that he will show the first and the best example of benevolence, by giving the assistance required as soon as possible, as the days are now getting sultry and the number of scholars are daily increasing. May God grant him the grace for getting his name immortalized by such an act of liberality."

The condition of vernacular schools all over India was far from satisfactory. It was reported in the Bombay *Guardian*[2] that the education of the masses was hardly advancing in other parts of India. The hundred vernacular schools established some five years earlier by Lord Hardinge in Lower Bengal had failed through sheer mismanagement and negligence. The vernacular schools in Bombay Presidency, the most advanced Presidency in India, were in a languishing condition and a feeling approaching despondency prevailed. This was the condition of education when Jotiba was struggling to promote education among the poor classes.

Jotiba was, therefore, tapping all possible sources, meeting donors, calling on high government officials and was naturally expected to contact one of India's eminent men of his time, Nana Shankarshett. A goldsmith by caste, he took a deep interest in the diffusion of useful knowledge among the people. He was also a philanthropist and well known for his catholic and patriotic generosity. He was a member of the Board of Education from its inception which was the extension of the Elphinstone Native Education Society. Nana Shankarshett's colleague, Dr. Bhau Daji Lad, a member of the Board of Education, a peerless medical practitioner of his day, too, took great interest in promoting education. A few days later both Nana Shankarshett and Dr. Bhau Daji took a leading part in establishing in August 1852 the first political institution in Bombay called the Bombay Association to promote and represent the demands and grievances of the people to the Government and the British Parliament.

This letter of the native observer referred to the Low Caste School which Jotiba had started in 1848. He had closed it and

2. The *Bombay Guardian*, 21 March 1851.

had, after some time, restarted it as already mentioned. Jotiba was spending a lot on it from his own pocket and from donations made by his friends and admirers. In May 1852 he gave it a broader base by forming a society for promoting the education of Mahars and Mangs, under the chairmanship of Sadashivrao Govande, his friend who had been in Government service either at Ahmednagar or at Bombay from 1848 to March 1852. Moro Vithal Walvekar became Secretary, Sakharam Yeshwant Paranjpye, treasurer, and Jotiba, and Babaji Manaji Dengale were ordinary members.

The *Poona Observer*, noting this school in its issue of May 29, 1852, says: "It will be no doubt very gratifying to the friends of native improvement to learn that a benevolent-minded Hindu of the Malee caste, has at his own expense, founded a school in Vittul Peit in the city of Poona, where Mahars, Mangs and Purwarees are taught the vernacular. This school has a large attendance of children and from the advantages it affords we should hope that considerable benefit may result to the community from its establishment." The *Poona Observer* further declared that "We are informed that the committee of the Management of the Native Female Schools in Poona have applied to the Board of Education for monthly allowance from the funds at its disposal for the support of these admirable seminaries. Major Candy and the Committee of the Dakshina Fund, we believe, intend proposing that some portion of it should be annually set aside for the maintenance of these schools."

Major Candy recommended the society for a grant-in-aid and the Government also, through its Dakshina Prize Committee, sanctioned a grant of Rs. 75 a month. Major Candy was em-powered to watch the expenditure and to make periodical reports to the Dakshina Prize Committee. Viscount Falkland, Governor of Bombay, in his Despatch of 1852 to the Directors of the East India Company, observes: "Some young men, who had a short time before established schools for native females at Poona, applied for a monthly grant towards the support of the schools from the General Fund for the encouragement of Native literature and education. We referred their application with strong recommendation in its favour for the consideration of the Dakshina Prize Committee under whose management the Fund has been placed and we are happy to say that they have awarded a monthly grant of Rs. 75 towards the maintenance of the schools and have expressed their willingness to increase the grant whenever the state of the school may seem to require."

"Your Honourable Court will no doubt peruse with interest the account furnished by Major Candy of these native female schools which forms an enclosure."[3]

II

The *Dnyanprakash* stated that while some murmured at this use of the Dakshina Prize Committee, the great majority were highly pleased with the arrangement. The Fund, however, observed the *Dnyanodaya*, could not have been appropriated to any object less in keeping with the original intention. Some of the old orthodox school of Hindus must think that matters had come to a sad pass when the money designed for the support of the Brahmins was expended on female education![4]

About this time young women joined the Low Caste School, but they were not willing to sit with young boys. So the girls were separated and a new school for low caste girls was established. The *Poona Observer*, commenting on the Low Caste Schools in its issue of August 21, 1852. said, "Jotee Govindrao Phooley has established two schools in Vittul Peit, one for the female children of Mahars, Dheds, Mangs, Chamars, and the other for the boys of the same classes. Both the schools are taught and superintended by Jotee himself, assisted by Brahmin teachers. These schools are supported by Jotee out of his private means, aided by subscription collected from Europeans and ent lightened natives. To these schools the Dakshina Prize Committee has liberally granted an allowance of Rs. 25 per mensem beginning from this month."

Having thus established his Low Caste School, goes on the report of the Board of Education, he (Jotiba) soon found a great desire manifested by the pupils for the establishment of a library, and again he devoted himself to the attainment of this object, and once more he succeeded. He has thus the credit of having been the main cause in establishing the first school for Mahars

3. Paragraphs 22 to 24 G.D. No. 117 of 1852, 10 November 1852, Despatch to the Honourable Court, pp. 362-363.
4 .The *Dnyanodaya*, 15 July 1852.

and Mangs in the same city, and the first Native library for these castes. He has thus in a three-fold manner devoted himself to the interests of his countrymen, but in justice to others we ought to add that he has been greatly assisted in his latter labours by several educated men in Poona.[5]

Jotiba was not an ordinary school teacher. He was a great teacher of the society. He gave his students the insight and power to think by preparing their minds for the reception of the seeds of thought and by digging, hoeing, and ploughing their minds; for instruction is related to knowledge and education to the faculties of the mind.

A Mang[6] untouchable girl of fourteen, who studied at Jotiba's school for girls of the low castes, wrote an essay on the condition of Mahars and Mangs. In her essay she observed: "The Brahmins say that the Vedas are their monopoly. They alone could study them. It is evident from this that we have no religious book. If the Vedas belong to Brahmins, it is their duty to conform their daily life to it. If we have no liberty to study books on religion, we are without religion. This is clear enough. O God, tell us which religion is descended from you so that we may follow it just as the Brahmins do their own."

"Formerly we were buried alive in the foundations of buildings. We were not allowed to pass by the Talimkhana. If any man was found to do so, his head was cut off playfully. We were not allowed to read and write. If Bajirao II came to know about such a case, he would indignantly cry: 'What! If Mahars and Mangs learn to read and write, are the Brahmins to hand over their writing work to them and to go round shaving widows with their bags hanging from shoulders?' God has bestowed on us the rule of the British and our grievances are redressed. Nobody harasses us now. Nobody hangs us. Nobody buries us alive. Our progeny can live now. We can now wear clothes, can put on cloth around our body. Everybody is at liberty to live according to his means. No bars, no taboos, no restrictions. Even the bazaar at the Gultekadi is open to us."[7]

This shows why the Untouchables, who laboured for ages under disabilities, naturally breathed a sigh of relief at the downfall

5. Report of the Board of Education for the year 1853-54, p. 18.
6. The Dnyanodaya, 15 February 1855.
7. Joshi, N. V., Poona: Ancient and Modern, Appendix II.

of the theocracy of the Peshwas. The new rule which had brought in the democratic principle of one man one value raised high hopes in them.

Jotiba's unflagging industry, perennial love and watchful care improved the tone of his schools, and these surpassed the work and worth of the Government vernacular schools. A note in the *Poona Observer* criticised the Board of Education for neglecting the Government Vernacular Schools and omitting one ot their important and responsible duties. It brought to their notice the deplorably bad condition of those schools which were put under the management of superannuated ill-educated men utterly ignorant of their duties. The guardians, it added, were exceedingly apathetic and the Government schools suffered for want of proper equipment. Contrasting the work of these Government vernacular schools with that of the female schools started by Jotirao, a native friend of the editor of the *Poona Observer*, wrote to him that the attendance in those schools was ten times more numerous than that of the vernacular schools.

"The reason assigned for this curious result," proceeds the *Poona Observer*, "is that the arrangements made for teaching the girls are infinitely superior to those for the tuition of the boys. One friend says that this matter is creating great despondency in the minds of the thinking portion of the male part of the community, for if things are allowed to go on long in this way, the girls will surpass the boys of the Government schools: indeed the former have already begun to look for victory at the very next examination and unless the Board exerts itself to the utmost we shall be disgraced to a certainty by having to admit the superiority of the females over the males, which will be very shocking to our ideas, and may be the cause of the girls' schools being suddenly closed!" However, the editor of the *Poona Observer* remarked that he had no such dread himself of any such result. If the girls' schools should go ahead of the boys for a time there would be no harm done eventually. This, he concluded, would put both the boys and the Board on their mettle.[8]

The superiority of men assumed by the Poona leaders was heroically maintained till 1920 when they opposed compulsory education for girls!

8. The Poona Observer, 29 May 1852.

III

It was now natural that the man whose hard and untiring labours in the cause of education of his countrymen, whose name had spread all over Maharashtra, whose work was reported even to the Court of Directors in London, should be honoured publicly by Government. The *Poona Observer* had given the news in its issue dated the 12th June 1852, saying that Jotee Govind Phooley, whose endeavour in the cause of native improvement had been recently noticed by it, "is, we hear, to receive a token of approbation by Government. A shawl of the value of Rs. 200, we are informed, is to be presented to him for his laudable exertions in favour of female education."

The Dnyatidprakasli,[9] furnishing this news to its readers, observed that Jotiba Phooley would be presented the next day with a pair of shawls. The old men, it added would, be displeased at this but the young would be glad about it. The Board of Education brought these exertions to the notice of the Government and suggested that a pair of shawls or some such honorary distinction should be awarded to him. The proposal was favourably received and accordingly Government purchased two shawls[10] for Rs. 193 and Major Candy, Principal of the Poona College, was deputed to make the presentation.

A meeting of the native nobility and gentry was convened at Vishrambagwada on November 16, 1852, for the purpose. Major Candy opened the proceedings by reading the letter of the Board of Education and then stating in Marathi the object of the meet ing, he presented on behalf of the Government a pair of shawls to Jotiba. Bapu Raoji Mande, Jotiba's friend and colleague, Moreshwar Shastri and Principal Pandit of Poona College, then delivered addresses on the importance of female education, and in appreciation of the great services Jotiba had rendered to the cause of female education. A class of girls was examined and the result gave them much satisfaction.

Then a young man of twenty-five with a handsome face, tyes, bright and kindly, nose sharp at the tip, shoulders broad, forehead high and broad, and jaws strong, rose to reply. He thanked his friends and admirers and sympathisers for the help they had

9. The *Dnyanaprakash*, 15 November 1852.
10. G.D. Index, 1852, p 82.

rendered him in his work. Concluding his speech, he feelingly said that he acted in conformity with the dictates of conscience and, above all, the will of God.

The *Bombay Guardian* published the report with great pleasure and directed the attention of its readers "to the progress made by young Jotee Phooley who for some years past had been indefatigable in his efforts to promote the education of his *country*."[11]

Giving the full report of the function, the *Bombay Guardian* stated that the proceedings were wound up in the usual fashion of native public assemblies by the presentation of garlands. Several European gentlemen and two or three European ladies were present. The *tout ensemble* was well calculated to impress the native mind both in favour of the young man in whose honour the assembly was convened, and the cause in which he had laboured.

Although Joti Govindrao Phooley, the *Bombay Guardian* went on, had been most prominent, there were other young men in Poona who had zealously supported him. "It appears," the *Bombay Guardian concluded*: "that many of the old school Brahmins are displeased that a present of shawls should have been made to a Sudra (Jotee Govindrao is a gardener by caste, although not by occupation) the Brahmins maintain that a man of his rank should receive the lower reward of money. Probably the feeling is that of displeasure that any reward whatever should have been given to him. We have the pleasure of knowing well the energetic native of whom we have been writing. Were all young Poona like him, it would be a matter of exceeding joy. That reckless infidelity which has laid waste so many of the young minds there, he trembles at as much as we do. Probably we may have occasion to notice him again, ere long. To have to chronicle such things is a delightful task."

The Brahmins who were displeased had harboured their wrath in their hearts. To them the very idea of a non-Brahmin being honoured in the Peshwa's palace must have been unbearable. Shawls were presented in those days to Sanskrit pandits most of whom did not know, to quote the Lokahitawadi, the meaning of what they recited. To them a man of learning meant a man well-versed in Sanskrit because Sanskrit alone was considered the

11. 26 November 1852.

repository of knowledge. Naturally they felt perturbed at this dire insult inflicted on them by Government by honouring a Shudra in their presence! They had a past before them; but they did not know that for them the present had ceased to exist. The conventions and standards by which their life had been regulated had come to an end. Old values and beliefs had fallen to pieces.

Jotirao was honoured in consideration of the great interest he had taken in the establishment of native female schools in Poona for low caste children. It was indeed a great day for Jotirao's friends who, amidst stress and storm, heroically stood by him. It was also a great day in the history of female education in India.

Sir Henry Sharp rightly observed that the chequered history of Indian Education in the nineteenth century 'was linked with the names of striking *personalities*'[12] like David Hare, Ram Mohun Roy, William Carey and others. Jotirao was one of them. Jotirao was rightly hailed as a liberator of Indian woman for whom he blazed a trail when M. G. Ranade was ten years old, when Vishnushastri Chiplunkar, leader of the reactionaries, was two years old, and before Gopal Ganesh Agarkar, the champion of social reform movement, Dhondo Keshav Karve, founder of Women's University in India, Pandita Ramabai and Mahatma Gandhi were born.

12. Hampton, H. V., *Biographical Studies in Modern Indian Education* (Preface).

CHAPTER V

Education and Equality

JOTIRAO PHOOLEY was thus a symbol of the revolution of social equality which was born of the impact of Western education and the great idea of equality brought by it to India. Equality as a force began to make for social, economic and national change all over India. In India the threads of religion were lockstitched into the social and economic privileges of the few. That socio-religious system called the caste system bred inequality.

Men of progressive opinions were starting girls' schools in some of India's big cities. The Students' Literary and Scientific Society, Bombay, whose first four presidents were European professors, started vernacular girls' schools on October 12, 1849, four Gujarati and four Marathi. In one of the Gujarati schools, at Murzban Street, Dadabhai Naoroji was a teacher. Deeply impressed with the importance of female education and anxious to devote themselves to its dissemination among the people of this country, the society started these schools.

In the schools of this society, the chief attention, announced the statement of aims and objects, would be given to the culture of the moral nature under which was included the formation of habits of order, propriety, and cleanliness; and this was proposed to be effected chiefly by means of moral tales. This was the first time a native institution, although presided over by Europeans, took to the education of girls in Bombay. A few days before the setting up of these eight girls' schools in Bombay, the Hon'ble Mr. Drinkwater Bethune, a Member of the Viceroy's Council at Calcutta, cited, at a meeting, the example of Lopamudra, and exhorted the Hindus to exert themselves in the cause of female improvement. So some energetic Hindus started a school for girls of the upper classes under a lady teacher. There was a general impression that although convinced of its importance they did nothing to promote it and until their mothers and sisters were educated, the Hindus would not be an en-lightened, happy people.

The school, however, languished after about six months, the supporters having broken their connection with it. Bringing this fact to the notice of the members of the Students' Literary and Scientific Society, the *Dnyanodaya* warned: "It may stimulate them to greater diligence and perseverance in the work which they are now undertaking. It is easy to begin a philanthropic work, but not so easy to preserve it in the midst of general indifference and perhaps opposition. Let them be warned by the example of the people at Calcutta. The cause of female education is one well worthy of continued efforts and *sacrifice*."[1]

On Bethune's death, Lord James Andrew Dalhousie, Governor-General of India, maintained the school. Babu Ishwarchandra Bose, a rich merchant, sent his daughter to this school. So his caste threatened to excommunicate him. On his surrendering his daughter was purified and restored *to caste*.[2]

All over India equality as a force was operating through the education of women and Shudras. When schools were thrown open to all classes alike and when girls' schools were established, news about them flashed across the country. These schools were visited and often publicly examined before huge crowds by even Governors and judges. When prominent and leading men sent their daughters to girls' schools this bold act of theirs was given wide publicity so that lesser men might follow their example.

Defenders of the lower classes fought their cause in the columns of newspapers. "It is one of the great defects of all our educational institutions in India," said a note in the *Bombay Guardian*, "that no provision is made for popular education. We educate the rich who are able to educate themselves and make no provision for the elevation of the Kunbee and Pariah." The poor ryot, the agriculturists from whose labours by far the greatest proportion of the revenue was deriyed were left uncared tor, in their native ignorance. One's heart, it bewailed, bled at the contemplation of the fate of the Indian ryot. The Brahman, the zamindar, the Government and the money-lenders all com-

1. The *Dnyanodaya*, 15 September 1849.
2. The *Dnytuwilnya*, 15 December 1851.

bined to degrade them. The ignorant peasantry were their slaves. Nothing could prevent the poor labourer and peasant from being defrauded, unless popular education penetrated the village and its inhabitants were taught their rights. No amount of material prosperity elevated a man who was the slave of ignorance and superstition.

"Let the Government," warned the note, "neglect the ryot, but he will not always be neglected. Some Indian demagogue, some Hindu O'Connel will one day start up and league the people against the Government, that neglected its first duty, the welfare of the labouring classes." While the work in the field of education was carried on by enthusiastic men, opposition was also voiced by the opponents of the education of girls and Shudras!

Orthodox Brahmins raised, in the name of religion, a violent opposition to non-Brahmins being given any education at all. They thought that the lower classes, if educated, would reap the benefits of education, their monopoly would be in danger, and consequently their position in society would be jeopardised.

When Poona Hindu College, popularly known as Poona Sanskrit College, was started in 1821 by Chaplin, the then British Commissioner, he kept it open only to Brahmins. In 1838 it was found that the Sanskrit College was worse than useless. On mature consideration and the acquiescence of some Brahmins, the Government threw it open to all Hindus. This aroused greatly the ire of the Brahmins in the city. The earth-born deities, the *Dnyanodaya* observed, were most unwilling that the fountains of learning should be opened alike to all. The Brahmin pandits trembled with alarm and anger. There was at once violent opposition organised by the pandits. They refused to teach the non-Brahmin students Sanskrit which, according to their scriptures, the non-Brahmin students had no right to learn!

A threat to the college was held out by the orthodox Brahmins. Major Candy, Principal of the college, gave the Sanskrit pandits time to think over the matter, and he took upon himself[3] the task of teaching Sanskrit to Sonar and Prabhu and other caste students in the class, while Brahmin students were being taught

3. The *Bombay Guardian*, 8 October 1852.

by Brahmih pandits. A majority of the Sanskrit pandits threatened to resign rather than teach the sacred language to non-Brahmin students.

II

The *Dnyanodaya* observed that this question had already been decided in all other parts of India. In Calcutta College all castes were admitted without distinction. It added:[5] "It is too late in the day for Brahmins to expect to indulge the idea, at the public expense, that they are peculiar favourites of deity, nay, gods upon earth. They, of course, are perfectly free to cherish these feelings and to act upon them, so far as they choose at their own expense. But it is idle to expect the British Government to expend its revenues in supporting these lofty pretensions. Public institutions must be free alike to all classes."

The *Prabhakar*,[5] criticising the intolerant attitude of the Poona pandits, said that the course pursued by them was very unreasonable and foolish. In Bombay hundreds of pandits taught Sanskrit and even repeated the Vedas, not only in the houses of the Prabhus and Sonars but also in the homes of Europeans, and it reminded its readers that the Poona pandits revised and returned to Government the *Rigveda* that it might be published in England. It sounded a warning to the pandits that their places would be occupied by others who were ready to accept them on much lower salaries.

It may be mentioned here that one Gangadhar Dikshit-Phadke, who eked out his living by teaching Sanskrit to Europeans in Bombay from 1820 to 1825, on his return from Bombay to Poona, was socially boycotted by the Poona Brahmins on the supposition that he might have dined with the Europeans. This poor pandit turned hermit and departed the holy world of the Brahmins.

The *Dnyanaprakash* voiced the grievance of the Brahmin pandits, by raising in addition a false alarm, that Government had introduced the Bible into Calcutta College. "The determination to teach," said desperately the *Dnyanaprakash* which meant the 'Light of Knowledge' "*the Shastras and Purann to*

4. The *Dnyanodaya*, 2 August 1833.
5. Quoted in the *Dnyanodaya*, 2 August 1853.

all classes in the Sanskrit College is even now being carried out. Why should not all unite in a vigorous effort to preserve our religious views and observances by founding a school for the Brahmins? Has all regard for caste and for our ancestral faith been extinguished?" *The Dnyanodaya* replied that the *Dnyana-prakash* was mistaken in saying that the Bible was introduced; into the Government College at Calcutta. The only trouble was, it observed, that students from all castes were admitted; and that was contradictory to Hinduism then so much the worse fork that religion. If Hinduism required that large masses of the| people should be assigned to ignorance and degradation, then it could not be from God. Neither could the masses be elevated! and blessed through its means.[6]

The *Dnyanaprakash*, attacking the pandits who taught the pupils of all classes in Poona Hindu College, declared: "Narayan Shastri Abhyankar and Gopal Shastri Gokhale have agreed to teach Sanskrit in Poona College to the youth of all castes without distinction. They entered upon this work onl the 1st April 1853 on which day we were present and saw these shastris teaching Sanskrit Grammar to Sonars, Shimpis, Parbhus, Parsis, and various castes of Shudras. Thus for thel sake of their bellies, they renounced the pride of caste and religion of their fathers. Alas! alas! what a shame! We are! truly astonished at beholding a proceeding so shameless and! wicked. The course pursued by these two shastris has caus a great excitement throughout the city. The minds of the Bhats and shastris and others are filled with indignation and the leading men among them are, we hear, about to summon a general meeting for the purpose of putting the offenders out of caste. Principal Bhats and shrewd shastri will doubtless turn this quarrel to good account."[7]

The *Dnyanodaya* said that it was not surprised at the indig nation of the Bhats; but was surprised to find such an article in *the Dnyanaprakash*, the Light of Knowledge. It was unworthy of its name as it upheld Brahmanical bigotry and intolerance. Another article by 'one of the enlightened' denouncing helplessly the work of the Sanskrit pandits who

6. The *Dnyanodaya*, 16 May 1853.
7. The *Dnyanodaya*, 16 May 1855.

taught Sanskrit to non-Brahmin Hindus as an evil, said that it was too late to arrest the evil; such was the downward tendency of things in the degenerate age! The *Prabhakar described* this subject as a fiercer controversy than anything ever known among the Poona Brahmins.

Later Nilkantha Shastri Bhat and live other professors who refused to teach Sanskrit to the non-Brahmin students were transferred to the Oriental Translation Office on lower scales of salaries. Four shastris Dhondashastri Baba Dengavekar. Shankar Joshi Vyavahare, Balshastri Deo and Krishnashastri Rajwade, were persecuted by orthodox Brahmins for teaching Sanskrit to non Brahmins, and Shankar Joshi was maligned for teaching *Yadnyavalkya*, the holy work, to Europeans! They faced the danger of being excommunicated.

The Brahmin pandits accepted work under the supervision of European beaf-eater, Major Candy, but their religion was in danger if they taught Sanskrit to their co-religionists! The ignorance and beliefs of the Brahmins tried Major Candy's patience. He was so kind and gentle that he was described unwisely as a simpleton. Candy prided himself on being an authority on Marathi. At first the Brahmin students and pandits did not allow him to enter Vishrambagwada in which the college was housed. One day when he entered the Wada the Brahmins purified it by the performance of a ceremony called *Udakshanti*. Then he was allowed to go as far as the parlour. If his presence there polluted the Brahmin students they went home and had a bath and rid themselves of the pollution.

Gradually it was conceded that Candy's presence in the college was unavoidable. This was remedied by changing clothes after being in his presence. The Brahmins saved their souls by a solution to the problem: that a king or a king's representative caused no pollution. Candy suffered their insulting behaviour with great patience. For some time he did not use shoes; nor did he have his lunch in the college.[8]

III

Although Poona Hindu College was thrown open to all Hindus, the scholarships were reserved for Brahmins. Thus a great in

8. Joshi, N. V., *Poona: Ancient anil Modern*, p. 70.

justice was done to the non-Brahmins. A correspondent, critical about this attitude, wrote in the *Bombay Guardian* asking Government whether the lowest classes were admissible to scholarships. "Nothing is said on this subject," he observed, "but we suspect the day is still distant when without regard to caste, creed or colour, equal justice will be dealt out to high and low by the Government of *India*."[9] Soon after, the Bombay Times published the news that scholarships in the Agra college were thrown open to all students, irrespective of caste, creed and colour, who conformed to the rule and passed *the test*.'[10] Till then scholarships were the preserve of Brahmins.

At Ratnagiri, a Sanskrit Veda *Shala*[11] was to be started about this time. The promoters convened a meeting to discuss ways and means to achieve their end. The non-Brahmins categorically told the Brahmins at the meeting that they could not contribute to any fund for the establishment of the Pathashala as their children were not to be admitted *to it*.[12]

This opposition of the reactionary and orthodox Brahmins to the new liberalisation, vindicated Jotirao's policy to the hilt. Brahmin opposition to the education of the lower castes was a prominent feature of the India of his day.

This was the fate of the Shudras; but the Atishudras, who were Untouchables, could not even dream of education. The orthodox section, which enjoyed the monopoly of education, was against it.

The leaders of the higher classes like Ram Mohun Roy and the Government policy-makers stood clearly for educating the upper classes, believing that education would filter downwards. On the other side, were leaders like Jotirao who clamoured for the education of the masses. It became evident that the British Government deliberately enforced the rule that education in India was to be a preserve of the higher classes.

The Honourable Court wrote to the Madras Government in 1830: "The improvements in education, however, which might effectively contribute to elevate the moral and intellectual condition of a people are those which concern the education of the

9. The *Bombay Guardian*, 8 October 1852.
10. Quoted in the *Dnyanodaya*, 12 November 1851.
11. School.
12. The *Dnyanodaya*, 15 October 1854.

higher classes of people, possessing leisure and natural influ¬ence over the minds of their countrymen. By raising the stan¬dard of instruction amongst these classes you could eventually produce a much greater or more beneficial change in the ideas and the feelings of the community than you can hope to produce by acting directly on the more numerous class. You are, moreover, acquainted with our anxious desire to have at our disposal a body of natives qualified by their habits and acquirements to take a larger share and occupy higher situations, in the civil administration of the country than has been hitherto the practice under our Indian Government."[13]

As regards the education of the low castes, the Government was not in favour of it. The reports of the Board of Education cited, in defence of their policy, Mountstuart Elphinstone, their ex-Governor of Bombay: "But here the wise reflections of Mr. Elphinstone, the most liberal and large-minded administrator who has appeared on this side of India point out the true rule of action. 'It is observed,' he says, 'that the missionaries find the lowest castes the best pupils; but we must be careful how we offer any special encouragement to men of that description; they were not only the most despised but among the least numerous of the great divisions of society and it is to be feared that if our system of education first took root among them, it would never spread further, and we might find ourselves at the head of a new class, superior to the rest in useful knowledge, but hated and despised by the castes to whom these new attainments would always induce us to prefer them. Such a state of things would be desirable, if we were contented to rest our powers on our army or on the attachment of a part of the population but is inconsistent with every attempt to found it on a more extended basis.'"[14] And yet Elphinstone has been extolled more as an enlightened ruler than seasoned statesman!

In their Despatch No. 49 of July 19, 1854 what is known as Charles Woods' Scheme, the Court of Directors directed that "useful and practical knowledge, suited to every station in life, may be best conveyed to the great mass of the people who are utterly incapable of obtaining any education worthy of the name

13. Report of the Board of Education tor the year 1850-51, paragraph 8.
14. Report of the Board of Education for the year 1851-52 paragraph 23.

by their own efforts; and we desire to see the active measures of government, more especially directed, for the future, to this object, for the attainment of which we are ready to sanction a considerable increase of expenditure."

Although mass education was now the policy of the Govern¬ment, it was more concerned with the consolidation of its empire than the salvation of the crores of its lower class subjects. Its high officials were never in favour of the education of the lower classes and always foiled any attempt made to promote it. Lord Ellenborough, President of the Board of Control, striking a note of caution to the Chairman of the Court of Directors, observed: "Education and civilisation may descend from the higher to the inferior classes, and so communicated may impart new vigour to the community, but they will never ascend from the lower classes to those above them; they can only, if imparted solely to the lower classes, lead to general convulsion of which foreigners would be the first victims."[15]

IV

In spite of this unsympathetic attitude to the education of lower castes, if some boys pursued their education, the Brahmins treated them cruelly and persecuted them. The Rev. Murray Mitchell narrates in *Recollections of My Early Missionary Life* an interesting incident. The Rev. Adam White went to visit a Government school near Poona. The Brahman Pantoji (teacher) was provided with a cane and he made good and frequent use of it. The Rev. Adam White asked the Pantoji why some clods were there. He replied: "I use my cane in the case of caste boys. If I struck the Mahar pollution from the outcaste boy would ; come along with the stick and my whole body would be pol¬luted. So when the Mahar boy is stupid, I just take a clod and let fly at him, and when I miss I take another."[16]

The Rev. Murray Mitchell tells a moving story of a boy sent to him by Jotirao Phooley. "My worthy friend Jotiba Govindrao Phooley, a remarkable man who laboured hard to benefit the Mahars—who are of the lowest caste, or rather of no caste at

15. Report of the Director of Education for the year 1857-58, pp. 10-11
16. Pp. 315-16.

all-one day sent a Mahar boy to us. He was sufficiently acquainted with his vernacular to allow us to receive him into the lowest English class.

"In a few minutes there came a deputation of Brahman boys, their dark eyes sparkling, and every gesture betokening emotion. 'We are going to leave the school; there are Mahars in it.' 'One Mahar, I think.' 'Yes; but one is as bad as ten.' 'Am I to drive the poor boy away?' 'We don't know; only, we go if he remains.' 'You need not touch him unless you like; you clever boys are near the top of the class, and the poor Mahar boy is at the foot. He is sitting on a different bench from you.' 'Yes, but there is matting on the floor; and it transmits pollu¬tion. We Brahmans are now all polluted, and must wash away the defilement before we eat.' 'You wish me then to remove the matting!' 'We must not have been in the class." 'Well, at any rate, I cannot and will not put the boy out of the class.'

"I was puzzled. I did not wish to drive away the Brahmans; yet I could not in conscience dismiss the Mahar. 'Wait till tomorrow,' I said, 'We are re-arranging the classes, you know, and perhaps you deserve promotion.' So, rather sulkily, the Brahmans retired. The Mahar boy never came back. I suppose he found himself like a fish out of water; the high and the middle castes, no doubt, stood firm; and I believe the teacher of that class did the same thing."[17]

The presence of a Christian teacher did not bring in pollution to the Brahmin students. For their own petty self they contravened the tenets and precepts of their religion, but they expected a rigid observance of their inhuman customs by their co-religionists.

At Madras some Pariah[18] students were admitted to an educational institution and immediately forty caste students left it rather than suffer contamination of the Pariahs' presence. Of the forty, more than twenty of them sought, with the most ample apologies, readmissions. They were readmitted. The caste students yielded, though with bad grace, to the firmness of the Government. The commotion then subsided.[19]

17. Mitchell, the Rev. Murray, *The Recollections of My Eaily Missionary Life*, pp. 314-15.
18. *Untouchable.*
19. *Friend of India*, 10 June 1852.

Early in 1852, four Billavar caste students belonging to one of the lowest castes in Canara, sought employment at the Judge's court at Mangalore. Findlay Anderson, Chief Justice, had declared two years earlier that in future learning would be the sole qualification for employment. Accordingly, the Billavar caste students were examined. They read and translated well. They were appointed candidates to learn the work and proceedings of the Court. Then a storm of opposition to their presence broke out.

The Brahmins had borne philosophically the announcement made by the judge two years earlier, but now they could not stand the presence of Billavar candidates. To them it was a deprivation of a dearly loved monopoly. The Brahmins said that if any one of them became head of the office, they would suffer the shame of serving under him and experience the contamination of his presence. Thereupon those clerks petitioned Anderson but he turned down their prayer. They appealed to Sir Henry Pottinger, Governor of Madras, but he upheld the decision of Anderson and said the proceedings of Anderson were praiseworthy.[20]

In the beginning of British rule, in the District Courts, the same kind of humiliating treatment was given to the lower classes. Brahmins sat on the floor before the judge. Shudras were ranged behind them. An outcaste stood at the window or at the door and bawled in his complaint or answer to the judge. This was soon done away with and the Mahar and Mang were allowed by the European beef-eater to stand before him, the rules of caste notwithstanding, and the holy Brahmins unwillingly consented.[21]

As this opposition to the non-Brahmins had sprung from the educated class, it became a continual affair. How Dhakji Dadaji, a member of the Bombay Native Education Society and a leader of orthodox section of society in Bombay, determinedly opposed the Shudras being admitted to schools has been already narrated. Next day children of Shudras, who attended schools of the Bombay Native Education Society in Bombay, had to leave the school. "The question of the admission of children

20. *Friend of India*, 26 January 1854.
21. The *Bombay Guardian*, 22 October 1852.

of Mahars and Dhers into Government schools," opined unsympathetically M. M. Kunte as late as 1882, "is not raised by the Mahars and Dhers themselves. It is not real, and has no practical bearing. It is a groundless agitation caused by sentimental English officials and unpractical native reformers."[22] Being a semi-reformist Brahmin, he made no bones about it.

The Brahmin teachers feared, Jotiba observed in his book *Slavery*, that if Untouchables were admitted to schools there would be at once a revolt. So Government, too hesitated to solve the question.

V

The revolution of equality was operating also in social affairs. Dadoba Panduraijg, a Hindu belonging to a lower caste, had given a stimulus to the thought of social equality in Maharashtra. According to Justice Ranade, Dadoba occupies a foremost place in the ranks of thoughtful inquirers after religious truth. A lover of the Bible, he had made Christianity the favourite study of his life. But he later expressed his unmistakable dissent from the philosophy and rationale of Christian doctrines. With the help of Durgaram Manchharam, a teacher in a Government Gujarati school at Surat, he had established the Mauav Dharma Sabha at Surat in 1844. Dadoba was an enlightened social thinker and had formed in Bombay a secret society called the Paramahansa Sabha in 1848. Its President was. Ram Balkrishna Jayakar, who was Head of a high school and who later became an Assistant Commissioner of Customs.

The members of the Paramahansa Sabha were native youngmen belonging to Shenvi, Sonar, Brahmin and Prabhu castes. They were drawn from Elphinstone Institutions, Christian schools and Government offices. It was a theistic society which believed in the fatherhood of God and the brotherhood of Man. They held weekly meetings for divine worship. The progress of the Sabha was rapid. The object of this society was to abolish caste, to secure prohibition of early marriage, to promote remarriage of widows and to introduce various other reforms in Hinduism. Its branch associations were established at Poona,

22. Report of the Education Commission, p. 514.

Satara, Nagar, Belgaum, Dharwar and Calcutta. It caused uneasiness among the orthodox Hindus regarding its character and object. The members of the Paramahansa Sabha ate European bread together and observed no caste rules; so they were denounced as foes of Hinduism, men of notorious conduct, a set of bastards.

Defending the members of the Paramahansa Sabha, the *Prabhakar* said that the editor knew that they were not men to indulge in indecent and licentious practices. The members of the Students' Literary and Scientific Society who were suspected of having subscribed to the view of this Sabha were turned out. Somebody stole the list of members, and the Sabha broke down in confusion. It became extinct about 1860. A critic expressed his opinion in the *Bombay Guardian* that the members of the Paramahansa Sabha did not have the courage of their convictions. Their object was not to do good to society but to gain a high name among Europeans and to distinguish themselves among natives.

The practice of divine worship Jotirao followed at the end of meetings, his close friendly associations with Keshavrao Bhavalkar and the dedication of his Ballads on Shivaji to Ram Balkrishna, President of Paramahansa Sabha, gave an indication of his connection in some form with this theistic and anti-caste society.

VI

About this time Hindus who were swept off their feet by missionary propaganda and profoundly influenced by the influx of Western ideas, embraced Christianity. Jotirao, although a critic of Brahminism, never thought of going over to Christianity. How grim the problem was can be seen from the cases quoted below.

Baba Padmanji, a Kasar Hindu youth of twenty-three, was an industrious intelligent student. He attracted the attention of his Christian teacher by his candour, and his zeal for the acquisition of knowledge. He was also acquainted with the Paramahansa Sabha. "But I found," he said, "that it could yield me nothing to satisfy the wants of my immortal soul; no assured hope of a blessed existence beyond the tomb. A rule of this society is that no religious views whatever are a barrier to admission." Under the guiding influence of his Christian missionary teachers in Bombay, which was then transformed into one of the strongholds of Christianity in India by the powerful and fearless personality of Dr. John Wilson, Baba Padmanji was swept off his feet, and he embraced Christianity, promising to endeavour to the utmost of his ability to promote the welfare of his motherland.

It was the fall of an inquiring mind, which perched on Christianity, with its vision and valour clipped. The fall of Baba Padmanji resounded throughout Maharashtra like the fall of a Maratha fort to the enemy in the seventeenth century. Baba Padmanji, friend and well-wisher of Jotirao, surrendered, but Jotirao stood irrevocably and heroically to his guns!

Not long earlier, Christians all over India had announced loudly and publicly the conversion of Maharajah Dulip Singh, who was the first Indian Prince to embrace Christianity. Born in 1837, he was hardly sixteen and it was declared that he had been neither coaxed nor frightened into Christianity. Echoes of the conversion of Gyanendra Mohan Tagore, son of Prasanna-kumar Tagore, the well-known pleader and for many years an intimate friend of Ram Mohun Roy, were heard throughout India!

Dhanjibhai Naoroji, whose conversion from the Zoroastrian religion to Christianity had shaken the Parsi community in Bombay, was thanking his singular fortune of converting two Dheds to Christianity on the anniversary of his own baptism!

About nine years earlier Narayan Sheshadri, a poor Deshastha Brahmin from Parali in the Hyderabad State, who was educated at a Scottish Missionary School, was baptised on September 13, 1843. His younger brother was living with him. As he was living under a Christian roof with his elder brother, his father Sheshadri Govind Parlikar wanted his younger son back. Sir Henry Roper, Chief Justice of the Supreme Court, Bombay, decided that the young Shripat must be restored to his father. Defiled as he was by intercourse with Christians, the question of his reconversion to Hinduism arose. The leaders of the society were divided. The orthodox leaders would not receive him back. Balshastri Jambhekar and Nana Shankarshett, leaders of the reformers in Bombay, could not succeed in restoring

Shripat to his caste. They sent Shripat to Kashi to obtain the support of learned Brahmins, but in vain.

The leader of the reformers, Balshastri Jambhekar, and several others, who had championed the cause of Shripat, came to grief. Balshastri had to make amends before his death. The Poona orthodox Brahmins had dealt a severe blow to these men of liberal views. According to their decision, the five products of the cow including its urine were administered to them and they were ignominiously deprived of their moustaches, Balshastri being the chief victim at the 'ceremony'! When Balshastri, the man of liberal views and great learning, died, the orthodox Brahmins said that his untimely death was caused by their curses.

The Brahmins had the keys to the salvation and purification of tradition-breakers and adjusted their meaning of the shastras to the size of the gift. Aba Kale who had been sent to London by Raghoba was not socially boycotted. His daughter was married to the son of Balaji Pant Natu. Ganesh Sitaramshastri Golvalkar, on his return from London, was invited to dinner by the Holkar at his palace and Golvalkar was not socially boycotted! The greater the gift, quicker the expiation.

Shripat Sheshadri's case had wide repercussions in India. Brahmins in Calcutta held a meeting on May 25, 1851. The question was then posed whether a Hindu who had broken caste by eating forbidden food could be absolved from his sin and restored to caste. The important enquiry was answered in the affirmative by an overwhelming majority, of the assembled pan¬dits. The next question was as to the mode of expiation. The gift to the Brahmins of some hundred cows was deemed a proper expiation. "Thus in Bengal it has been ruled that money alone without any degrading corporeal penances can restore the offender to caste. Even should the outcaste have eaten the flesh of the cow, the gift of some hundred cows, or we suppose, some lakhs of cows will atone for his guilt."[23]

Five years after Shripat's case, a Poona Brahmin who suffered social boycott for having lived in the same house as an untouchable woman was restored to caste by Brahmins after receiving a substantial gift in the form of money. Those Brahmins, who did not have shares in the booty, were angry at this. It proves

23. The *Bombay Guardian*, 13 June 1851.

that religion and custom were utilised by Brahmins for selfish ends. Such abominable practices had a tremendous effect on Jotirao's mind and loaded the guns of his revolt against priestcraft and Brahminism. Both these cases were hotly discussed in Poona.

The missionary influence and exertions had by now swept the first educated generation off their feet. In 1831 the rage among the students against religion had reached its climax. The students at the Hindu College at Calcutta became bolder and expressed their hatred of Hinduism. Some wrote parodies on the holy *mantras*, and broke their sacred threads. A wild band of the boys feasted on roast-beef and flung the fragments into a Brahmin's house. This reckless gesture filled all Hindus with horror.[24]

Sensible and patriotic men of liberal views were seeking a way out to reintroduce into society those who hated Hinduism but did not actually embrace Christianity. So they established a society at Calcutta in August 1852 for the deliverance of Hindu apostates. Its object was to reclaim for society, on the performance of certain ceremonial rites required by the *shastras*, those young men who by the evil counsels and wiles of the missionaries might become Christians.[25]

Although impressed by the missionary ideals of service, love, brotherhood, Jotiba had not come yet in closer contact with the missionaries who, in spite of their devoted and inspiring services in the sacred cause of Indian education and enlightenment, harboured dangerous designs of proselytisatiqn. He was moving in the field of education. This could not have escaped his notice. The primary object of the missionary, said Lord Elinborough, was proselytism. A missionary gave education, he observed, because by giving education he hoped to extend Christianity. Lord Elinborough warned the Court of Directors that aiding the missionary schools was not only a danger to the success in education alone, but to the peace of the Empire.[26]

It is well known how Macaulay, the first author and organiser of the educational policy of India in 1835, expected in India

24. The *Bombay Guardian*, 3 September 1852.
25. The *Bombay Guardian*, 24 September 1852.
26. Lord Elinborough quoted in the Report of the Director of Public Instruction, 1857-58, pp. 11 and 12.

the emergence of "a class Indian in blood and colour, but English in tastes, in opinions, in morals and in intellect."

On October 12, 1836, Macaulay wrote to his father that "the effect of this education on the Hindoos is prodigious. No Hindoo, who has received an English education, ever remains sincerely attached to his religion. Some continue to profess it as a matter of policy; but many profess themselves pure Deists, and some embrace Christianity. It is my firm belief that, if our plans of education are followed up, there will not be a single idolater among the respectable classes in Bengal thirty years hence."[27]

27. Trevchan, Sir George Otto, *The Life and Letters of Lord Macaulay*, pp. 329-30.

CHAPTER VI

An Attempt on Jotirao's Life

THE SCHOOLS set up by Jotirao gradually made progress. He did his utmost to provide the pupils with proper equipment. What his schools had attained contained a pledge of still greater progress in times to come. The female pupils of his schools were publicly examined on Saturday, the 12th February 1853. At four o'clock the sight presented was a very interesting and animating one. The quadrangle had been prepared for the occasion, carpeted and with sofas and chairs properly arranged. It was filled with the most respectable persons of the European and Indian communities while the surrounding verandahs were occupied, on one side, by the girls of different schools and on the other by the students of Poona College. The windows of the College looking over the quadrangle were crowded with heads, and a vast multitude had collected outside Poona College. It was the largest meeting ever known in Poona; the number of persons in the quadrangle, during the afternoon, could not have been less than 3,000, and there was a still larger number outside.

Among those present were Brigadier Trydell, Mrs. Trydell. E. C. Jones, Mrs. Jones (Patroness of the Schools), Major Candy, Principal of Poona College, Prof. Fraser, Sardar Appasaheb Dhamdhere, Prof. Kero Luxman, Prof. Krishnashastri Chiplunkar, Jagannath Sadashivjee, Bapoo Raojee Mande and others.

Bapurao Mande then read the Annual Report on the state of female education in Poona. Before entering into details regarding the seminaries, whose purpose was to emancipate the fair section of the natives of the country from the bonds of ignorance and superstitions, he took a rapid review of their establishment and growth.

"Impressed with the necessity and importance of female education to the cause of improvement, progress, and enlightenment of their countrymen and resolved to make a beginning," the Report observed, "a few educated natives established in July 1851, the first Girls' School in Poona. The timely liberality of the Honourable Sir Erskine Perry, that philanthropic and disinterested friend of the Hindus, whose departure from India is universally regretted, enabled them not only to provide it with what was indispensably necessary to its success, but also to establish another school immediately. The number of girls under tuition at the time of the last annual examination, which took place on February 17,1852, amounted to upwards of 50. The progress then exhibited by the girls, who had attended the schools since their foundation, was far greater than that made in any of the Boys Schools during the same period, and called forth unqualified commendation of the exertions of the teachers."

"Suffice it to say," the Report proceeded, "and we say it with pride and pleasure, the Government took notice of the disinterested and patriotic exertions that are made, and at a public meeting held in this Hall but a short time ago, presented a pair of shawls to Joti Govindrao, to whom and to his colleagues Keshavrao, Jagannathjee and Anna, the first Girls' School owes its foundation."

"Some opposition was at first apprehended from a few native gentlemen, who took a wrong view of the change sought to be effected by female education in the condition of the females of this country. But this was put down, in some measure, by the independent spirit of the founders and friends of the schools and much more by the lively interest taken in them by many gentlemen and ladies, whose liberal support and frequent visits, made the enemies of these schools afraid of injuriously interfering with them."

"The prejudices against teaching girls to read and write, which is all the natives understand by education, began to give way to the general desire of mothers to get rid, during the time of work, of the annoyance of their little ones, which was very easily done by sending them to school. The good conduct and honesty of the peons attached to the school, in conveying the girls, who are generally loaded with ornaments, to and from school, removed every obstacle in the way, and really parental treatment and indulgent attention of the teachers, made the girls love the schools, and literally run to them with alacrity and joy."

Narrating the difficulties that came in the way of female education, the Report further said that most of the girls ceased to attend in consequence of their marriage and the whims and caprices of their fathers-in-law and mothers-in-law. Women did not permit their daughters-in-law to receive education.

"It will thus be seen," the Report concluded, "that the custom of early marriage offers the strongest opposition to female educa¬tion in this country, and it is of the utmost importance to do something by which the evils arising from this custom may be lessened and removed. The committee, therefore, propose introducing into the schools under their management the system of stipendiary scholarships, to induce the poor parents, or fathers-in-law and mothers-in-law, to allow their little girls to attend the schools. This is, however, a particular remedy."

Annasaheb Chiplunkar, who took a keen interest in the female education and had been bold enough to provide accommodation to a girls' school in his own house, made a vigorous speech in Marathi on the occasion, on the importance of female education. The Hindus thought it contrary to their religious faith that women should study religion and receive education and be respected on an equal footing with men. They cited authorities from ancient scriptures, he observed, which prohibited women from educating themselves and from aspiring to equal status with men. Blind obedience or servile submission to the husband was the mission of their life. This was a wrong notion. It was the speaker's belief that education would help them to perform their domestic duties efficiently and enable them to bring up and look after the welfare of their children in the proper way.

Annasaheb then thanked all the guests, especially Sir Erskine Perry, Ex-Chief Justice of the Supreme Court, Bombay, and Pre-sident of the Board of Education, who donated before his de parture for London a sum of Rs. 50, and J. G. Lumsden, Secretary to Government, and Brown, Judge, who gave a present of Rs. 100 each. The Secretary was happy and the number of girls in the three schools 'was about 275 as against 90 the previous year. The Dakshina Committee paid a grant of Rs. 75 a month, he added.

Chiplunkar said that it was a matter of shame for him to observe that Europeans donated generously to the cause of female education in India while educated and prosperous Hindus did not give any thought to the question. They would be punished by God for this neglect. They should help the cause of female education in the interests of their grand-children and great-grand-children.

Major Candy requested Prof. Fraser to thank the ladies for the trouble they had taken in attending the function. Prof. Fraser said: "In the efforts now made by the Government, the missionaries, and the natives themselves, in the cause of female education, we see the day-spring of India's social elevation and permanent civilization. You are not insensible to the inevitable blessings, personal and social, which education has conferred on you; nor need you be ignorant of the grand fact that the progress of human civilization has only kept pace with the progress of female education and that the elevation of your sex is intimately and essentially associated with the elevation of the race. The degeneration of woman among the ancients accounts, in fact at least, for the instability of early civilization. It is impossible for society to be permanently elevated whose woman is debased and servile."[1]

II

The annual examination of Jotirao's Low Caste Schools was also held on March 21, 1853. "The public examination of the Poona low caste male and female school," said a writer in the newspaper, "founded by the zealous and benevolent Joti Govindrao Phooley, was held in the court of the late Peshwa's Taleemkhana, Peit Shukrawar, on Monday morning, the 21st March 1853 at 7 o'clock. A large and most respectable audience assembled even at that early hour to witness the results of Jotirao's educational efforts among the low caste children."[2]

"Among the European and native ladies and gentlemen, we observed Mrs. Trydell, the wife of Brigadier Trydell, Mrs. Collurn, Judge Keays, Asstt. Judge Lloyd, Major Candy, Principal of the Poona College, Rev. J. Michell, Missionary, J. Keith, Esquire, M.D., Civil Surgeon of Poona, Captain H. Gillmore,

1. Printed Report attached to G.D. Vol. 27 of 1853, pp. 1 to 10.
2. The *Bombay Guardian*, 16 December 1855.

Aide-de-Camp to General James, Professors Frazer, Nilkant Shastri and Kero Laxman of the Poona College, the Principal Sardar Amin, Annasaheb Chiplunkar, Anna Sahasrabuddhe, Wamanrao Paranjpey, Sadashiv Ballal Govande, Moro Vithal Walvekar, Sakharam Yeshwant Paranjpey, Babajee Manaji Dhengale, Krishnajipant Saranjame and others. Judge Keays presided over the function."

On behalf of Jotirao Phooley his statement was read on the occasion by his colleague Wamanrao Paranjpey in which Jotirao had traced the history of the growth and development of his schools.

Jotirao was scrupulous in maintaining the accounts of the schools. He gratefully mentioned a list of the noble donors of whom several were Europeans in high offices who had taken an active interest in the education of the low caste schools. For want of funds, he observed, the schools could not make the desired progress.

"The principal subjects taught in these schools were reading and writing, writing to dictation, and grammer, geography of the world generally and India particularly, and history of the Mahrattas."

Owing to the exertions of Lowjeebin Rangaroot Mang and Ranba Mahar in collecting children, liberal donations and subscriptions from several charitable gentlemen, Government aid through the medium of the Dakshina Prize Committee, and above all owing to the blessings of God, this school, he observed, through innumerable difficulties had gone on doing good, good up to that day, and humbly prayed to God to grant it success in future also.

"I am greatly obliged to all the ladies and gentlemen well-wishers of the natives for their help and also for having honoured this meeting with their presence. I doubt not that the conviction thus communicated of the appreciation of their education by the ladies and gentlemen here assembled will furnish with a great motive to those children to be still more assiduous in their studies. I hope the day will soon come when they will themselves pray God for their benefactors."

In those days topmost officials paid visits to schools and encouraged the teachers with a view to promoting the cause of education. John Warden. President of the Board of Education, paid a visit in the last week of June 1853 to the female schools started by Jotirao under the auspices of the society. The schools had earned fame. "When I visited the first girls' school with its female teacher," he said, "it was a small school established by stealth; but now you have these schools. The total number of girls whose names are borne on the rolls is 237 and the average attendance in the three schools is 200." "That time," Warden observed, "we heard stories of one girl having read herself blind, and of another who had died from the effects of study." "There are," Warden added, "at the Presidency eight girls' schools, of which three are Marathi, one Gujarati and four Parsi, the total number of girls being five hundred. We have no official returns of the girls' schools in the mofussil, they are principally at Poona and Ahmedabad and may be roughly estimated at 500."[3]

About this time Sardar Amin Rao Sahib Krishnarao Vinchurkar was praised publicly for his courageous and exemplary act in sending his daughter to the girls' school. "It is gratifying," observed the *Dnyanodaya* joyfully, "to see men of his standing thus practically exerting their influence in favour of female education. A few years ago such a person would have been thought insane, had the report obtained credence among the people that he had sent his daughter to school. But a brighter day is dawning."[4]

Shortly after, a meeting of the Society for the Education of low-caste Hindus was held on September 10, 1853. Jotirao held that there was no other work of greater interest and importance than the promotion of education among the Mahars and Mangs. Jotirao therefore had placed the school under a Society so as to bring more energy and aid to the task.

Speaking at the meeting, Sadashiv Govande said that because of their colossal ignorance his countrymen had sunk into superstitions and slavery. Ignorance was, he observed, a dangerous disease and it must be rooted out by the proper medicine. It was in the fitness of things that it should be begun with dispelling the ignorance of the lowest classes, who were the worst victims of the caste system and suffered untold hardships. The

3. The *Dnyanodaya*, 15 April 1855.
4. The *Dnyanodaya*, 2 May 1853.

meeting terminated after Jotirao had led the prayers. Nothing was more praiseworthy than thus to seek to enlighten the ignorant and elevate the degraded, observed the *Dnyanodaya*, paying aglowing tribute to Jotirao for his unrelenting struggle and noble aims.

Jotirao's success was now becoming an eye-sore to some Poonaites. The *Dnyanaprakash*[5] a moderately reformist journal jn social matters, sincerely paid its meed of praise to Phooley for his role, sacrifice and zeal in the field of education. It, however, said with some acerbity that Phooley was well aware the *Dnyanaprakash* generally believed with most that the higher castes under the influence of Brahmins had deprived the low castes of education and wealth. It regretted, however, that Brahmins alone were represented as the foremost party to it. It was no use repeating those views any longer. But such being the case it was necessary on the part of Phooley to praise in his report all persons, especially the Brahmins, for whatever assistance they had rendered him.

A few colleagues of Jotirao were Brahmins and they courageously and unselfishly supported him, and their names were mentioned, for they were office-bearers in the institution he founded. Jotirao's growing popularity was the source of this taunt by the *Dnyanaprakash.*

H. W. Reeves, then Revenue Commissioner, Southern Division, announced a donation of Rs.15 per mensem for the schools of Mahars and Mangs. It can be seen from this that Jotirao's work for the low castes was appreciated more by the liberal Europeans than by his compatriots, barring a few colleagues who stood by him till his death. The Europeans generously contributed towards the fund for the low caste schools. Excepting Jotirao's Brahmin colleagues, the native educated and well-to-do men contributed poorly. The Lokahitawadi paid a subscription of Rupee one per mensem, Professors Krishnashastri Chiplunkar and Kero Luxman Chhatre paid four annas each per miensem.

Naturally, overwhelmed by the appreciation and assistance given by the Europeans, Jotirao mentioned their names gratefully in his Report and many were irritated at this. So even

5. The *Dnyanaprakash*, 5 December 1853.

after twenty years Jotirao wrote in his fiery book Slavery: "I shall never forget the assistance H. W. Reeves, Revenue Commissioner, rendered to the schools. He not only rendered financial help but also visited off and on the Mahar Mang schools, made inquiries about the progress made by them and struggled hard to encourage them in every way. Low caste people will be under his everlasting obligations which it would not be possible for them to repay. I am exceedingly grateful to various other Europeans who helped me in the spread of educa¬tion among the Mahars and Mangs."[6]

Notable personalities were being attracted to Jotirao's school for the low castes. It was considered an epoch-making event in India. Moro Waman Dhamdhere, a Munsiff from Tarapore, District Thana, paid a visit to the school in June 1853, accompanied by Tatyasaheb Bhide, a lawyer in the employ of Maharaja Scindia, and Appasaheb Chiplunkar, a rich landlord of Poona Dhamdhere was mightily pleased with the progress of the students and sent a sum of Rs. 5 as a gift. The visitors highly praised Jotirao for his great humanitarian and patriotic work. The newspapers gave publicity to such visits and asked wealthy men to emulate their examples.

III

Moro Vithal Walvekar, Secretary to the Society for Promoting the Education of Mahars and Mangs, applied on December 16, 1853, to the Governor of Bombay, Rt. Hon'ble Viscount Falkland, for a plot of land and for money to build a school house on it. Taking into consideration, Walvekar stated, "the distressing circumstances of the Mahar and Mang School, the Governor should grant a sum of money to the society sufficient to build a school room that would accommodate about 150 boys and 100 girls and direct the Collector of Poona to make over to it a suitable plot of land for its erection."[7]

The Governor was of the opinion that every encouragement should be given to the society formed for the improvement of Mahars and Mangs which he was happy to observe had a native for a secretary while another native had established the school.

6. Phooley, J. G., Slavery (Marathi), p. 167.
7. G.D. Vol. 22 of 1854, p. 63, and G.D. Vol. 38 of 1858, p. 181.

therefore sanctioned a plot of land known as Trimbakji s Dengla's Tophkhana for the erection of the proposed school house. In May 1854 he asked the Collector of Poona to advance Rs. 5,000 in case that amount was not available from the Dakshina Prize Fund. Eventually, as the chief executives in the departments concerned were not keen on the education of Mahars and Mangs the amount remained unpaid, but a plot of six acres and 33 *gunthas* was made over to the Society early in 1857. The place was known as Bhokarwadi where the school stood for years.

By now the policy of Government as regards the education of Untouchables had undergone a change. The Court of Directors in their Memorial Despatch of 1854 which is called Woode's Despatch, declared that "no boy be refused admission to the Government school or college on the ground of caste". Woode's Despatch has been hailed as the great educational charter. So far the Government had not allowed the Untouchables to share in the blessings of education. In August 1855 certain inhabi¬tants of Ahmednagar prayed for the establishment of a school for the education of the low castes. Accordingly, in November 1855, Government opened there a school. "It is the first occasion," said the Report of the Board of Education, "on which we have established a school for these castes."

Thereafter, in June 1856, the Headmaster of the Government High School at Dharwar refused admission to a Mahar boy, and after much correspondence on this issue between the Government of Bombay and the Government of India the latter said that the boy would not have been refused admission to any Government school in the Presidency of Bengal. The Court of Directors in London passed an order on the subject saying that "the educational institutions of Government are intended by us to be open to all classes."[8] The Government of Bombay, which, for the sake of a few individuals, was always afraid to interfere with the prejudice of ages, was brought to its senses, and it declared that "all schools maintained at the sole cost of Government shall be open to all classes of its subjects without distinction."[9]

8. Report of the Director of Instruction for the year 1856-57, p. 88.
9. Report of the Director of Instruction for the year 1856-57, p. 93.

These circumstances show the magnitude and complications of the problem Jotirao had handled heroically and unselfishly. On the one side lay an unsympathetic Government afraid to interfere in the education of the low castes and on the other were men of the upper classes who opposed female education and were against the education of the low castes.

Most of Jotirao's colleagues were Brahmins. They humanely and courageously stood by him. Jotirao was a social revolutionary in the true sense of the word. So he stood unflinchingly for the rights of the poor peasants and the landless low castes. His aim was to re-build a society in which this vast population would enjoy all human rights. A Whig was a liberal who stood for greater social and political reforms. But 'was any king in England a Whig? Kind Brahmins took pity on the Untouchables, as did the saint-poet Eknath some three hundred years earlier.

Jotirao's colleagues were motivated by humanitarian ideals as were the English humanitarians of their age. But a humanitarian may not necessarily cherish a love for social and religious equality. This was the difference between Jotirao and his benevolent colleagues. A man who inwardly clings to the idea of superiority of his high caste over others, from which he derives social prestige, privileges and power, cannot be a social revolutionary. Socially, a Brahmin cannot be a social revolutionary, barring some brilliant individual examples of great men, just as a British king cannot be a socialist by instinct. Jotirao wanted to impart education in such a way that the lower classes would be prepared to fight for their rights of liberty and equality. At this time, some differences of opinion appeared to have arisen between them on the content and nature of education to be imparted to low caste children. The girls' schools started by Jotirao were running smoothly under the management of the committee. He was also required, he observes, for certain reasons to place the schools for the Mahars and Mangs under a committee.

Now that Jotirao had placed all the schools under societies, in the conduct of these schools the will of the majority came to prevail. Jotirao's colleagues did not like the interpretations he put on the holy *puranas*, scriptures and history and were afraid these would filter down to the lower caste pupils. He bitterly exposed the motives ot the makers of laws and social injunctions. The matter was discussed at some meetings and many differences came to the surface. A large majority of his colleagues favoured only instruction in the three R's for the low castes, whereas Jotirao insisted that they should be imparted such an education as would give them knowledge of what was right and what was wrong. He wanted them to fight for their rights and be able to guard their interests. If, by the tolerance and kindness of the British, they became educated, Jotiba's colleagues thought, the low castes would denounce those who had heaped insufferable disabilities on them for ages and would side with the British rulers. Whether or not this fear was in their minds while they were considering the question of the education of the low castes, Jotirao says, he was not sure.

For these reasons Jotirao says that he decided to withdraw gradually from these societies. The schools were now well-established. Moreover the question of earning a livelihood was pressing hard on him. Both Jotirao and his wife had been serving the schools without any remuneration, nobly and selflessly. He passed some years fully engrossed in this work, which demanded close and unremitted attention. His father had driven him out of his house and he now felt the need of a job. He accepted the post of a teacher in a Scottish Missionary school in Poona. It was a female boarding school started in July 1854 in the compound of the Mission. The institution consisted of an orphanage, or home for destitute children, and a boarding school for the female children of converts whose parents could not rightly or fully train them and such other children over whom the mission could exercise a control.

The report on the working of these schools observes: "At present we have 13 boarders. During the day they are joined in their lessons by 40 day-scholars. We have been happy in securing the aid in their instruction (for nearly four hours a day), of one of the most zealous and accomplished teachers in Poona— Jotee Govind Rao Phooley—a native philanthropist whose persevering efforts on behalf of the education of females and of the low castes, have called for the warmest commendations of the Board of Education and of Government itself. He has fulfilled our highest expectations; the progress of the girls has been most satisfactory."[10] Jotirao was running also a tailoring shop which was managed by a servant. Besides, in her leisure hours Savitribai, with the assistance of some maidservants, used to make thick quilts for sale. Jotirao, who had now grown a beard, would visit his father occasionally, but he was not yet fully reconciled to him.

IV

The Brahmins deteriorated yet more feverishly from their sub¬lime height of fidelity to the scriptures and were now introducing garbled versions of the Puranas, and manufacturing new ones. The story of Satyanarayan was one of their newly created myths, a new god used to exploit the ignorance of the poor classes. So, with a view to breaking the shackles of the mental slavery of the Shudras, Jotirao made another attack on their superstitions. He wrote in the year 1855 a drama called *Tritiya Ratna*, exposing the claims and beliefs expressed in the Puranas in the name of God. It depicts how a Brahmin priest on his rounds in the village tells a farmer's wife who is pregnant that her coming child would be a danger to her husband. She takes fright at the prediction. He consoles saying that the danger can be warded off if he offers up prayers and makes intercession for the family. She consents. While the prayers and feasts are going on at the house of the farmer, a Christian missionary steps in. A debate ensues. The cunning of the Brahmins is exposed. The conclusion is that knowledge is better than worship of idols.

The farmer and his wife are advised to attend the Night School which Jotirao had started at his house for adults. Jotirao and his wife imparted free education to farmers and their wives at their house in the night for two hours a day.

Jotirao submitted this drama to the Dakshina Prize Committee, which of course rejected it. The drama was opposed, Jotirao said, by the Brahmin members who dominated the Dakshina Prize Committee. This committee, he expressed much later his opinion on it, was the younger sister of the Poona Municipality. Neither institution cared to light the path of the Shudras and to serve their cause.

10. *Oriental Christian Spectator*, February 1855.

Those who had received Western education were not held much in respect in those days by the general orthodox population. Jotirao had terribly shocked them by his innovations, such as female education and low caste education and now by accepting a teacher's post in a missionary school. Any man who said that Hinduism and Hindu customs or traditions should be reexamined was condemned in those days as a Christian. "When a Hindy says anything," observes a writer, "against his own religion or finds fault with it in the least, people at once without any consideration call him a missionary or a worshipper of Christ. But I do not perceive what necessary connection there is between finding fault with his own religion and becoming a disciple of Christ. Why not say, that he has become a Mohamedan? It would seem that they call him a Christian because of his studying English."[11]

The times were so difficult for educated Hindus that even a slight sign of an innovation or a deviation on their part would bring on criticism or excommunication. For example, somebody told young V. N. Mandlik's father[12] that he had become a reformer. His father, an orthodox Brahmin, shuddered at this news and so asked his son what that word "reformed" implied. In those days a reformer meant a man whose conduct was not regulated by strict, obstinate traditions. But by reform young Mandlik meant research into religion for restoring it to its pristine purity. At such a time Poona, the stronghold of Brahmins, was naturally enraged at Jotirao's conduct which they condemned as debunking and sacrilegious. Hot heads among the reactionaries planned to put an end to Jotirao's life. They hired two men, one Ramoshi named Rode and the other Dhondiram Namdeo Kumbhar, both low-caste men, to achieve their ends.

These two men entered Jotirao's house at dead of night with naked swords in their hands. He turned over in his bed. The sound of the intruders' steps and some whispers fell on his ears. He was started up out of his sleep and was soon fully awake. He sat erect as he saw in the dim light of the metal-lamp two dim figures. "Who is there?" "Who are you?" inquired Jotirao, getting up. The flame of the lamp was brightened. Terrified,

11. The Dnyanodaya, April 1849.

12. Havaldar, G. R., *Biography of Raosaheb V. N. Mandlik* (Marathi), p. 280.

his wife stood, baffled, bewildered by his side. "We have come to finish you," blurted out the Ramoshi. "We are sent to put you to death," growled the other. "What for? Have I wronged you in any way?" he asked with great poise and composure. He raised his voice a little and repeated, "Have I sinned against you?" "You have done nothing to us. Certain men have set us on you," came the answer. "Do you gain anything by this?" asked the man of the people with calmness. "We have been promised one thousand rupees each," came back the reply. "If you are to be profited by my death, here is my head before you! It is my glorious fortune that the poor men I have served and loved to serve should cut my throat. Hurry up! My life is for the poor. After all the poor are benefited even by my death!"

He was prepared to die for the benefit of the poor! The benefactor's presence awoke the god in the conscience of his murderers. They saw his face glowing with equanimity and resignation, betraying neither pain nor anxiety of any kind. They came to themselves. They fell at his feet in reverence and exclaimed, "Permit us, oh! Tatyasaheb, to go and put your ill-wishers to death." Jotirao was a godly man, a real saint walk¬ing the earth. He ordered them not to utter a word to anybody of what had happened, nor to harbour any ill-feelings or ideas of revenge against the men who had hired them. He said: "They did not know what they were doing. Let them live long!" Pardon is the most glorious kind of revenge.

But the two men who had come to murder Tatyasaheb—Jotirao was now called by this name by his people—became his de¬votees. They joined Jotirao's Night School. The Mang became his body-guard, and the Kumbhar, Dhondiram Namdeo, became a Pandit. Afterwards, Dhondiram became a pillar of the Satya-Shodhak Samaj, wrote some books, and preached its message. On the title page of his famous book Vedachar is the following:

"Satya Shodhak Samaj—*Vedachar* by S. S. Pandit Dhondiram Namdeo Swami of Jest Shrengari Kudalgi and S. S. of S. Shankaracharya's estate, and printed and published by Laxman Rao Gopal Rao Savant for the information of the backward class."

CHAPTER VII

On Indian War and Hindu Widow

THE SCHOOLS for the low castes worked smoothly. The Dakshina Prize Committee, some natives and many European gentlemen supported them. No low caste boy was charged a fee. Books and slates were given gratis. There were four Brahmin teachers and two low-caste. Jotirao's name is mentioned as founder in the report of the Director of Public Instruction for the year 1855-56. On August 29, 1856, the schools were examined publicly, when H. W. Reeves presided. After this Jotirao's interest in the girls' schools slackened. It was found that there were no girls in the low caste schools. There were eight teachers and about 300 pupils on the rolls of whom some belonged to other castes.

A rebellion broke out on May 10, 1857, for the overthrow of British rule in India, and soon it assumed the proportion and magnitude of a War of Independence. In Maharashtra proper there were some stray incidents. The Poona Brahmins of Bajirao II who mustered strong at Poona for gifts were taking things lying down. The prominent leaders of the revolution were Maharashtrians though the fields of battle were outside Maharashtra.

The Crimean war had left an impression on the minds of Indians that the English were not invincible. The conquest of the Punjab was the work of Indian troops. Dalhousie who unified and modernized India by cutting her off from her medieval moorings, pulled down some Indian States through the doctrine of lapse and loaded with hatred the guns of Princely India, which was seething with discontent and revenge. A belief caught the imagination of the common man that a century of English rule was about to come to an end.

The spark, however, was ignited by the growing fear among the sepoys of the christianization of India when it was rumoured that cartridges were greased with cow's and pig's fat, the cow sacred to the Hindus and the pig hateful to the Muslims. The support of Sir Salar Jung, Minister of the Nizam, the passivity of the Sikhs and the hostility of Nepal to the revolutionary leaders saved the Indian empire for the British. The English won by the skin of their teeth. On the fall of Delhi in 1857, the Governor of Bombay telegraphed to the Resident at Hyderabad: "If the Nizam goes, all is lost." "Had the Nizam openly avowed sympathy," said Colonel Briggs, "the whole of southern India would have been in a blaze," for the British. When Salar Jung visited England in June 1876 he was hailed there as the 'saviour of Indian empire'.[1]

Jotirao was firm in his' convictions. Because the Hindus were divided by caste system, he seemed to have thought, there was disunity and lack of real patriotism. And, therefore the British had succeeded in imposing their rule on India. He was not sympathetic but apathetic towards the revolutionary struggle that was raging all over northern India for the overthrow of British power. Yet, because of his patriotic antecedents and independent spirit of mind, he was shunned during the days of this rebellion by European friends and admirers. They must have watched his activities with no little suspicion. Since that time Jotirao resolved not to visit Europeans except on invitation, and later he never sought interviews with them.[2]

The response of Jotirao to the failure of the revolutionary war was not that of a patriot. He breathed a sigh of relief when the revolt led by Nanasaheb was suppressed. An agonizing fear had seized his mind. If Nanasaheb succeeded, Brahmin rule would have been again established in Maharashtra, and serious social and religious restrictions would have been imposed on non-Brahmins as had been done during Peshwa rule. "British rule is there today," Jotirao remarked, "it may not be there tomorrow. It may not even outlast us. Nobody can be sure about its permanency. But as long as it is there, the lower classes should educate themselves and release themselves from the age-long thraldom of Brahmins, which had kept them bound with ignorance and deprived them of social and personal and human dignity."[3]

It was Jotirao's firm belief that the existing rule was favourable

1. *Indian Statesmen,* G. A. Natesan and Co., Madras, p. 10.
2. Phooley, J. G., *Slavery* (Marathi), pp. 155-59.
3. Phooley, J. G., *Slavery* (Marathi), pp. 155-59.

to social reform and progress. Two decades later, G. G. Agarkar,[4] a leading figure in the social reform movement, too, said that the existing times were favourable for social reforms. God was merciful, he thought, to the Shudras that He frustrated the attempts of Nanasaheb Peshwa.

Jotirao did not help the British either. He was aloof, lonely, believing that the rebels would not succeed as he seemed to think that it was not a war of the people. Southern India was partly indifferent, partly lukewarm and in Poona not a Brahmin rose in revolt. Jotirao did not believe, it seems, that good Govern¬ment is no substitute for self-Government. Frankly and boldly, he preferred British rule to Brahmin rule. He had such a dread and hatred of Brahmin rule that he totally failed to look at the revolution from a broader angle which even the *Bombay Times* described as 'a deadly national rebellion'.

Revolution is a vehicle of change, as is a social or religious movement. With it come new values and new ideals. Jotirao was not a political thinker. Vishwanath Kashinath Rajwade, Maharashtrian historian, expressing his views on this rebellion which aimed at the overthrow of British power, opined that the men of that generation were incapable of realising the significance of the great struggle; therefore, there was no question of their joining this or that party. Rajwade condemned the leaders of that generation as worthless men who were a disgrace to the society and nation! At the same time he branded the revolutionary leaders as a brand of thoughtless men who were more of a philosophic and world-negating bent than realistic![5]

The public examination of the Mahar and Mang schools was held at Babaji Munagee's Coal Factory, opposite the Queen's Hostel near the City Hospital, on Tuesday, the 2nd February 1858, in the evening at half past four. A large number of European and Indian gentlemen assembled. C. M. Hajrrison, Judge of Poona, presided. Among the gentlemen assembled were Edwin Arnold, Principal of Poona College, Mrs Arnold, Lt. C. J. Griffith, Inam Commissioner, The Rev. J. Mitchell, Bapu Raoji, Framji Nusserwanji, Annasaheb Chiplunkar, Noolkar and other officials.

4. Agarkar, G. G., Essays, Part I, p. 131.
5. Aitihasik Prastavana (Marathi), p. 356.

A report was read showing the progress made by Mahar and Mang children from September 1856 to January 1858 by the Jt. Secretary Waman Prabhakar. A few advanced scholars of one of the schools were very kindly permitted by the Free Church Missions to attend their English institutions, but from causes which would be tedious to detail, the report said, most of the scholars had discontinued at that seminary. It was also related that in rainy and winter seasons attendance became very precarious as they had no clothes to protect themselves from rain and cold. Scholarships of higher value should be given, and these scholars should be formed into a normal class. An Industrial department should be attached to the schools to teach them useful trades and crafts, to enable them, on leaving school, to maintain themselves comfortably and independently.

"The Government have also sanctioned," observed the Report, "the grant of a liberal sum of Rs. 5,000 for the erection of a new school, the building of which will ere long be commenced. They have also kindly made over to the Society a site to build the school." The war of 1857 had its effect on the European donors of the school. The Report says: "Several European and Native Gentlemen have of late withdrawn their monthly subscriptions and these have fallen so low that it will be the painful duty of the society to shut up at least one of the three schools under their direction."

At a time when the Mahar and Mangs had become alive to the utility of education and were demanding better teachers, the society would have, the Report stated helplessly, to shut up one of the three schools, if benevolent persons did not come forward with a liberal hand and prevent the extreme step.

C. M. Harrison, Judge of Poona, made a very moving speech. Concluding his speech, he said: "The disinterested efforts of the Founder of these schools and of the native gentlemen who are acting with him and who form the committee are, I consider, worthy of all praise. They have my entire sympathy and they shall have all the countenance and support it is in my power to afford them."

This reference to Jotirao by the judge testifies to the fact mentioned by Jotirao in his statement submitted to the Hunter Commission: 'I continued to work in them (schools) for nearly nine or ten years and that I and my wife worked together for many years.'[6]

Jotirao finally withdrew himself from these societies when they were properly established, and when the cleavage between the committee and him widened. The Dnyanodaya was sorry that the natives of Poona were not helping the schools. It noted with regret that the Europeans had ceased helping the schools and added that it was a disgrace to the liberal and patriotic men of Poona that they were not helping the schools.

The Director of Public Instruction, however, held the view that a different kind of teaching was required for the low castes and as he wished to have one individual school in every district for the benefit of those who found book-learning above them and useless, he concluded in his Report on these schools: "My views on the subject have been confirmed by witnessing the signal failure of the Mahar and Mang schools, in Poona, from which Government aid was withdrawn a year ago."[7]

The school house could not be built as the money sanctioned by Government could not be secured, either on account of the downward trend and tone of the schools, or the dwindling interests of the committee. Sadashivrao Govande became the first General Secretary of the Sarvajanik Sabha in 1870, which mainly voiced the political grievances of Maharashtra.

The school met in a cottage on the site which Government had donated. Later, under Resolution No. 5421 of 24th September 1874 the school was transferred on a special grant to the Local Fund Committee and in 1894 Government, under Education Department Resolution 1921 of November 13, 1894, ultimately made it over to the Poona Municipality. The other schools continued to work until 1869, when a mention was made in the report of the Director of Instruction for the year 1868-69 as follows: "Four Marathi Girls' schools at Poona which receive a grant from the Dakshina Fund are not prospering."

II

Jotirao's mind was now engaged in another important and vital social reform. A practical reformer, he destroyed all religious

6. *Education Commission, Bombay, Vol. II,* p. 141.
7. Report of the Director of Public Instruction for the year 1861-62, p. 44.

dogmas that were against reason and opened the door to forms. His aim was to reconstruct society on the basis of equality, liberty and reason.

Enlightened by the sparks of Western education and thought India had begun to march with the times and was throwing away her outworn cruel customs and obstinate traditions. Haunted and pressed by a personal grief caused by the death of his brother's wife on the pyre of his brother, Ram Mohun Roy had helped the Government to abolish the practice of Sati. Govern ment put an end to it in 1829. Yet, it seems, the cruel practice had not entirely disappeared until 1852. In the *Telegraph and Courier*, Bombay, news appeared in November 1852, that English officers pulled, at Bhuj, an unfortunate woman off pyre. She was quite willing to be saved; but the attendant Brahmins dragged her back, and on her second attempt to escape they dashed out her brains.

There were many more cruel superstitions yet crying for solution. Exposure of the sick on the banks of the Ganga had been regarded in Bengal as a religious duty and a high proof of the relatives' affection for the dying man. The sick were not allowed to die in peace at home. It was the belief of many that if at the hour of death one thought about the Ganga one would attain a place in heaven. This pernicious custom was no less criminal than Sati, widow-burning, or infanticide of girls. The *Calcutta Review* published the horrifying accounts of these ghat murders which involved crime and distress. The medieval customs of infanticide lingered in some lower sections of Hind society, but British rule put a stop to it.

Superstitious women counted rice or wheat grains day and night till the full measure of one lakh of grains was complete and then the whole thing was offered in worship to God. Wicks of various kinds numbering a lakh were offered to God. To offer grain or seeds devoutly to cows and eat the remnan's which were excreted was a religious act. Brahmin priests would thrive on such superstitions of the people, and a period of such austerities would always end in a costly feast to Brahmins! All these superstitions Jotirao was preparing himself to attack.

The power of Maharashtrian Brahmins, with the loss of thctt| political supremacy, came under a critical review. Under Britis rule their religious and social power began to diminish. In

1827 the Shankaracharya visited Poona and demanded as *dakshina* any amount he chose. Some represented this matter to the British Collector of Poona who ordered that the Shankaracharya should accept what people offered him willingly.[8] During Peshwa rule the Shankaracharya named any amount he pleased for his dakshina. Brahmins, too, were now made amenable to the law. They were now punished even at Kashi where for years together these tiny gods on earth tried to escape punishment before the law.[9]

The new modes of transport, new roads, Western education, railways and transfers of officers to different towns and centres gave a rude shock to the rigidity of old Indian customs and prejudices, and smote hard the old system of joint family, it hegan to crumble. Educated men began to think of having educated girls as their partners. For completing their primary education, girls naturally required some time. So the question of the minimum age for marriage arose. And along with it the question of widow-remarriage, too, pressed for a solution.

Though liberated from self-immolation on the funeral pyre of her husband, the widow faced from her young age widowhood till her death, the cruel tonsure of her head and the unjust laws of inheritance. A sad life, dependable on the head of the family, was her lot ordained by Hindu traditions and customs and the *shastras*.

Down to the ninth century the custom of tonsuring the widow was not in vogue. Only nuns and monks tonsured their heads. Tonsuring gave the widow an ascetic appearance. She was expected to lead a celibate life. So it was necessary to destroy her beauty.

Remarriage of child widows was allowed upto the year 1000. Earlier, widows were allowed to keep their hair but not to oil it. It became general from the year 1200. Originally, the custom of tonsuring was confined to Brahmins, but gradually it spread to the upper classes as a whole, and was prevalent more in northern India than in southern India. Shri Vaishnavas vehemently opposed the custom in southern India.[10]

8. Govande, Dr. V. B., *Trimurti Darshan* (Marathi), p.43.
9. Phatak, Prof. 9. N. R., *Biography of Mr. Justice M. G. Ranade* (Marathi), p. 111.
10. Altekar, Dr. A. S., *Position of Women in Hindu Civilization*, p.188.

The presence of the widow was regarded as a symbol of inauspiciousness. Early in the morning the sight of the widow was shunned as an ill-omen. Nobody would willingly see her face in the morning. She could not walk about freely at home. Regarded as impure, she remained humiliated and ostracised in a corner. She was deprived of her ornaments and was forbidden to dress well or to attend the marriage ceremony even of her own children or the thread ceremony, or any other auspicious function. She would waste away in a dark nook. She became an eyesore even to her parents. They often said that had this unfortunate girl died instead of her husband, they would have given their son-in-law another of their daughters in marriage.

The reformers said that only the marriage locket should be taken away from the widow after her husband's death. Other things such as bangles, hair, the vermilion mark, and the hair-knot which she used in her virgin state, she should retain; she had a right to them.

Poet after poet then sang of the terrible fate of the widows who either perished in utter sorrow and misery in a corner or ended in debauchery with their hands full of crimson blood of the embryos, bringing disgrace upon the families from which their fathers, mothers and husbands sprang.

The propaganda for widow remarriage was started in Maharashtra as early as 1840. By writing a booklet in Marathi on widow remarriage, Vishnushastri Bapat, the pioneer in this field in Maharashtra, championed the cause in Poona. Remarriage of two Brahmin widows took place at Belgaum in 1842. These marriages escaped, however, unnoticed. The Lokahitavadi said that the prevailing condition of widows was unbearable, and setting aside the injunctions of Manu and Yajunavalkya, they should relieve widows from the tragic fate and miserable life. In the last week of October 1853 a meeting of the Hindu community was held at the general assembly institution in Bombay "to consider the advisability of introducing the custom of remarriage of Hindu widows." Over five hundred persons assembled. Gangadhar Appa Shastri was to have presided over the meeting: but he was absent owing to a fear of persecution even though he had advocated the remarriage of widows in his writings. Bhawani Vishvanath occupied the chair in his place. Orthodox Shastris had mustered strong to oppose the reform; and so the meeting broke up after a heated debate.[11]

The Widow Remarriage Act was passed by the Government of India on July 25, 1856. By this Act XV of 1856 any Hindu widow was free to marry if she liked, and her progeny would be looked upon by the law as entitled to succeed to her property as other Hindu children could. England was preparing for the Divorce Act and the British Parliament passed it in 1857. In 1857 the Rev. Baba Padmanji wrote a novel entitled *Yamuna Paryatan.* This first Marathi novel put before the bar of world opinion the sorrows of the Hindu widow.

In 1854 the Shankaracharya decided a case of a young widow, who had morally gone astray. On receiving some money as dakshina, he ordered her father to perform the holy rites by administering him water made pure by bathing his toe in it, and by five products of the cow. When however, the Brahmin asked for the purification of his daughter who was pregnant, the Shankaracharya ordered that the young widow should be kept in the hollow trunk[12] of a tree and the trunk should be burnt all round. Then, if alive, the widow should be tonsured and reclaimed to the society after a feast was given to one thousand Brahmins. Every religious or social rite or ritual prescribed a feast or the distribution of money to Brahmins!

The cruel practice of tonsuring widows long persisted, although it began to break down rapidly in the first quarter of the twentieth century. The story is told of a Brahmin's widowed sister who, in due course, died. As she had not undergone the rites of shaving her head, Brahmins refused to attend her funeral. Barbers would not shave the head of the dead body. So she was consigned to flames by her Shudra neighbours. As late as 1930s, a similar case of a Brahmin widow from Nasik was reported by Anant Hari Gadre, a champion of social equality and annihilation of untouchability in Maharashtra, in his famous weekly, *Nirbhid.* Because the widow had not had her head tonsured during her widowhood, the Nasik Brahmins refused to carry her dead body to the crematorium. They got the

11. The *Bombay Guardian,* 28 October 1853.
12. Phatak, Prof. N. R., *Biography of Mr. Justice M. G. Ranade* (Marathi) pp. 110-11

head of the dead body pitilessly shaved, and then the corpse was carried away and burnt.[13]

III

Although this problem of remarriage of widows was confined to Brahmins and some other high caste Hindus, Jotirao was moved by the miserable condition of the widows, and often by their immoral behaviour. Sometimes they were involved in child murder. A man of flaming indignation against injustice, Jotirao actively supported the movement for widow remarriage. He wanted to liberate the woman from her age-old shackles. The Indian woman was now at the crossroads.

The remarriage of a Shenavi widow took place in Poona on March 8, 1860, with a Shenavi widower. The widow was about eighteen. The *Dnyanprakash*[14] published the news of the widow marriage and stated that it was not necessary for it to express its opinion on it. It is said that Jotirao encouraged the marriage of a Shenvi widow in 1864, and it seems this must be the marriage often referred to. Great reforms are the result of a series of small pioneering efforts.

Later, Vishnushastri Pandit, rightly called the Ishwarchandra Vidyasagar of Maharashtra, resigned his job in 1864 and devoted his life to the cause of widow remarriage. Moved by the tragedies and crimes which sometimes resulted from the misdeeds of widows, Jotirao, a wonderful combination of a dreamer and a man of action, who attached more importance to deeds than words, resolved to found an orphanage where widows would secretly come either for delivery or for keeping their babies. Consequently handbills advertising this bold announcement were pasted on the walls of houses in Poona. They read: "O you widows! come and deliver here safely and secretly. Take your child or leave it here at your sweet will. The orphanage will do the looking after!" This news sent the Poona orthodox wild. They asked one another who its author could be. The reply often was: "Who else can It be! No person except Jotiba. The perfidious villain!" Orthodox Hindus became red in the face the moment they heard Jotirao's name. "It is a disgrace

13. *Nirbhid*, 22 March 1936.
14. The *Dnyanprakash*, 12 March 1860.

the way he is behaving," they said indignantly. Great social changes do not occur accidentally. They are willed by men of action.

This social institution was the first of its kind in India. It was conducted by a non-Brahmin boldly, humanely, benevolently, especially for Brahmin widows, to save them from disgrace, avert the killing of embryos and children, and to save the lives of the widows who often either committed suicide or were involved in criminal proceedings. Although meant for pregnant widows the orphanage was indirectly guided by one great motive. It saved orphans from going over to Christian missionaries.

This time Jotirao formed no committee. He was conducting the orphanage without the help of Government or any Brahmin colleague. His experience in conducting the girls' schools and schools for the low castes under committees composed of Brahmins had burnt his fingers. So he scrupulously avoided placing the orphanage under a committee of Brahmin members. The men who could not save their sisters and mothers from mental tortures and from tonsures were quite unfit, he said, to become members of that Institution. Several widows delivered their children safely in this orphanage. Thus Jotirao became a saviour of the unwilling sinners. The orphanage continued its noble work, and eminent men showed keen interest in it.

Just then Jotirao's father fell ill. Govindrao's other son Rajaram lived with him. He looked after the property, and his household affairs were running smoothly. Yet he was grieved that Jotirao had no child. The old man advised him fervently to marry a second time, so that he might have children. He tried to impress the point through Jotirao's father-in-law. That family also agreed. But when they asked Jotirao to consider their suggestion and insisted that he should respond to it, Jotirao was perturbed. He said that if a pair had no child, it would be unkind to charge a woman with barrenness. It might be that the husband also was unproductive owing to his defects. In that case if the woman went in for a second husband how would her husband take it? Would he not feel insulted and humiliated? According to him, it was a cruel practice for a man to marry a second time because he had no issues from fist wife.

Jotirao lived up to his philosophy. But that was not the case with his generation. Describing the moral condition of generation of Krishnashastri Chiplunkar and pointing to life of this Pandit, Lokamanya Tilak aptly said that the generation of Chiplunkar had made vice[15] fashionable in poona. Jotirao stood head and shoulders above his contemporaries respect of high moral conduct, and so he outlived the dangerious attacks made by the rabid reactionaries. So Jotirao did marry a second time and fulfil his father's desire. His decision came as a sore disappointment to his father. His illness be prolonged, and he died.

Jotirao did perform the obsequies of his father, but not as ordained in the Brahmin *shastras*. In accordance with rational view of life, he performed them. He did not believe in offering lumps of flour to crows as an oblation to the deceased and his ancestors! Instead he stood a dinner to poor, cripple people and distributed books and other articles to students! On the death anniversary of his father, he gave a dinner to poor people and distributed books among poor students.

There were some family bickerings and disputes about property but he refused to fight over them with the family of uncle. Children were the wealth of the nation and the wealth of the nation was his wealth. He looked after them in orphanage. For money he had no love. He tried to live by his own hard work, never leaned on others for his livehood For ages it was the practice of the Shudras who rose to eminence by virtue of their learning or abilities to join the higher da to assimilate themselves with the Brahmins and to forget neglect the class from which they sprang. Almost all India ancient famous saints and seers afford such illustrations. But Jotirao was the only eminent man from the lower classes who had ample opportunities to attain prosperity and to shine in galaxy of the brilliant men of the upper classes, and yet he neither joined them nor made common cause with them. The eduction and welfare of the lower classes absorbed his thoughts.

Jotirao's wife Savitribai looked unflaggingly after the children in the orphanage as if she were their mother. She had no child; but with her kind and generous disposition she tenderly

15. Lokamanya Tilak's articles from the *Kesari*, Part IV, p. 291.

lovingly cherished the infants. It was her practice to invite, from time to time, all neighbouring children to dinner. She was happiest and smiled her sweetest when she was left among children. So dearly she loved children. She would invite her female neighbours to help her to dress and feed the children. For several years she had worked in the girls' school conducted by her husband. One can imagine the significance of her work when one knows that until 1873 a woman's appointment to the post of teacher was noted in leading papers like the *Native Opinion* as a matter of respect and pride.

CHAPTER VIII

Priestcraft Exposed

JOTIRAO HAD so far made a living as best as he could. His income however was not sufficient for his livelihood and to meet the expenses of his different activities. After his father's death, Jotirao thought of augmenting it. Serving the Government was out of question. Service of the people was his aim in life. A man of his education and ability, integrity and industry would have risen high in Government service. But he wanted to earn his living independently. About this time Government had come out with a big project for the building of the Khadakwasala Tank. It was a gigantic construction. Jotirao contracted to supply the Government with stones. Sakharam Yeshwant Paranjpay with whom he had been friends since boyhood, became his partner in this contract. Gyanoba Krishnarao Sasane, son of Jotirao's cousin, helped him in this work.

Jotirao believed in honestly working for his livelihood. Almost the first public man in modern India to devote his time to serving the masses, he never thought of becoming a whole-time public man. He never thought of exploiting public resources for his own purpose or for his followers and at the same time trying to preach the ideal of plain living and high thinking! He cherished no false ideas about sacrifice. A sacrifice that is clad in insufficient clothes but rolls in untold bank balance breeds hypocrisy and corruption in the land.

The year 1860 witnessed a great change. It was in this year that James Wilson's Income-Tax Bill became law on July 24, 1860. He founded India's financial system and established the budget system. And in the immediate 'post-mutiny' years the new construction works were started by the Indian Government as, in the words of a British-owned newspaper: "nothing has been done for public works, nothing for education. The Police has not been reformed, the road system has not been organised, civilisation has not advanced and the administration has not improved."[1]

The contract with Government brought Jotirao into touch with labourers and Government officers, low class servants and especially engineers. A man intensely interested in the welfare of workers and of an upright nature, he guarded the interests of the workers, explained to them their duties, the benefits of education, and the mental slavery imposed on them by the Hindu socio-religious system. He enjoyed the company of the labourers and organised them. He pointed out to them the examples of clerks and high officials working there and said that if their children were educated they, too, would improve their sad lot and lead a better life. Thus in his leisure hours he held discussions with them and sometimes gave lectures to them.

In this situation Jotirao studied for two or three years how corruption was practised by high officials and engineers. He knew well how they made up accounts by showing false attendance of labourers and how they divided the profits among themselves.

The clerks, who were mainly Brahmins, pressed the *mistry* to connive at the false numbers on rolls and the false attendance register. If the mischief came to the notice of any incorruptible officers, they made a scape-goat out of the *mistries*. They utilised for their household work the services of women who were Government servants. They made them cleanse utensils for them. The labourers tended their horses, made their beds, pressed their legs. The clerks asked policemen to visit their houses, took their Brahmin acquaintances and friends with them on the day of payment to receive wages for which they had not worked, and gave their higher officers bribes by regular instalments.

The European high officials, while on duty, often went hunting and returned to their tents at the construction place dead tired. They signed papers in a hurry with full faith in the Brahmin clerks under them, and leaving the work to them, relaxed with glasses of beer and brandy. Soon they dozed off with some newspaper in their hands. They seized the workers poultry and embezzled their money. If there was a shortage in

1. The *Times of India*, 7 August I960.

the treasury they asked the contractor to make good the deficit by adding mud to the construction instead of stones. Jotirao said that he was reminded of Peshwa days where hundreds of the beggar population of Brahmins were fed from the revenue collected from the peasants. Thus these Brahmin clerks and Brahmin supervisors reduced the Kunbis to penury although they toiled endlessly. They themselves earned substantially and resigned their jobs if they were likely to be found out.

Jotirao observed in his songs that what he was narrating was from the experience he had gained in his work. So he suggested to Government that workers from all communities should be selected for employment. If the Government stood for justice and the welfare of all communities it should stop the exploitation of poor labourers.

Jotirao had a consuming hatred of oppression, corruption, nepotism and jobbery. A man of fearless character and spotless life can raise such a hue and cry against these vices which exploit the labourers, defraud Government and undermine national reconstruction. Since Jotirao, Lokamanya Tilak was the only leader who once remonstrated with the Mamlatdars against using unfair means to gain favour and promotions. These two leaders fearlessly attacked corruption in officials, but Jotirao more indignantly and ruthlessly than any other leader in his day.

Jotirao attacked the European officers with equal fury and fire. He attacked the clerks and supervisors under them not because they were Brahmins but because they were corrupt. He did not condemn the whole Brahmin community, but he did condemn these Government servants, as at that time the Brahmins were chiefly and prominently the Government servants, engaged in executing its policy and carrying out its orders. Power breeds corruption. Men with an impartial bent of mind, of integrity and of national character are found in every community. Jotirao knew this. That is why he clamoured for justice for all with malice for none, and praised even a Brahmin if he was impartial, just and honest.

Jotirao, seeing that, if honestly and industriously used, contracts gave him adequate money to conduct his household and to help other people, entered into a new contract with the Government to supply mortar for the construction work of

Yeravada Bridge. There also he gained ample experience and watched the activities of the Government officers and the habits and characteristics of the working classes. He was now thorough¬ly convinced that the employees of the Engineering Department harassed the workers and squeezed as much money as they could out of them.

II

Though he was engaged in the contract business he was now reading in his leisure hours and at night the works of the saint-poets of Maharashtra and works by William Jones and by the Christian missionaries on Indian history and literature, Henry Mead's *Sepoy Revolt*, and several other books. He also accorded his consent to Tukaram Tatya Padval to use his name as publisher of the second edition of his book *Jatibhed Viveksar or Reflections on the Institution* of Caste. Tukaram Tatya, keenly interested in the revolution of social equality, had written that thought-provoking and volcanic book. It shows how Brahmins have managed to preserve the monopoly of learning and leadership and have kept below them the ladder of the descending steps of the caste system. The book reveals how the Brahmins regarded themselves as personifications of superiority-godliness and sacredness on earth, and how, according to the scriptures, however debased a Brahmin was he was to be respected more than any non-Brahmin, howsoever learned, brave or virtuous.

The first edition of Tukaram Tatya's book had been published in August 1861 in the name of Wasudeo Babaji Nowrange as publisher. Distinguished for a life of simplicity, piety and benevolence, Nowrange was exceedingly truthful, and courageous in practising what he preached. He paid all his creditors in London, although his partners in India had asked him to collect their dues and return to Bombay without disclosing the fact of their insolvency to the English businessmen concerned. On his arrival Wasudeorao Nowrange became one of the founders of the Prarthana Samaj and his example illuminated the pages of the history of the Indian social reform movement. A very sincere reformer, he married a widow in 1870. Wasudeorao Nowrange was in London in 1863, doing business. It was through Mama Parmanand that]otirao came into contact with Wasudeorao Nowrange, who secured for Jotirao an agency of mattrices. Jotirao prospered in this business for a number of years.

The author, Tukaram Tatya Padval (1838-1898), was Bhandari by caste. Considering his times, he wrote and spoke Marathi and English well. He had a passion for reading. His father died early and he was adopted by his brother's wife and brought up in Bombay where he had been born. He served in the Railways and in the Walcot company. He was associated with all progressive movements of his times. He had risen himself, in the words of the *Indian Spectator*, from the humblest origin to a position of honour and independence. He was a homeopathic doctor of repute and he conducted a charitable dispensary. His charity was catholic. All classes loved him alike.

Padval's life was, in many ways a standing protest against priestly domination and the iron bonds of caste. He was thoroughly convinced that caste system was the root of all the miseries of the lower classes. Therefore he believed that there was no task more sacred than to wake up the lower classes to their sad lot and to deliver them from the thraldom of the caste system. With that end in view he wrote the book and gave Nowrange's name as publisher of the first edition. The author remained anonymous saying that if he was convinced that his name would add to the prestige of the book, he would reveal it.

As the author, Tukaram Tatya, was a friend of Jotirao, the latter agreed to put his name as publisher of the second edition of the book as no other person came forward to do so. The second edition of the book was published in 1865. Later Tukaram Tatya himself became a famous publisher of several religious books on Hinduism and counter-balanced the propoganda of Christian missionaries in India. He was one of the founder members of the Prarthana Samaj.

The author, Tukaram Tatya, dedicating the book to his countrymen, observed:

"My Countrymen!

I dedicate this essay to you in the hope that it will be of some service to you. If it succeeds in convincing even one of you of the nature and consequence of the system of caste prevailing in Hindu Society, I shall have reason to consider that I have not laboured in vain.

Believe me, as ever,
My dear Countrymen,
Your humble well-wisher,
A Hindu."

"The book is printed and published by Mr. Joti Govindrao Fulle of Poona. 1865. Price—Annas Fourteen."

The name of Jotirao must have acted as fuel to the fire in the book. It was condemned as an outrage on Hinduism. A Poona Brahmin, commenting on the first edition, had said that the author was an enemy of the Hindus under a Hindu roof.

Jotirao agreed to give his name as publisher of the book as the book described how in the name of religion Brahmins shielded their self-interest, their selfishness and their narrowness: how they walled oft and divided Hindu life into narrow and isolated grooves. A note of revolt sounded most clearly behind all Jotirao's work, and he courageously launched this attack against the orthodox and the reactionaries. His aim was to establish a social order on the basis of equality, freedom and reason and the caste system was the negation of these principles.

It seems from an issue of the *Dnyanprakash*, Poona, that a Devrukha Brahmin reader was offended by the account given in the *Jatibhed Vivekasar* of the origin of Devrukha Brahmins. He drew attention to the quotation from *Sahyadri Khand* given in the book with regard to Chitpavan Brahmins.

III

Meanwhile the orphanage continued and men of progressive leanings took a keen interest in it, paying visits to it and appreciating its meritorious mission. In the *Dnyanprakash* it was observed in February 1871 that a benevolent gentleman had built an independent house to shelter the orphans and pregnant widows. Jotirao thus saved the widows from disgrace from persecution by society. Out of the children delivered there a few survived. One of these children was a boy born in 1873 of a Brahmin widow named Kashibai. In his Will Jotirao says that this woman was living in the house of Kesopant Sindi in Ganja Peth. Savitribai had cut his navel string, and Jotirao and his wife had performed the ceremony of naming the boy on the twelfth day after his birth. He was named Yashwant, one who brings success. Savitribai looked after the boy with the care and affection of a mother and brought him up very tenderly. Jotirao and his wife both treated him as their own son.

Men like the Lokahitavadi, Vinayakrao Bhandarkar, trustees of the Prarthana Samaj, Madan Shrikrishna who became judge of the Small Cause Court, Mama Parmanand, Wasudeorao Babaji Nowrange, Tukaram Tatya Padval and others who were deeply interested in all social movements, sincerely appreciated Jotirao's work and held him in high esteem.

On his arrival in Poona in 1871, Ranade became Jotirao s admirer and showed great interest in his social activities. Impressed by Jotirao's significant contribution to society and the success of his orphanage, Ranade and his friend Lalshankar Umiashankar Trivedi established in 1875 such an orphanage at Pandharpur. Because of his angelic heart, Lalshankar was called 'Dev Munsiff'.

The problem of widow remarriage to which Jotirao wanted to give an impetus, was now boldly taken up by Vishnushastri Pandit, who in his student days, had supported Jotirao in his pioneering efforts to promote female education. He was a member of the Committee established by Jotirao to promote education of girls. On his resignation from Government service, Vishnushastri accepted the editorship of the *Indu Prakask.* Like the *Subodha Patrika* of the Prarthana Samaj. it was a mouthpiece of the social reformers. He wrote fiery, thought-provoking articles on the subject, made fervent speeches at important centres in Maharashtra and published a chain of booklets on it.

Vishnushastri at last founded on January 28, 1866, a society for the promotion of widow remarriages whose branches sprang up at Ratnagiri, Ahmedabad, Poona and at other places. Under the auspices of this society the marriage of one Pandurang Vinayak Karmarkar with a widow girl named Venubai, daughter of Prabhakar Bhat Paranjpye, was celebrated amidst pomp and joy. The invitation to the marriage was issued over the signature of seven sage-like men. They were Gopal Hari Deshmukh, the great champion of social reforms, Vishnushastri Pandit, Vishnu Moreshwar Bhide, Shrikrishnashastri Talekar, Vishnu Parashuram Ranade, Mahadeo Govind Ranade and Janardan Sakharam Gadgil. Vishnushastri had deposited in the name of Venubai a sum of Rs. 2.000 out of the funds of the society, and presents worth Rs. 3,000 were showered on the newly-wedded couple.

News of this marriage divided Maharashtra into two camps, and the battle was fought at Poona in 1870. A debate was held to decide the issue of widow remarriage. Both sides fought furiously. But one of the jurors from the camp of the reformers, for fear of persecution, slipped off, and the party of reformers lost the battle by two votes. Afraid of being excommunicated, some of the reformers surrendered to the orthodox. Among those who surrendered was the Lokahitavadi. However, Vishnushastri did not give up the fight. He knew well that reactionaries and tradition-mongers are always in a majority. It is interesting to note that Dr. R. G. Bhandarkar, the eminent Indian scholar, was disqualified on grounds of caste from participating in this debate as a juror, he being a Saraswat Brahmin![2]

Jotirao believed that example is better than precept. Undaunted by the curses of the orthodox, he courageously threw open his own cistern in 1868 to .the low castes. A daring deed indeed! It provoked the orthodox. There was again a stir in the city. A man who had braved so many dangers during his youth was not afraid to face many more in order to promote the cause he so dearly loved. His own castemen threatened him with excommunication. The whole orthodox town condemned him as a Christian; for, only the missionaries did not regard the touch of the Untouchables as a pollution!

Well did the Lokahitavadi write in his famous letters: "The Brahmins hold the Mahars in contempt and will not touch them, but they are willing to associate with the English on the most friendly terms. This is quite astounding when it is considered that according to the Shastras it is less improper to associate

2. Phatak, Prof. N. R., *Biography of Mr. Justice M. G. Ranade*, p. 149.

with Mahars than with the Europeans. But these Brahmins are fools, they will not understand this."[3]

The Lokahitavadi also advised Brahmins that they should not say that a certain man was a Mahar and they would not see his face. The Mahar, wounded by the haughty words of such Brahmins, went straight to the British and said: "The Brahmins are haughty and puffed up. I will punish them.'"

The reason why there were low caste people in British army was that the Brahmins regarded them with contempt, gave them crumbs of food to eat and treated them worse than dogs.[4] The Lokahitavadi was right. Insults beget their own avengers. But the Brahmins never understood this. They simply washed off their sins by saying that the Mahars and Mangs were not patriots! The Lokahitavadi laid down the precepts.

Jotirao was alone in practising what he preached and in giving a lead to Maharashtia. He was fearless, frank, straightforward, selfless and had the boundless moral courage of a maker of history. He could open new paths and achieve success because he was a man of mission and had the courage of his convictions. His opponents were orthodox, but had power, wealth, brains and educated men of their caste on their side. Jotirao had truth, the invincible weapon, on his, and a group of devoted followers and friends. They prided themselves on being associates of a man who was a symbol of plain living and high thinking. He was, in crude way, the living image of the goddess of learning, the incarnation of the soul of the depressed Shudras of the ages gone by.

IV

Jotirao himself published, after some time, a book of ballads, depicting how the Brahmins fleeced the poor classes by making them observe various religious rituals. From the pungent and biting review of the booklet that appeared in the Vividhadnyan Vistar it seems that he was greatly helped in this work by his boyhood friend Vinayakrao Bhandarkar, the Rev. Mr. Baba Padmanji and Gangadharshastri. This was the first little

3. The *Dnyanodaya*, 1 August 1849.
4. Lokahitavadinchi Shatapatre (Marathi), edited by Tikekar, S. R., p.420.

book of ballads which was the result of Jotirao's reading books by early European authors on Indian history and literature. The *Vividhadnyan Vistar* ridiculed the so-called research done by Jotirao. From this stage onwards Jotirao clung to the idea that the Brahmins alone were the Aryans, and they had ruthlessly and cruelly reduced the Kshatriyas, who constituted the Shudras and the Atishudras, to penury and slavery. This became the refrain of all his books, the burden of all his songs.

But Jotirao's attacks on Brahmins, who heartlessly exploited the Shudras. were irrefucable. His writings, have much social content, and he graphically describes the prevailing social milieu. He narrates how the Brahmin teachers of his day deliberately discouraged the low caste pupils or frightened the low caste pupils into leaving schools; how the Brahmin Educational Inspectors supported Brahmin teachers by submitting false reports to the effect that the poor classes had no liking for education.

Jotirao exposes the doings of Kulkarnis, the village accoun¬tants, and those of other officers who were all without exception Brahmins. They were in league with Brahmin clerks and with revenue officers like Mamlatdars who all worked under British officers. These Brahmin officers sometimes cheated their British officers by omitting, while reading the complaints or the cases to them, the main statement of facts or arguments from the peasants' letters or applications! Thus the administration of law was partial and unjust, full of malpractices and corruption. The patil, the village police officer, was a non-Brahmin, but a helpless tool in their hands.

Kulkarnis sowed discontent and discord and fomented quarrels among the villagers. Brahmins secured posts of clerks, Kulkarnis, Mamlatdars exclusively for Brahmins. They dispensed justice, administered laws, decided cases in favour of Brahmin money-lenders and convicted poor peasants. Brahmin officers fawned on low caste prostitutes, but hurled shoes at Mahars and Mangs and did not care to stand for justice or humanity. Thus the Poor low caste did not get a fair deal from the Brahmins who were in authority.

The peasants formed the main source of revenue to the Government; yet their children were illiterate, ill-clad and ill-fed. On top of it all, Brahmin teachers preached treason in schools. So

Jotirao entreated Queen Victoria in his ballads to take pit the poverty-sticken peasants, rescue them from the inh Brahmin tyranny and save her rule from corruption and practices. He suggested that teachers, magistrates and cle should be appointed from other castes also, so that the of these tyrants might be broken. If Queen Victoria made per arrangements for the education of the peasants' chil seaired them jobs in the administration and justice in court of law and protected their rights, they would sing glory.

Brahmins were far ahead in education partly because of tradition of learning and partly because of the favoured ment they were given by the British rulers, who wanted reconcile them. Moreover, the theory of filtration, w expected education to filter down from the higher classes to lower classes, failed absolutely and education remained con to the higher classes and mainly to Brahmins. Brahmins constituted five per cent of the population of the Province either creditors; clerks, teachers, Mamlatdars or in positions power in the whole Presidency of Bombay.

Ten years later, in July 1879, Sir Richard Temple, Gove of Bombay, in his Report to the Governor-General, observe "If indeed education had had the effect of throwing em ment into the hands of other castes then the Brahmins w have been jealous. But such is not the case; they have not to complain of on this count. On the contrary they being intellectual qualities transmitted through many generate much'the cleverest of all the people, get altogether the best it in every thing that depends on education."[5] When, 1 the non-Brahmin leaders as directed by their master Jot took up the thread and began to replace Brahmins in ment service, shrewd and selfish Brahmins began to that the non-Brahmins were begging for jobs; they were patriots!

Jotirao laid emphasis on representation being given to other castes, so that there should be a check or control Brahmins' anti-social behaviour. Those who were benefited the existing arrangements andadministration were bound to ridicule Jotirao

5. The Hindustan Times Weekly, 8 July 1962.

and, although themselves rank communalists, they denounced him, on the pretence of maintaining progressive views, as a communalist. Yet, in some of his songs, Jotirao said that Christians, Muslims, Mangs and Brahmins should all be regarded as brothers.

The *Vividhadnyan Vistar*, which was meant for 'ladies and. gentlemen', was very unsympathetic in reviewing the booklet. It could not grasp the reasoning in it. There was at that time no idea of social justice or social equality that could be a guiding factor in thought and conduct. The trend of Jotirao's ballads was, the journal thought, against the higher classes, especially the Brahmins; so it must be against religion and good taste! It was good taste and good religion, the journal seemed to have thought, to regard a co-religionist as an Untouchable and to fleece an ignorant man of his money in the name of religion and to keep him forever in a servile condition.

The missionaries, for their own objectives, and government for its own reasons, hated the Brahmins. Jotirao, the *Vividhadnyan Vistar* said, swayed by the prejudical research of European scholars, used their conclusions for his own purpose. Much of Jotirao's interpretation of history failed, but the facts remained. This booklet of Jotirao is not available today. The poems quoted by the *Vividhadnyan Vistar* are found neither in his *Priestcraft Exposed* nor in his *Life of Shivaji in Poetical Metre*.

After his meritorious service in the field of education, Jotirao was not spending his time idly, as was described by Narayan Vishnu Joshi in his book Poona: *Ancient and Modern*. He visited Raigad, the old capital of Shivaji, with great admiration and curiosity. It was Jotirao who first discovered the tomb of Shivaji in a dilapidated condition covered with dry leaves and stones. He composed a ballad on Shivaji and published it in June 1869. Though mixed with Jotirao's novel interpretation of Parashuram's life and the illgotten supremacy of Brahmins, 'he ballad is inspiring. The title of the ballad is *Life of Shivaji in Poetical Metre*, composed in the interests of the people. The author Joti Govind Phooley inscribes the ballad "to the memory of Rao Bahadur Ramchandra Balkrishna, President of the Paraahansa Sabha, late Assistant Commissioner of Customs and Justice of Peace, as a mark of profound respect and testimony of sincere affection by the author."

The ballad is spread over forty-five pages. Jotirao is at more with poetry than with prose. The poet describes himself as *Kulwadi Bhushan*, an honour to the Kulwadi. He is of opinion that because of the wars with Parashuram and his caste, the Kshatriyas, the warrior classes, were weakened and India vulnerable to foreign invasion.

Jotirao was the first leader and poet in Maharashtra under British rule to sing the glory of Shivaji who has been regarded in the history of modern India as a symbol of courage, self respect, patriotism, and heroism. A liberator and founder of an Empire, he has been a source of great inspiration to numerous Indian patriots and revolutionaries. Jotirao, the poet, describes the invasion of India by the hoards of Muslim fanatics as under :

Leaves Kabul, dips in Sindhu,
Wears a beard, harasses Hindus,
Shaves Brahmin tuft, cuts off organs,
Breaks Shiva images, hammers temples,
Eats beef, leaves pig,
Destroys paintings, ruins sculptures,
Uproots idols, sends to Kabul,
Thrashes Hindus, rails at religion,
Imprisons kings, flays bodies,
destroys temples, builds towers

and Jotirao the poet sings in a patriotic vein how Shivaji assisted by his faithful, fearless, brave lieutenants, and inspired by his mother, unfurls the flag of Hindus.

Then Jotirao depicts the whole thrilling life of Shivaji as a glorious battle for a holy cause. He pays glowing tribute to Shivaji's cautious nature, his daring deeds, his peerless charactor as regards his famale captives, his insight into human and his foresight in establishing a Maratha Navy. Shhi accepted Ramdas as his preceptor, Jotirao adds, just to win affection of the people. The darling of Jijabai, sings Jotil became a terror to the Mogul invaders.

Jotirao was thus the first leader in his generation to draw the attention of Maharashtra to the achievements of Shivaji Three years later M. K. Kunte, who was a scholar and orator, a friend and colleague of Ranade and a semi-social reformer, tried to compose an epic on Shivaji; but after completing six cantos, he gave up the august attempt. Jotirao's *Life of Shivaji in Poetical Metre* and Kunte's *Rajashivaji Kavya* were submitted to the Dakshina Prize Committee. The latter was awarded the prize.[6]

V

Another series of poems Jotirao published at this time was on the economic exploitation of the ignorant, superstitious Shudras by the Priests. The title of the book is *Priestcraft Exposed.* It was published in the same year, i.e. 1869. Many customs and superstitions attacked by Jotirao have now been abolished, some have worn themselves out with the passage of time; but it may be imagined how terrible they must have been in those days. The poet Jotirao narrates the following:

If the Brahmin priest does not give alms to a Chandal, how does his religion allow him to receive alms from a Shudra? Then he describes how the Brahmin priest squeezes a lot of money out of a peasant. When a peasant's wife delivers a child, he frightens the peasant into performing some ceremony or other, or offering prolonged prayers just to propitiate the deity and to avert the approaching imaginary death of the child. In doing so his sole aim is to feast on the fortunes of the peasant, such as they are.

At the time of concluding a marriage and performing it the Brahmin priest has the upper hand; more often than not he has the last word in the matter. His astrology and whims do or undo the marriage offers. The destinies of men and women are in his hands. Often in the marriage settlement his voice is heard in both the families. In the meanwhile the priest urges them to offer some long prayers for propitiating the planets. He is the chief mover and monitor! Jotirao therefore, asks his men to select few persons from among the relatives and friends of both sides, and get the marriage settled among themselves and to perform joyfully the marriage ceremony with fervent prayers to God. There is no necessity of a Brahmin priest. He should be dispensed with.

Then there is the ceremony to be performed by the husband of a girl-wife on the attainment of her puberty.

6. D.P.I. Report 1869-70, Appendix CP—P-285.

The officiating priests and their relatives and friends have a grand dinner in the names of God and religion. As a result the peasants who cannot stand such economic strains are drowned in debts!

Sometimes there is the ceremony to be performed when the occupation of a newly-built house takes place. Again a dinner for Brahmin priests is given and respect to them is paid. The owner of the house and the carpenters and masons sit mutely in a corner awaiting their turn at the food after the terrestrial gods have finished their sumptuous dinner.

A clever Brahmin reads at a Shudra peasant's house a religious book and creeps into his confidence. Then he takes charge of the recovery of the dues, and for a time impresses the peasant with his efficient management by bringing in more money from the tenants. On winning the confidence of the master, next time he files suits against them for failure to pay the dues. Having frightened them into submission, he clandestinely meets the peasants one by one and promises them a way out if his hand is greased. The poor creatures compromise for fear of a greater disaster. The master, too, is wheedled into meeting the poor tenants half way and thus the victorious villain goes home merrily whistling a tune! In addition, there are different seasonal religious functions at which he is there to be their guide to heaven! The poor peasants at last bend, physically and economically, under the religious pressure of the gods and the priests.

There is also another trick played on the peasant to fleece him of his money. An old peasant reduced to a skeleton is sinking fast. A fleet of country doctors extract money from the family with bated breath and hot haste. The news of his sad serious illness reaches the ears of a Brahmin priest. He sweeps across the way and sits reading at the peasant's house a religious book to ward off his death! After a while the poor wife of the peasant is bamboozled into giving gifts to the Brahmin to save her husband's life. If a gift of the cow is not possible, the priest is content with the gift of a pair of new shoes. The sobbing wife is asked not to interrupt her husband's sleep, although he is at death's door. She is asked to speed up her gifts. She offers gifts to God through the priest. But God does not grant her prayers. At last the man breathes his last.

For ten days the officiating Brahmin priest harasses his son and extorts whatever he can from the family. The relatives and castemen in the village are given a dinner, the Brahmin is given pots, a pair of shoes and an umbrella, if not a cow; and the crows are given rice balls.

The peasant's son runs into debt. The Brahmin priest himself becomes his money-lender and after some days, in order to be able to pay the instalments of interest, a fresh deed is signed. The farmer's old wife, now without teeth and with hardly enough food to eat, is deprived of her farm. She quivers like a lizard without a tail. She dies from hunger and her son becomes a pauper. "Oh, Queen!" goes on Jotirao's fervent prayer, "Educate this Shudra, impart knowledge to him, and save him from his tragic fate!" On the occasion of an eclipse, the Brah¬min priest collects his yearly tax on the death anniversaries of the fathers of the living farmers. Besides, he is at the places of pilgrimage to collect dakshina. Thus at every place and at every stage the peasant's superstitions were exploited.

The Brahmin priests wear their sacred threads, but they cannot change their nature. They take ablutionary baths, say prayers daily, apply sacred ash to their foreheads, but they remain essentially irreligious.

With the sacred cloth Brahmins become themselves Untouchables. Even the touch of a clean hair of a Shudra causes pollution to them. The Shudras are prohibited from hearing the Vedas recited; but the Brahmins teach Europeans to read the same. Masquerading as earthly gods themselves, they fall at the feet of prostitutes. They throw food at Shudras: but drink wine as members of the *Shakti cult*. They give the Shudras water to drink, making it sacred with a dip of their toes in it; but kiss the tongue of the worthless concubines of even lowest caste or even of a different religion. The illiterate Shudra has become shameless; he licks the feet of Brahmins. So Jotirao exhorts the Shudras to think over their degradation and struggle to improve their lot.

We of the twentieth century will not be able to understand. Jotirao unless we know the social conditions of his times. It was the social conditions that drove him mad. His soul was wrung with pain at the heartless and pitiless exploitation of the poor peasants done in the name of religion. His approach was as rational as it was humanitarian. It was based on justice as well as on morality.

Priestcraft Exposed was a restatement of the views Jotirao had expressed in the drama he had submitted to the Dakshina Prize Committee. He published it at his own expense. One of his friends tried to persuade the officers in the Education Department to purchase some copies of Jotirao's book, but to no avail! Who would, to say nothing of the Brahmin officers, introduce such a controversial booklet into schools and create an uneasy atmosphere there? It was like recommending the reading of Luther's articles in Catholic schools. Jotirao. when asked why he did not exert his influence over the Dakshina Prize Committee, replied that evil means should not be used for attaining a good object.

CHAPTER IX

Slavery

THESE SLEDGE-HAMMER blows delivered by Jotirao shook to their foundations the citadels of prejudices and privilege, ignor¬ance and oppression. The cracks of his whip resounded through¬out Maharashtra, and Jotirao, accustomed now to the storm and stress of public life, came forward to give a still greater shock to those who were capable of thinking and reflecting

Maharashtra was awakening to new and progressive ideals. In Bombay, after the breakdown of the Paramahansa Sabha, which was socially a revolutionary institution, it was reborn on March 31, 1867. in a more mild and evolutionary form as Prarthana Samaj. Most of the leaders and advocates of the Paramahansa Sabha were the founders of the Prarthana Samaj. Institutions are children of ideas, said aptly Carlyle.

The Paramahansa Sabha, a theistic society, laid emphasis on equality in social relations whereas the Prarthana Samaj, although believing in social equality, was more inclined to spiritual ideals. It was the difference between Dadoba's temperament and that of Dr. Atmaram Pandurang Tarkhadkar, Waman Abaji Modak, M. G. Ranade and Dr. R. G. Bhandarkar. In their preliminary meetings some of them thought of laying emphasis on social matters like abolition of the caste system, encouragement of widow remarriage, promotion of female education and abolition of childmarriage; but in the end it was decided to lean more towards spiritual than towards social ideals. Although he was one of its inspirers and pillars, Ranade joined the Prarthana Samaj in 1870. The founders of the Paramahansa Sabha were chiefly social reformers whereas the founders of the Prarthana Samaj were mostly spiritual reformers.

Naturally Jotirao did not join the Poona branch of the Prarthana Samaj when it was started on December 4, 1870, by its Poona workers some of whom were his friends and sympathisers. He was a believer in theism, the fatherhood of God and the brotherhood of man; but he did not join an institution which turned mainly to the pulpit and to prayer, and not to the masses. Though these angelic leaders were, in the words of Sir Narayan Chandavarkar, who was himself one of the worthies of the Prar-thana Samaj, associated with all that was good and noble and led a life of piety and service, almost all of them were Government servants and armchair-liberals having no active interest in the uplift of the masses. Jotirao knew this well.

By now Poona had undergone a change. On April 2, 1870, the Sarvajanik Sabha was founded in Poona and its two stalwarts, Ganesh Vasudeo Joshi alias Sarvajanik Kaka and Sadashiv Govande, took upon themselves the task of representing the griev-ances of the people and of the Press. Moro Vithal Walvekar and Sakharam Yeshwant Paranjpay, two of Jotirao's colleagues, went to Bombay in search of service. Sarvajanik Kaka—Public Uncle—and Govande did their utmost to represent the grievances of the people. Their prestige and fame became so powerful that they boldly organized the Indian Press against Lytton's Press Act, took to Swadeshi propaganda, first of its kind in India, and gave expression through the Sarvajanik Sabha to the people's ills.

Jotirao's friend Govande was now turning to the philosophy of Vedanta, a world-negating attitude. His father had turned a recluse and had rested eternally in the court-yard of his house. Govande later was entangled in the coils of a certain recluse and lived the rest of his life with a world-negating attitude. Yet Govande had developed into a very influential leader with his colleague Sarvajanik Kaka, who was a man of boundless energy, patriotic spirit and bubbling originality. On his arrival in Poona in 1871, Ranade, with his scintillating personality and his all-round philosophy, gave a fillip to the work of the Sarvajanik Sabha.

Poona had established, early in the year 1852, its first political institution called the Deccan Association. Britain was then con-sidering the nature of constitutional changes to be effected in India in 1853. This first political organisation in Maharashtra was mostly dominated by Sardars, Jagirdars and young patriotic men. They had received a liberal English education and wanted to represent, on behalf of the natives of India, the grievances of the Indian people to the authorities in England. Government, however, passed a wedge through it by offering some members better prospects on their transfer. And it died out within four months.

Much earlier, one Moreshwarshastri Sathe had established an institution called Kalyanonnayaka Sabha. According to it, only Sanskrit literature contained the best and most useful knowledge in the world. Its members were bitter opponents of widow-remarriage. They wished Hindu widows to give up salt-eating and waste away fasting and praying.

There was a political association called the Poona Association established in 1867; but it ended its life without creating much stir and gave place to the Sarvajanik Sabha.

An institution named Veda Samachar was started in 1865 at Madras. Its birth was the result, as was the birth of the Bombay Prarthana Samaj, of a visit to Madras by Keshub Chandra Sen who was a great revolutionary leader of the Brahmo Samaj. The Veda Samachar had nothing to do with the Vedas. Its members wanted, without evoking the least resistance, to reform social customs. They breathed and preached gradualism. This was the picture of social reform movement in India in Jotirao's time.

Jotirao had no faith in the ideals or philosophies of these organisations which were interested in the grievances of the higher classes and could not care to understand the ills of the lower classs, who never appeared in their programme and propaganda. It was, then, no wonder that he should describe the Sarvajanik Sabha as the Bhat (Brahmin) Sabha.

M. G. Ranade was in the meanwhile growing to be a man cf great vision and great thought. He was the doyen of Indian thinkers and reformers. His broad-minded outlook brought him in contact with Jotirao. They both visited each other's home. They held each other in respect. When Ranade visited Jotirao's house he was paid the honour which he deserved so eminently. Ranade activised one hand of the society in Maha-rashtra through the help of Sarvajanik Sabha and the Prarthana Samaj while Jotirao activised the other. Ranade was naturalchy interested in the activities of Jotirao and offered him help and sympathy.

Both Jotirao and Ranade welcomed new thought and were on the right path to the salvation of the nation. Each held a torch of reform in his hand. Both were intellectually and spiritually fresh and alert. Ranade was a man of light, learning and fore sight. Jotirao had insight, valour and vision. Ranade wanted to remove the social ills and liberate the society and not to remould the social structure. Jotirao wanted to pull it down and build anew. Both believed in making society better fitted for a new life. Both had respect for human dignity and had faith in essential equality between man and man. In their scheme of things nobody would be below; everybody would be with you and not against you. They obeyed the dictates of conscience, the divine spark in them.

But why Ranade, one of the greatest men of his day in India, was drawn to Jotirao can be seen in the former's social and political ideology which fully justified the movement started by Jotirao for social equality and social justice, for promotion of rational thinking and removal of social injustice. "You cannot have," observed Ranade the great sage and seer, "a good social system when you find yourself low in the scale of political rights, nor can you be fit to exercise political rights and privileges unless your social system is based on reason and justice. You cannot have a good economic system when your social arrangements are imperfect. If your religious ideals are low and grovelling, you cannot succeed in social, economic or political spheres. The interdependence is not an accident, but is the law of nature."[1]

In January 1871 a social institution called the Stree Vicharawati Sabha was established in Poona by Saraswatibai Govande, wife of Sadashivrao Govande and friend of Savitribai Phooley, and Saraswatibai Joshi, wife of Sarvajanik Kaka. At the instance of Ranade" and assisted by Sarvajanik Kaka, Poona women held a function on April 25, 1873, to distribute vermilion. The depressed class women were given it at an isolated place while the non-Brahmin women, who were at first suspicious of the treatment they would receive at the hands of Brahmin women, joined them there. This was a unique function. It is not known whether Savitribai Phooley attended it.

Immediately after the establishment of the Stree Vicharavati Sabha, female students of the Native Female Normal School at Calcutta established an institution and held their first meeting on April 14, 1871. It was attended by twenty women. Babu

1. *Miscellaneous Writings of the Late Hon'ble. Mr. Justice Ranade*. pp. 231-32.

Keshub Chandra Sen urged them to be prepared to work for the uplift of the natives.

II

Jotirao had been preparing the ground for a social reform move-ment. With a view to freeing the lower classes from ignorance, prejudice, illiteracy and caste-feeling, and from the thraldom of Brahminism, he had written books and pamphlets on the subject. He was busy writing a book, parts of which he completed in August and December 1872. The first part of the book contained his proclamation under which he challenged Parashuram to appear before society as he was described by Brahmin scriptures and puranas to have been living for ages. This was unmistakably a dig Jotirao had at the Brahmins as he wanted to annihilate the doctrine of incarnation in Brahminism.

The other part comprised his manifesto relating to his readiness to regard any man as a member of his family and to have food with him if he was convinced that the man led a virtuous life, had faith in God and was following an honest calling. Jotirao declared that he himself had broken the shackles imposed upon him by Brahmin scriptures and come out of the prison of slavery. He denounced all Brahmin scriptures and their teaching which had condemned the Shudras as the slaves of Brahmins, and he declared as his brothers all those who treated him as his equal, even if from another country.

Those who by their behaviour imposed humiliation on others he would leave to act as they liked; but he himself refused to discard the God-given, sacred rights of Man. If any Shudras willing to break the shackles of Brahmin thraldom, informed him of his desire to do so, he would be grateful.

Referring to the manifesto issued by Jotirao, a Brahmin journal of Poona, *Lokakalyanecchu*, sarcastically observed: 'Our well-known Jotirao who is a man of great learning and great thoughts, a great research scholar and a grant philosopher, sent a letter for publication. The letter was full of self-praise and Brahmin hatred. We have no place for this letter for which we hope Phooley would excuse us!"

A Christian journal called *Shubhavartamana* from Kolhapur published Jotirao's manifesto as no Hindu editor would publish it. Although his Hindu contemporary might think it reviling, in its view it was a worthy and brave announcement. As Jotirao did not believe in caste system, he had courageously declared that he would have food with anybody. The journal expressed a hope that the number of such men would increase in the land.

These two announcements were parts of his book *Slavery within the Indian Empire, under the cloak of Brahminism*. It was published in June 1873, and it at once became a controversial book. It is for the first time here that Jotirao who previously signed as Joti now signed and put his name on the book Jotirao.

It was a sequel to his three books on the same subject. Liberty, equality, and fraternity is the burden of his books. Liberty is essential to every man. To bestow, the book observes, liberty on a man who does not enjoy it is the duty of every good man under the sun. It is a great achievement to recapture the God-given rights of every human being who has been deprived of it. A self-respecting man would not falter to do this act. Every human being needs proper rights for his or her happiness. To confer freedom on every human being by liberating him from injustice, is the main object of noble men who undertake such great tasks at the risk of their lives.

Jotirao sang the glory of the American heroes and statesmen who nobly and untiringly fought for the liberation of the Negroes. The poet in Jotirao imagined the divine satisfaction that prevailed on the day when Negro mothers met their sons and daughters, wives their husbands, sisters their brothers and men their relatives! It must have been a glorious spectacle, he imagined.

The brutality which skinned their backs, burnt their skins and broke their limbs had diminished in the land of the new world, Jotirao rejoiced to note it. He visualized a society in which the peasant and worker were freed from the Brahmin thraldom that crushed them under its various forms—dark superstitions, colossal ignorance, endless religious rites, never-ending debts, and the fear of God.

Inspired by the glorious triumph achieved by Lincoln, who had abolished slavery in 1863 in America, Jotirao dedicated the book

To

The good people of the United States
As a token of admiration for their
Sublime *disinterested* and *self-sacrificing*
Devotion in the cause of Negro
Slavery; and with an earnest desire,
that my countrymen may take
their noble example as their guide
in the emancipation of these Shudra
Brethren from the trammels of
Brahmin thraldom.

The book opens with a quotation from Homer: "The day that reduces a man to slavery takes from him the half of his virtue." The book is written in dialogue.

It is divided into sixteen chapters; the first nine explain the history of Brahmin domination in India as interpreted by its author.

The Brahmins invaded India, the original cradle of their race being an arid, sandy and mountainous region. They were imbued with every notion of self, extremely cunning, arrogant and bigoted. They fought the Kshatriyas who comprised the Shudras and Atishudras. The Kshatriyas were a hardy brave people. They offered heroic resistance to the Aryan invaders, but were defeated. Their best, beloved, equitable, just, brave and powerful king was Bali, whose empire stretched from the Himalayas to Ceylon.

Then came Waman, leader of the Brahmins. According to *puranic* scriptures the four preceding incarnations of Vishnu perhaps related to the evolution of Man. There is a story that Waman tricked Bali out of his empire either at a game of dice or in the form of a Brahmin beggar who asked for three paces of land; the two paces occupied heaven and earth and the third he kept on the head of Bali and Bali was pushed down into the internal region of the earth. Jotirao ridiculed the idea, asking the *puranic* authors whether Waman was greater than earth and heaven!

Jotirao said that Bali, his hero, fell fighting in a battle with women Bali became an immortal king. The later Brahmin scriptures incorporated his name in a list of seven immortal personages—Ashvatthama, Bali, Vyas, Hanuman, Bibhishana, Kripa and Parashuram. The non-Brahmins have been reviving their dreams of a Bali raj every year saying on Dassara day: "Let all troubles and misery go, and the kingdom of Bali come". The last of the Aryan leaders Parashuram, the sixth incarnation of Vishnu, who butchered myriads of men and defenceless innocent children and pregnant women of the Kshatriyas. was so selfish, infamous, cruel and inhuman that the author Jotirao was of the opinion that the cruelties perpetrated by Nero and Alaric sank into insignificance before his ferocity. So he held that Parashuram was more a fiend than a god.

The Aryan Brahmins, opined Jotirao, held the Kshatriyas in great aversion; their hatred divided the Kshatriyas into Shudras and Atishudras in order to weaken their forces, and they subjugated them. According to Jotirao, Shudras and Atishudras belonged to one race. Because they bitterly opposed Brahmin suzerainty, they were dubbed Dassyus, Asuras, Rakshasas and Mahars, whereas they regarded themselves as Devas! They forbade the Shudras to touch Atishudras, and the Atishudras being deprived of the means of livelihood, were obliged to eat carrion.

Then the Brahmins composed works. They prohibited the Shudras and Atishudras from reading scriptures, amassing wealth, and from following certain occupations or professions. They added from generation to generation incredible legends to the fabricated tales in their holy books. Jotirao therefore denounced *Manusmriti* as an unholy book.

The Brahmins established the caste system arrogating to themselves the position of earthly gods, the possession and enjoyment of the rarest gifts of fortune, and the highest rights and privileges. The commonest rights of humanity were denied the Shudras. Thus they reduced the Shudras and Atishudras to slavery and penury. They forbade them to read their holy works, so that the hidden blasphemous lies of the Brahmin scrip¬tures should not be exposed and their myths exploded.

III

According to the Brahmin *shastras*, observed Jotirao, Brahmins were not subject to the law. It was enjoined that "if a Brahmin kills a cat or an ichneumon, the bird chasha, or a frog, a dog, a lizard, an owl, a crow or a shudra," he was absolved of his sin by performing a sort of fasting penance, perhaps for a few hours or a day requiring not much labour or trouble. On the other hand, a Shudra killer of a Brahmin was put to death, for the killing of a Brahmin was considered the most heinous crime one could commit. The power and prestige of the Brahmins is shown by a story in which Bhrugu, n. Brahmin sage, gave a kick on the breast of the god Vishnu!

Jotirao congratulated the British Government on having set aside the preposterous, unjust and inhuman penal enactments of the Peshwas and on having established equitable laws.

Jotirao cited from various Brahmin scriptures instances in which the superiority or excellence of the Brahmins was en¬joined on pain of divine displeasure. These were the divine rights of the Brahmins:

"The Brahmin is styled the Lord of the universe, even equal to God Himself. He is to be worshipped, served and respected by all.

A Brahmin can do no wrong.

Never shall the king slay a Brahmin, though he has committed all possible crimes.

To save the life of a Brahmin any falsehood may be told. There is no sin in it.

No one is to take away anything belonging to a Brahmin.

A king though dying from want, must not receive any tax from a Brahmin, nor suffer him to be afflicted with hunger, or the whole kingdom will be afflicted with famine.

The feet of a Brahmin are holy. In his right foot reside the holy waters of all places of pilgrimages, and by dipping it into water he makes it as holy as the waters at the holiest of shrines.

A Brahmin may compel a man of a servile class to perform servile duty, because such a man was created by the Almighty only for the purpose of serving Brahmins.

A Shudfa, though emancipated by his master, is not released from a state of servitude; for, being born in a state which is natural to him, by whom can he be divested of his natural attributes?

Let a Brahmin not give temporal advice nor spiritual counsel to a Shudra.

No superfluous accumulation of wealth shall be made Shudra, even though he has the power to make it, since a se man who has amassed riches becomes proud, and by his insolence or neglect he gives pain even to Brahmins.

If a Shudra cohabits with a Brahmin adulteress, his life is to be taken. But if a Brahmin goes even unto the lawful wife of a Shudra he is exempted from all corporal punishment."

The main object of these injunctions, ordinances and prohi tions observed Jotirao, was to dupe the minds of the illiterate and ignorant and rivet firmly upon them the chains of bondage.

"This mass of legends and idle phantasies and blasphemous writings were palmed off on the ignorant masses as of divine inspiration, or as the acts of the Deity himself. The most immoral, inhuman, unjust actions and deeds have been all attri buted to that Being who is our Creator, Governor and Protector and who is All Holiness Himself."

Jotirao attributed to the caste system based on the selfish superstitions and bigotry of the Brahmins, the evils under which India had been groaning for ages past.

The Indian *ryot* consisting of mostly Shudras and Atishudras Jotirao observed, had been a proverbial milch cow. Those held sway over the *ryot* cared only to fatten themselves on products of the sweat of their brow, without caring for their welfare or condition.

The Brahmin despoiled the lower classes not only in his capacity as a priest, but also in the capacity of a Government officer, as the Brahmins had monopolized all higher places of e moluments. He was the master, the ruler, the village hereditary accountant, the village police Patil being a tool in his hands. He was the temporal and spiritual adviser of the *ryots*, the money-lender in their difficulties. He set them by the ears fomented trouble among them. In the capacity of a Mamlatdar, a supervisor in the Engineering Department, an officer Revenue and Public Works Departments he was there to exploit him, in league with the Kulkarni, or the lawyer or the leader who were Brahmins. So there was nepotism, bribery and jobbery because of the domination of one caste in the administration. Jotirao condemned this gang of officers as village demons. He suggested to Government to appoint Englishmen on basis of *Inum* lands or pensions to report on village matters.

The Western ideas and civilization were exercising their influence over the Brahmins, and they were not as superstitious, cruel and intolerant as they were under Peshwa rule. "Is the Brahmin," he asked, "inclined to make atonement for his past selfishness? Perhaps it would have been useless to repine over what has been suffered and what has passed away had the present

been all that is desirable." l"We know," he observed, "perfectly well that the Brahmin not descend from his self-raised high pedestal and meet his kunbi and low caste brethren on an equal footing without a struggle. Even the educated Brahmin who knows his exact position and how he has come by it will not condescend to acknowledge the errors of his forefathers and will not willingly forgo long cherished false notions of his own superiority. At present not even one has the moral courage to do what duty demands, and as long as this continues, one sect distinguishing and degrading another sect, the condition of the Shudras will ain unaltered, and India will never advance in greatness or prosperity."

IV

Jyotirao therefore appealed to Government to provide the Shudras educational facilities, and to dispel their ignorance and prejudices. The Government should care for the education of lower classes. It was its duty to do so because most of its revenue came from the labour of the *ryot*, from the sweat of his brow. It was anything but just and equitable to expend pro a large portion of Government revenue on the education of the higher classes who, it was believed, would in time vend learning without money and without price. According to Jotirao the theory of filtration was wrong and its philosophy utopian. The best way to advance the moral and intellectual welfare of the people was to spread instruction among the masses,

Demanding then the abolition of the virtual monopoly of the Barhmins in the administration, he advocated the recruitment of the candidates from other classes. He suggested that candidates from the lower classes should be selected, trained and appointed to the posts of Kulkarnis, Patils, and teachers. He raised no objection to Brahmins getting posts in proportion to their population. He said it was agonizing to see that there was not a Mahar or Mang graduate. Brahmin teachers had brought disgrace upon the Education Department by creating this situation.

How Jotirao was justified in making his attack can be seen from the fact that until the year 1881-82 there was no student from the Atishudras in either any of the high schools or colleges of the Bombay Presidency. He also demanded the establishment of village schools without Brahmin teachers because they either discouraged the lower class pupils or frightened them into quitting the schools.

Jotirao urged the necessity of nominating men from the lower classes to Municipal bodies to look after the interests and amenities of the lower classes, such as adequate supply of water and light. It was his experience that because of absence of representatives of the lower classes on Municipal bodies, the poor classes were not provided even the minimum supply of water. When the Atishudras and the poor classes of Poona started using cisterns in the localities of the Brahmins, they obtained a supply of water for their own cisterns. He felt that it was the bounden duty of the Municipality to provide proper lighting and an adequate water supply to the lower classes.

Jotirao wrote that the practice of calling the roll for the criminal tribes who committed robberies was not improper; but he held the view that the same practice would have been not improper in case of pregnant Brahmin widows whose crimes were more sinful and harmful to society. Jotirao further observed that had the Brahmins been real patriots they would not have reduced the Shudras and Atishudras to slavery and regarded even pure spring water at their hands as more impure than the urine of animals.

Jotirao observed that the Brahmins were brothers, but he was ashamed to call them so. He would accept them as brothers even though they had harassed the Shudras in the past, if they would thenceforward be just in their dealings by giving up their selfish motives. It was his firm belief that the press manned by Brahmins would never help the lower classes by exposing the black deeds of Brahmins. The lower classes, who were in the main illiterate, did not know whether the printed word was man or donkey.

Jotirao believed that the Vedas were not God-inspired. They were man-made. The Vedas fomented divisions in society. The theory that the Brahmins sprang from the mouth of Brahma, Kshatriyas from his arms, Shudras from his feet was a galling and flagrant myth. As, according to him, Narada stirred up quarrels among the Kshatriyas and made the world safe for the Brahmins, he condemned him as a villain. He condemned *Manusmriti* as an unholy work which prescribed slavery for the Shudras. He had nothing but praise for the mighty personality of the Buddha. The Brahmins, in order to establish their supre¬macy again, gave up beef-eating and wine, and absorbing some tenets of Buddhism, they revised their holy works and ultimately defeated Buddhism by cruelly persecuting its followers.

Jotirao denounced the Maharashtrian saints Mukundraj, Dnyaneshwar and Ramdas who did not have the courage to condemn the wicked acts of the Brahmins. These saints described the wickedness of the Brahmins as *Karmamarga* and their Vedanta as the path of knowledge and did not raise their finger against the exploitation of the Shudras by the Brahmins. So his verdict was that these Maharashtrian saints helped to perpetuate the hold of the Brahmins over other classes.

The message, through his book, to the Shudras and Atishudras was that they should educate themselves as long as British rule was there in the land. It was not certain how long that rule would last. But during that time they should be all educated and prepared to fight their battle for liberty, equality and fraternity by dispelling ignorance and prejudices, destroying the coils of slavery entwined around them by the Brahmins. It was God's wish, he observed, that Nanasaheb Peshwa was defeated in the revolt of 1857.

"My object in writing the present volume," observed Jotirao : "is not only to tell my Shudra brethren how they have been duped by the Brahmins, but also to open the eyes of Government to their pernicious system of high class education, which, broad-minded and highly sympathetic statesmen like Sir George Campbell, the present Lieut. Governor of Bengal, are finding to be highly mischievous and prejudicial to the interests of Government. I sincerely hope that Government will before long see the error of their ways, trust less to writers or men who look through high class spectacles only, and achieve the glory of emancipating my Shudra brethren from the trammels of bondage which the Brahmins have raised around them like the coils of a serpent."

"The Shudras are," Jotirao concluded with confidence, "the life and sinews of the country, and it is to them alone and not to the Brahmins, that the Government must ever look, to help them in their difficulties, financial as well as political. If the hearts and minds of the Shudras are made happy and contented, the British Government need have no misgiving about their loyalty in the future." He cried vociferously for mass education and loudly denounced the theory of filtration, but in vain!

V

Jotirao's proposition that the Shudras were originally Kshatriyas was amply proved by no less a scholar than Dr. B. R. Ambedkar. It was the confirmed view of Jotirao that the ancient history of India was nothing but the struggle between Brahmins and non-Brahmins. The meaning he attaches to the non-Vedic deities is very important from the sociological point of view. According to Jotirao the festivals of Dassara and Diwali, and the sacredness of Sunday are non-Brahmin in their origin; Khandoba, Jotiba, Bahiroba, and Martand Malhar are the gods of non-Brahmins.

In the supplement to the *Government Gazette*, Bombay dated the 25th December 1873, some details regarding the book *Slavery* are given. A Government officer, probably helped by a Brahmin assistant, described the book as a philippic on Brahminism, a discourse full of invective. Jotirao issued one thousand copies of the book. It contained one hundred and seventeen pages demy 12 mo. It was printed at the Poona City Press. It was registered for copyright. The price of the book was annas twelve; for Shudras and Atishudras it was annas six.

As the Government officer described the book as a philippic—one of the three orations of Demosthenes against Phillip of Macedon, his remarks were blatantly censorious. The *Government Gazette* further observed: "It is a most virulent production, mostly consisting of the most wild and ludicrous fancies. In a few places it is even indecent." The language of Jotirao in *Slavery* is crude in some places. But the Government reviewer lacked insight and therefore missed its social content. It casts also a revealing light on the mind of the Government employees against whom Jotirao so furiously fought.

The book was reviewed by R. B. Gunjikar in the *Vividhadnyan Vistar*. This monthly magazine was for 'ladies and gentlemen'. The book was meant for peasants, the Atishudras and their tyrants. So the task of the reviewer naturally became pungent. He reminded his readers of similar booklets issued by Jotirao. The reviewer piously said that this book was, as all Jotirao's previous books were, foolish and full of invective. It was apparent, Gunjikar opined sarcastically, that such a book betraying such a colossally incomparable knowledge of language, religion, history, and logic must have been born out of the brains of a jealous, disappointed, dwarfish Christian, newly converted but frustrated, and Phooley must be a mere tool in his hand.

The reviewer emphatically said that the book wanted to destroy Brahmins root and branch, that they should not be given shelter of any kind, whatsoever; that they should be deprived of all their rights, and that Christian missionaries should be invested with these rights. He condemned the book, saying that it was full of invective, indecent expressions and false statements.

The *Vividhadnayan Vistar* got an opportunity to have a tilt at the *Satya Dipika*, Bombay, a Christian weekly, in which Jotirao's book was advertised. The shree on the front page of the *Vividhadnyan Vistar* had become a disturber of the Biblical beatitude of the *Satya Dipika*. So the reviewer seized the opportunity of blaming the editor of the *Satya Dipika* for having published in his journal an advertisement of Jotirao's book which was according to *Vividhadnyan Vistar*, full of wicked thoughts. The editor of the Satya Dipika, Gunjikar added, had boasted of its rules of moral conduct and had already published a notification that only good books, excluding novels, were advertised at cheap rates. Gunjikar asked the editor of the *Satya Dipika* whether Jotirao's book was more valuable than a novel because it abused the Brahmins.[3]

A reader wrote to the Dnyanprakash complaining of Jotirao

3. The Vividhadnyan Vistar, November 1873.

who had priced *Slavery* at annas twelve for Brahmins. He himself had been to Jotirao's shop and purchased a copy for annas twelve although the price was annas six for the Shudras. Jotirao recognised him as a Brahmin customer and therefore charged him annas twelve. On reading the book the Brahmin realized why its price was kept at annas twelve for Brahmins.[4] The Brahmin reader was not surprised that the book was not discussed in the *Dnyanprakash* or in any other paper, as it was modelled after missionary booklets written to condemn the Brahmins. But if, the reader of the *Dnyanprakash* said, the author had sold it at low price as did the missionaries theirs, the book would have had a wide circulation and Jotirao would easily gain his object. The Brahmin customer of Jotirao was fully justified in his complaint against him. Being a Brahmin, he never imagined that slavery would cost so much!

Jotirao's message to do away with an intermediary in religious ceremonies was practised by a goldsmith at a village near Dapoli in Ratnagiri District. He performed the obsequies of his relation with the help of Sanskrit works. Some letters appeared; in the *Dnyanprakash* protesting against this adventurous pandit!

As to Jotirao's violent opposition to the theory of filtration, he proved to be in the right. Ram Mohun Roy, Macaulay and other prominent educationists of Jotirao's day were in favour of the theory of filtration. "In many respects," observes Mr. H. V. Hampton, "Ram Mohun Roy was far in advance of his age, but in so far as he believed that education must begin at the top and spread downwards, he was in agreement with the prevalent opinion of his day. With many others he considered that culture and useful knowledge would inevitably 'filter' down from above and, gradually at first and then more rapidly, would reach the masses. Subsequent history has shown that those who; pinned their faith to the filtration theory were too optimistic."[5]

Jotirao was no research scholar, he was no pandit, he was no philologist. He wanted to condemn the theory of incarnation, which was not in existence until the days of the *Mahabharat*. He had no knowledge of theology. His stand that the Chitpavan Brahmins came from the east coast of Africa or from Iran; or

4. The *Dnyanprakash*, 8 September 1873.
5. Hampton, H. V., *Biographical Studies in Modern Indian Education*, p. 67.

Egypt or Palestine, was not refuted by any historian. On the ontrary, historians and research scholars have given proofs and corroborating facts. V. N. Mandlik in his article in the journal of the Bombay Branch of the Royal Asiatic Society in 1865, R.B. Gunjikar in his book *Saraswati Mandal*, Lt.-Col. Mark Wilks in the *Historical Sketch of the South India*, Edward Moor in the *Hindu Pantheon*, the Rev. William Taylor's *Oriental Manuscripts* and several others have upheld the same view.

Apart from historical corroboration or otherwise, if this argument used for attacking the Brahmins is applied to non Brahmins, as against the Hill Tribes of India, who would remain there to boast that they were original inhabitants of this land?

The bitterness in the tone of the book was the reaction of the mind of Jotirao to the prevailing social condition. For this bitterness, the background of Peshwa rule was responsible. Jotirao revolted against priestcraft, the gods of the Brahmins, the scriptures, the *puranas* as he thought they were dripping with tears and the blood of generations of Shudras and Atishudras who had been their victims for ages. British rule had brought with it justice, an independent judiciary, and scientific outlook, and stood in bold relief against the background of unrest, arson and injustice of Peshwa rule.

Jotirao was happy to see that British rule had brought education, science and justice for all; but he overrated its blessings. He could not realize that the British god of Progress was sitting on the Indian caste system from which he did not care to alight, and so there would be no equitable progress for all the classes in India.

Jotirao believed with Ranade and the Lokahitavadi that God had sent British rule to India to reform the Hindus by correcting their foolishness, dispelling their ignorance, and by removing their prejudices. That was no mean gain. Jotirao was sure that some day British rule would end.

Jotirao's fight for the emancipation of Shudras and Atishudras, who were peasants and landless classes, was against their exploiters, and in those days they happened to be Brahmins. The men who were running the administration of the British were almost all Brahmins. The money-lenders and Government officers such as police-officers, *Shirastedars*, Mamlatdars and Assistant Judges were Brahmins. They all combined to keep the lower classes in bondage and exploited them jointly. Brahmin priests, money-lenders and lawyers were always there in every village to fleece them of money. Their lands and property were? defrauded by this trio. So the fight assumed the colour of com-munalism, though its trend was economic and social.

The title of the book is more colourful than outlandish. Slavery connotes a condition of bondage in which human beings are bought and sold, and forced to work without payment. That kind of slavery was abolished in the British Empire in 1833, in Russia in 1863 and in America in 1863. This was not exactly the case in India. Jotirao attacked and exposed the religious and social slavery practised in India by Brahmins under the cloak of religion. He himself tells us that: "My object in writing the present volume is not only to tell my Shudra brethren how they are duped by the Brahmins......" Under the cloak of religion the Shudras and Atishudras were made to slave for the Brahmins; the Untouchables, a section of their coreligionists, were treated worse than slaves; but they were not, bought and sold.

Jotirao derived inspiration for his drive against social injustice from the struggle in the U.S.A. The Lokahitavadi pointed out to American freedom struggle and said that if the British did not yield power when the people of India would be able to govern themselves, they would do what the Americans had done in America to throw off their yoke. The impact of the freedom struggle of the U.S.A. and of her declaration of the abolition of slavery on the minds of Jotirao's generation was tremendous.

Jotirao made the Brahmins, especially the Chitpavans (without mentioning them), the target of his attack. The Chitpavans are not mentioned in the Vedas. The Vedas were not their creation. It is not certain whether they were responsible for all scriptures and *puranas*. Until the seventeenth century their names do not appear in history. During the days of Shivaji and Sambhaji they had no political power. They were not treated as their equals by the other Brahmins in Maharashtra. They ran errands and were also cooks by calling.

It was on the advent of Balaji Vishvanath as Peshwa on the scene of Maharashtra politics that they found themselves emerging as a respectable and powerful community. It was all right till the accession to the gadi of the Peshwa Balaji Bajirao. He pressed the other Brahmins to give a status of equality to the Chitpavans. The Brahmins, who had kept their holy books their rituals, dogmas and ideas of highness and lowness in their houses, opened out now and began the *karmakandas* which had been suppressed since the days of the Buddha's rise, and the rise of Mahanubhava, Gosavi, Nath and Bhagwat sects. The communal tension, even among the Brahmins of different lines, thus became aggravated, and the situation rapidly deteriorated after the death of Peshwa Madhavrao. The other castes, too, were harassed by the Chitpavan Brahmin rulers. The Nasik Brahmins had forbidden Bajirao II to visit a certain sacred Ghat.

In Northern India, the Brahmins did not differ from the Kshatriyas and Shudras in their dress, food and behaviour. But in Western India, to the South of the Narmada, Brahmins completely turned to vegetarian life, regarded other castes as Shudras, and when they won political power in western India, the unification of these two powers in them, priestly and political, came to be hated by other castes. Jotirao's life was a reaction to this situation.

CHAPTER X

Satya-Shodhak Samaj

HAVING WRITTEN a book ol advice addressed to the lower class, Jotirao resolved now to launch a movement in Maharashtra for their liberation from Brahmin thraldom. A revolutionary leader like Jotirao required an institution, an authoritative credo, and a platform for the propagation of his ideals. During the previous fifteen years he had been propagating his views, preaching at public meetings, through leaflets and booklets the importance of education and exhorting the lower castes to educate their children, and to redeem themselves from the evil customs, wicked prejudices and wily precepts imposed on them in the name of God by the Brahmin priests and their religious works.

Jotirao impressed upon their mind that their slavery was not inborn, inseparable and preordained or a divine dispensation as described in the Brahmanic scriptures. Awakening self-respect in the peasants and toiling masses, he infused courage in them to stand up against the poverty and social injustice, and against the oppressive, unjust and inhuman Hindu priestcraft and the caste system. He also imbued them with new thoughts, new ideals of human dignity, equality and self-salvation. His writings and his speeches focussed Government attention on the grievances of the peasants and of the workers engaged by Government Engineering and Public Works Department.

Jotirao wanted now to organise his followers and workers, so that they might assimilate his rational ideas and bring them into effect. It was his aim also to show the Government how the peasants were being exploited and how they were suffering from a desperate, grinding poverty and glaring social inequality. He strove hard to raise the Atishudras to the level of the Shudras. Lost rights are not secured without a struggle. Jotirao knew well that the upper castes, especially the Brahmins, would be not only unsympathetic but also intolerant, and that the tradition-mongers would not easily give up their privileges, position and power. There was no question of their expecting to get any political rights as they had no strength and organization behind them. So he decided to set up an organization to preach his ideology.

Accordingly, Jotirao convened on September 24, 1873, a meeting of all his admirers and disciples at Poona. About sixty men from many important centres of Maharashtra assembled. Jotirao made an impressive introductory speech and impressed upon his followers the necessity of a central institution for the guidance of the movement. After some discussion and several other speeches, it was agreed to form an institution. There was much enthusiasm among the chosen lieutenants of Jotirao. They decided to organize the mission and to spread the message of the movement. Jotirao named this institution Satya-Shodhak Samaj—Truth-Seeking Society.

It must be mentioned here that Jotirao's three Brahmin friends, Vinayak Bapuji Bhandarkar, Vinayak Bapuji Dengle and Sitaram Sakharam Datar helped Jotirao and his colleagues to establish the Satya-Shodhak Samaj.[1]

Jotirao was elected first President and Treasurer of the Satya-Shodhak Samaj and Narayanrao Govindrao Kadalak was elected its first Secretary. The objects of the Samaj were to redeem the Shudras and Atishudras from the influence of Brahmanical scriptures under which the Brahmin priests fleeced them, to make them conscious of their human rights, and to liberate them from mental and religious slavery.

A member at his initiation into the Samaj had to take an oath in the name of god Khanderao and declare his allegiance to British rule. It may be mentioned here that even the Servants of India Society of G. K. Gokhale had frankly accepted the British connection as ordained in the inscrutable dispensation of Providence for India's good. The urban class alone, which had received Western education, was at that time praying gently for political rights.

Much later, after the death of the founder of the Samaj, the goal was summarised as follows: (a) all men are the children of one God. who is thus their parent (b) As there is no necessity of an intermediary to approach the mother or to please the

1. *Navashakti*, 24 September 1972.

father, there is no need of an intermediary such as a priest or a preceptor to enable the devotee to offer his prayers to God. (c) Anyone accepting that principle is qualified to be a me of the Satya-Shodhak Samaj.

Membership of the Samaj was extended to all castes including Brahmins and Mahars and Mangs, and even Jews and Muslims were its members in its early stage. The weekly meetings held on Sundays at the places where branches of the Satya Shodhak Samaj were established. In Poona, at the house of Dr. Gavade in Somawar Peth, weekly meetings were held. The subjects discussed were the necessity of temperance and compulsory education, encouragement of swadeshi goods, dislodging the Brahmin priest from the position he held in the religious field, making arrangements for performing marriage at minimum expenses, and freeirig men from the beliefs in astrology, ghosts and demons. The main attack was upon the caste system and idol-worship. Emphasis was also on the principle of the father hood of God and the brotherhood of Man.

The Brahmins, desiring to destroy the movement in its early stage, began to propagate their views against the Samaj. The poor ignorant masses, frightened by the Brahmin priests, came to Jotirao and asked him how their prayers would reach God if they were said in Marathi. Jotirao said that it was wrong to suppose that prayers said in Marathi, Gujarati, Telugu and Bengali did not reach God. God read the human mind and understood the yearnings and prayers of every human being. Did not the prayers said in Latin, English and French reach God? Did not the prayers of Tukaram, Namdeo, Eknath, Chokhamela and Savata Mali reach the ears of God?

The Brahmins brought pressure upon the villagers not to be members of the Satya-Shodhak Samaj. Those who became members were harassed, and some of them lost their jobs in Goverment service as Brahmins used to be their Government supervisors. Narayanrao Kadalkar, the Secretary, too, was transferred to Mahabaleshwar. Then the Shudras were told that if they performed their ceremonies without Brahmins their families would be extinct or would perish on account of the curses of Brahmins and their gods.

II

The difference between the Satya-Shodhak Samaj and the Prarathana Samaj or between the Brahmo Samaj and Satya-Shodhak Samaj worth considering. It shows why Jotirao, the peasant philosopher, felt the necessity of an independent institution! The Arya Samaj was not born until 1875.

Both the Prarthana Samaj and the Brahmo Samaj believed in theism. So did the Satya-Shodhak Samaj. According to these three institutions, all men were the children of one God. They discarded all kinds of intermediaries such as a priest or a preceptor to enable the devotee to offer his or her prayers to God or to help him in the performance of any religious ceremonies. All three held weekly prayers and meetings. Ram Mohun Roy started with 'Brahmo', the Prarthana Samaj with 'Prayer', Jotirao, with 'Truth', and later Dayananda with 'Arya'.

The Brahmos and Prarthana Samajists prayed for spiritual welfare and believed in the efficacy of prayers. Such emphasis was not laid by Jotirao on prayers and spiritual welfare, Jotirao was not God-intoxicated.

Jotirao's Samaj believed neither in the caste system nor in the basic four-fold division of society. He prescribed few religious rites and did away with priestly intermediaries. The Brahmo Samaj recognised theoretically no distinction of castes and prescribed no rites and ceremonies. The Prarthana Samaj had much the same principles as the Brahmo Samaj. All three prohibited idol-worship.

But at meetings of the Brahmo Samaj, only Brahmins had beenallowed to officiate[2] as priests since Ram Mohun Roy. It was a holy preserve and privilege not contaminated by non-Brahmins. Keshub Chandra Sen, a non-Brahmin by birth and a brilliant leader of reforming zeal, got the Brahmos to renounce the sacred thread of their Brahmanical badge for which Ram Mohun Roy and Devendranath Tagore had constitutional partiality, and he got them to concede the right of officiating as priest to the non-Brahmins. "The Principle that the Brahmo Samaj had followed since Raja Ram Mohun Roy, namely, never to allow anyone

2. Gajendragadkar, Mr. Justice P. B., former Chief Justice, Supreme Court, in his Foreword to *A Century of Social Reform in India*—By S. Natarajan.

but respectable Brahmins to officiate at the pulpit, was surrendered."[3]

The Prarthana Samajists also renounced the sacred thread, and any member was allowed to officiate at the pulpit. In June 1867 Bhikoba Laxman Chavan, a Bhandari teacher, was allowed to officiate as priest in Bombay. Simple, pious, and generous, Bhikobadada was a man of liberal views and a perfect theist. A Christian convert, Shahurao Cookde, editor of the *Dnyanodaya* was scandalised to see Bhikobadada leading the prayers, and he criticised it in his journal. "The caste in the convert awoke said the historian of the Prarthana Samaj in giving his opinion on Cookde's remarks.

Raja Ram Mohun Roy, founder of the Brahmo Samaj accepted Christ's ethical teaching but repudiated his divinity. He maintained and believed in the infallibility[4] of the divine origin of the Vedas. Jotirao had no faith in the divine of the Vedas. Nor did he consider any religious book such as the Bible, or the Koran, a revelation. He regarded them as man-made. The title of Raja was conferred upon Ram Mohan Roy by Mogul rule, and he believed in the British raj as a divine dispensation.

Keshub Chandra Sen, who was attracted to the mighty personality of Christ, was attacked as a Christian more for his revolutionary social views than for his admiration for Christ The Prarthana Samaj, though dominated by higher classes, tried to flavour its philosophy with a little sprinkling of Tukaram in order to draw the common man to its teachings. It tried to be on the side of the angels and sought a spiritual refuge in Bhagvat Dharma, turning away from the masses to the gods of eqality in the spiritual world!

These twins, Brahmo Samaj and Prarthana Samaj, had no popular appeal. Their activities were confined to the intelligensia gentsia in the cities who afterwards participated in the debates of the Social Reform Conferences. Their gowns, their places of worship, their music, their language differed from those of Satya-Shodhak Samaj. They believed in social evolution

3. Mozoomdar, P. C., *The Life and Teachings of Keshub Chander Sen,* p. 156.
4. Gajendragadkar, Mr. Justice P. B., former Chief Justice, Supreme Court, in his Foreword to *A Century of Social Reform in India.*

as the Satya-Shodhak Samaj wanted a social revolution. The leaders of the Prarthana Samaj were mostly intellectuals; but they lacked moral courage. On account of their great learning, their deep devotion to God and their elevation to high posts in Government administration, they could not come into contact with the masses.

The Satya-Shodhak Samaj lacked the support of major intellects. Their philosopher was a simple and honest peasant. A man of the world, he was endowed with keen perceptions, and a rational outlook. The Satya-Shodhakites were moved to social action by their hearts. Their language was the language of the people, their places of propaganda were the corn-gathering places. The dress of the preacher of the Satya-Shodhak Samaj consisted of a blanket, a turban and a dhoti, and he had a drum in his hand. He referred to their debts, to injunctions and rites the peasants suffered from and told them how the little money they had was drained away by the cunning and selfish Brahmin priests! He urged them to send their children to schools so that they might learn what was law, what was religion, what was god. They were men of farmer's stock, and they could not bring to their task learning and reason, although they displayed much energy and earnestness!

To have founded an institution which matched with the institutions founded by Ram Mohun Roy, Ranade and Bhandarkar, and later by Dayanand Saraswati was no mean achievement. Moreover the leading characteristic of Jotirao's institution was that, unlike their institutions, it struggled for the uplift of the masses. The Satya-Shodhak Samaj was thus the first institution to launch a social movement in modem India. It raised its voice against social slavery and demanded social justice. It was the shrill voice of a long-suppressed people in India.

III

Jotirao later denounced the Brahmo Samaj and the Prarthana Samaj as a ruse born of the Brahmin brains to cloak the political disigns their forefathers had preached in ancient holy works such as the Vedas and the Gita. And indeed the Gita was, said Jotirao's disciple, Dr. B, R. Ambedkar, a political document.

Immediately on the foundation of the Satya-Shodhak Samaj,

Jotirao started translating its resolutions into action. He called for applications of students for scholarships and granted scholarship to ten students. This was greatly appreciated and applauded by the non-Brahmins. He next turned his attention the religious aspect of the mission of his Samaj.

One of Jotirao's relatives was working at his shop. He was on illiterate man and a young widower. Jotirao taught him in leisure hours to read and write. A few days later, he got his marriage settled and decided to solemnise it in conformity with the rules and resolutions of the Satya-Shodhak Samaj. The poor man agreed.

The news of Jotirao's decision as to the nature of that marriage spread in the neighbouring villages. The Brahmin prients were stirred to action. They instigated some rude ignorant persons to scare away the father of the proposed bride from such a performance of marriage without God and Brahmin, which they said was a disgrace to the community and a sacrilege. But the mother of the bride was a friend of Savitribai Phooley. she stood firm. The marriage took place on December 25, 1873. It was a very simple affair with expenses confined to the of betelnut. The main feature of the ceremony was that bride and the bridegroom declared their allegiance and took vows composed by Jotirao. The guests blessed the couple in a chorus. Members of the Samaj attended the ceremony in large numbers. A lot of presents were made to the couple. The marriage ceremony came off safely! A Hindu marriage without a Brahmin priest! A great event indeed!

Jotirao was let off as a breaker of law for the first time; but when he decided on another marriage in the same style, the Brahmins strained every nerve to frustrate his object and to humiliate him. They sent men on horseback to the village of the bridegroom to convince Gyanba Sasane, the proposed bridegroom, of his folly. The village ruffians pursued him. They threatened him with excommunication and other dire consequences.

Sasane ran in consternation to Jotirao and pleaded that he would rather remain a widower for life than face persecution. Since his youth Jotirao had been dealing with such opposition. Encouraging him. he said that the British Government was there to protect his rights. Upon this Sasane sadly pointed out that the Government offices were manned by Brahmins. Jotirao cheered him saying that most of the European officers and the reformist Brahmins were exceptions to the usual mentality.

At this time the Brahmins instigated Jotirao's relatives including his cousins to take some action against him. They had their family friends, but they had no prestige. So with the backing of the Brahmins they thought they would gain some prestige if they could successfully browbeat Jotirao. These hirelings and stooges circulated a rumour among their castemen that Jotirao some day would throw them suddenly into the fold of Christianity. They not only did this, but also were itching for a clash with Jotirao on the day of Sasane's marriage. With that end in view they arranged marriages between children of two or three. Jotirao, through his friend Polani Rajanna Lingu, a lawyer, and Gangarambhau Mhaske, a public man, both influential men in Poona, managed to arrange for police protection on the day of Sasane's marriage.

The ceremony took place at Jotirao's house on May 7, 1874. Some hours before it the bride was, for fear of being kidnapped, left in Jotirao's charge. A big crowd consisting of young Brahmins and non-Brahmins witnessed the marriage being celebrated in a new, simple way, without much expenses but in great gaiety. All had a hectic time. Jotirao's Mahar and Mang followers had thronged the place, eager to defend their great leader and liberator. News about this marriage appeared in some newspapers under the title: "Hindu marriage without a Brahmin priest!"

The success of these two marriages put the Brahmin priests to consternation all over the district, and they made angry protests against the marriages. They laid their heads together. The non-Brahmins felt elated at their success.

New activities of men of action always attract new lieutenants. Knshnarao Pandurang Bhalekar (1850-1910) then an energetic, able and courageous young leader joined Jotirao with his band workers. He was born at Bhamburde, now called Shivaji Nagar and came of a Mali family. His mother died early, and his father who was serving in the District Court of Poona, died in 1866 when Krishnarao was only sixteen. For want of any support he had to abandon his studies. Two years later he was appointed a candidate in the District Court. His restlessness over and sincere sympathies for the poverty-stricken masses, however, made him a staunch, fearless leader in the movement. Poet editor, Bhalekar was a powerful speaker and soon became spokesman of the Satya-Shodhak Samaj.

On pressing invitation, Jotirao went early in 1874 to Bombay to open a branch of the Samaj. At several places he made speeches and urged the lower castes to stand by his Samaj help and expand the movement which promised to liberate them from Brahmin thraldom. He wanted them to become men, and not to waste away their lives as hewers of wood and drawers of water, as had been their lot for ages.

During his stay in Bombay, Jotirao gave a turn to the philan thropy of Vyanku Kalewar and Jaya Karadi Lingu, who were well-known contractors in Bombay. They promised to the stop spending money on feasts to Brahmins and donated the money to the Satya-Shodhak Samaj for the promotion of education. Anothe Telugu contractor, Narasinha Saibu, presented Jotirao with dress of honour, but Jotirao gave it away to a poor man. The movement inaugurated by the Satya-Shodhak Samaj was hailed by educated non-Brahmins all over Maharashtra. One worker writes in *Dnyanodaya* that since the rise of knowledge among the lower castes they knew what was proper and what was proper, what was religion and what was not. The Satya Shodhak Samaj was spreading this light. Its leader was Jotirao. Several well-to-do and generous-minded donors were ing forward to help the movement with money, printing press and other things. This was an indication of a great change the Hindu society was undergoing.

Men of wealth and influence now gathered under Jotirao banner. P. Rajanna Lingu was one of such influentialment. He hailed from the Telegu Mali community. In Bombay they were called Kamathis. This whole community backed Jotir Another important leader was Ramayya Vyankayya Aiyyavaro A rich man and a devoted worker, he followed Jotirao througt thick and thin. These Telugu Mali leaders financed Jotirao's every project and supported his movement. The other valuable support to the Samaj came when Ramsheth Bapusheth Uravane, a wealthy and leading Poona merchant, joined the Samaj Marutrao R. Navale, father of Dr. Annasaheb Navale, was of the staunch advocates of the Samaj.

Another assistant was Dr. Vishram Ramji Gholay. He was

then an assistant surgeon and afterwards was appointed Honorary Surgeon to the Governor-General of India. He was Gawli by caste. His great grandfather, Gopalrao Gholay, commanded the Fort of Anjanwell during Peshwa rule. His grandfather Sambhaji lost the command of the Fort in 1818 when the Maratha Empire came to an end. Vishram's father was a Subhedar in the army. Having served in different capacities in his youth, Vishram Gholay (1838-1900) passed the examination of Assistant Surgeon at the Grant Medical College, was appointed by Government in 1870 an Assistant Surgeon at Kumtha, and was transferred to Poona in 1874. A great donor and a man of wide reading and catholicity, he became, at the age of 35, a pillar of the Satya-Shodhak movement and an asset to Jotirao in many ways. He was an eminent physician and surgeon of his day and a leading personality in Maharashtra. The first anniversary of the Samaj was celebrated with great eagerness and enthusiasm. There was a slight change in the office-bearers of the Samaj. Narayan Tukaram Nagar was elected Secretary and Bhalekar and Seth Ramuseth Uravane were elected members of the managing committee. Some young non-Brahmins like R. V. Dhamnaskar, V. L. Birje, Dr. Santuji Ramji Lad and Narayan Meghaji Lokhande, who afterwards became noted men in various fields, were members of the Samaj. Some Brahmins including Jotirao's old friends Sadashivrao Govande and Sakharam Yeshwant Paranjpey and friends like Tukaram Tatya Padval and Vinayak Bapuji Bhandarkar were also members of the Satya-Shodhak Samaj.

IV

The sincerity and drive of the Satya-Shodhak Samaj evoked a tribute to its workers from a journal which said that the widow remarriage institution in Bombay should take a leaf out of the Samaj's book. And indeed it was a proper reminder to the ideologues of social reforms.

The social reformers were mostly a batch of protesting men without the courage of true Protestants. Jotirao had two occasions to rebuke Ranade severely for his defeatist and timid leadership. The first occasion came when the question of the marriage of Ranade's widowed sister cropped up.

When M. G. Ranade, on his arrival in Poona in 1871 told Jotirao that he had a widowed sister, Jotirao said that he was grieved to hear the news of the sad loss of his sister's husband. However after a pause, Jotirao said: "But it is a reformer's sister that is widowed. You can make the best of this sad lot. God has given you an opportunity to practise what you preach! Make bold to give effect to your vow by getting your sister remarried. No good is obtained without a struggle. Social re¬form does not come of itself. You have to practise it and make people accept it by your courage and suffering." Upon this Ranade replied that if his sister's remarriage took place, his father would be utterly grieved and the Poona Brahmins would excommunicate him. This invited a severe rebuke from Jotirao. He, in a severe retort, said angrily, "Raosaheb, then don't pretend to be a social reformer!"

The second occasion arose when M. G. Ranade lost his wife in October 1873 and married at the age of thirty-two a girl of eleven years. All the reformers drew in their horns. Jotirao again reprimanded Raosaheb Ranade for the betrayal of the cause he so solemnly espoused.

"Oh, the utter degradation and rottenness," sadly cites the *Vividhadnyan Vistar* a quotation from a contemporary about six years after this second marriage of Ranade and bewails: "into which the India's sons are wallowing! It cannot admit of a question that Mr.................. has given a severe blow to the

cause of widow marriage. If grown-up men, educated in the highest degree and occupying the position of leaders of their generation blessed with uncommonly high qualifications of the head and heart, cannot withstand, in critical times, the importunities, and threats of their fathers, and patiently undergo the consequent ill consequences, when these importunities and threats are subversive of the most serious public reforms, which they have deliberately and solemnly espoused before God and man, they and the people they are by their position to lead must forever continue as children and all their efforts end in worse than child's play."[5]

Another contemporary reformer, Lokahitavadi Gopalrao Deshmukh, underwent an expiation for having sent his son to

5. Vol. II, No. 9

England for education. Not only that, when he was asked by Government whether he would go to England to give evidence before the Finance Commission, he informed Government that he was prohibited by Brahmins from undertaking a voyage to England, and as he feared excommunication, discredit and disgrace, he would not cross the black waters! And the Lokahita-vadi was extolled to the skies as a herald of social reforms in Maharashtra! Thereafter the Lokahitavadi crowned his career with an anti-climax by performing marriages of his grand-children when they were six or eight years old! Jotirao had rebuked the Lokahitavadi for his cowardly conduct!

Native Opinion, criticising Gopalrao Deshmukh, aptly observed: "The word 'reformer' has become very cheap amongst us; but after a very careful examination into the documents, we cannot hold that this officer has yet proved his title to be a reformer. We hope he may become one, as years roll on; but it will require a life-long self-sacrifice and untiring labour and perseverance on his part before we can admit him into the roll of our Luthers and Tukarams!"[6] If this test is applied to the social reformers in India, how many of them would remain on the roll of reformers? Of the remaining few, Jotirao towers above his contemporaries.

Emerson said that good thoughts are no better than good dreams unless they are executed. So did Romain Holland when he said: "Thought is action, and only action can make thought of any value."

In times of crucial tests, the leaders of the social reforms, except the brilliant protagonists Wasudeorao Nowrange, Sada-shiv Pandurang Kelkar, and Vishnushastri Pandit, showed lack of moral courage. That was their bane. In spite of their protestations and Sunday social philosophy, which also showed little concem for the majority in. society, they performed the thread ceremony of their sons in the old fashion, celebrated the marriages of their children when they were very young and thus became a reproach to the philosophy of social reform. That is why Vishnushastri Chiplunkar and Lokamanya Tilak could mercilessly attack them.

The brilliant exception, as said already, to this pitiable plight

6. *Vividhadnayan Vistar*, Vol. XI. No. 11.

of the Hindu reformers, was Vishnushastri Pandit. A man of great learning, dauntless courage and unimpeachable character, he showed an irrevocable faith in his mission. He was the only leader who was invariably as good as his words. When most of his colleagues betrayed the cause of social reform, Vishnushastri heroically married a Brahmin widow in December 1874, after the death of his first wife. Vishnushastri Pandit was, therefore, praised by his foes and friends alike.

Jotirao's sympathies were with the social reformers and helped them in times of difficulties. However, he had not much faith in their social reform activities as the reforms they espoused were confined to Brahmins alone.

On invitation from Ranade, Swami Dayanand Saraswati went to Poona in July 1875 from Bombay where he had just established the Arya Samaj. A seer and sage, Dayanand had toured the whole of north India and Bengal, making triumphant speeches, conquering institutions and personalities, inspiring and revitalising the Hindus with his virile message. Dayanand Saraswati (1824-1883) sponsored a religious and national move¬ment for the liberation of Hindus from the rigidity of the caste system and of untouchability. Believing in the divine origin of the Vedas, he was of the opinion that there was no knowledge beyond the Vedas, as did the Muslims hold that there was no knowledge beyond the Koran.

In Maharashtra the Arya Samaj did not take root as the caste system was dominating the lives of Hindus, and its rigidity was tightened by the Brahmin Raj of the Peshwas. Moreover, the Vedic religion of Dayanand was not understood by the masses, nor did the preachings of the Prarthana Samaj permeate to the masses in Maharashtra. Eight years after, Ranade, its guiding philosopher, held that the Brahmo Samaj constituted a part and parcel of Hinduism.[7]

The Poona orthodox were seized with reactionary spasms and fears. Whosoever stood for a change, for reforms, for new knowledge, for abolition of untouchability, for social justice and for social equality was denounced by them as an enemy of the Hindu religion and of the country. Dayanand delivered several lectures in Poona. Orthodox Hindus found fault with Daya

7. The *Subodha Patrika,* 21 February 1881.

nand's Sanskrit and his philosophy. For about two months the voice of the sage echoed throughout Poona.

The reformers decided to take out a procession in honour of Dayanand. The Poona orthodox resolved to break it. On September 5, 1875, the battle was joined. On the previous day, the reformers had contacted Jotirao for help. Dayanand's ideas of social equality, and especially his struggle for the abolition of untouchability were akin to his own mission. Although the lower castes failed to take any interest in the message of the seer, Jotirao agreed to help the social reformers by joining the procession with a party of his followers. Dayanand was seated on a decorated elephant; the holy works were being carried in a palanquin; the country drums, bands, and conches blared in front of the procession. Jotirao participated in the procession, walking along with Ranade and other social reformers. Jotirao's men had joined the procession in large numbers to give protection to the social reformers.

The Poona orthodox and hooligans had decided not to allow the procession to go undisturbed and unmolested. They decorated an ass, named it *Gardabhanand*, followed him in procession and made an ass of themselves. Just after the Dayanand procession had reached its destination, the procession of *Gardabhanand* reached there and a free fight ensued between the two parties. Ranade had arranged for police protection. They made a lathi charge and the crowds dispersed in confusion.

Ranade was a friend of Jotirao. He was also a friend of Ramji Sakpal, the father of Dr. B. R. Ambedkar, who regarded Jotirao as one of his three *gurus*, Buddha, Kabir and Jotirao. To recognise greatness in others one must possess greatness one self. Ranade recognised the greatness of Jotirao. Later Dr. Ambedkai waged a war with the orthodox in India for two decades and more, over the abolition of untouchability and the establishment of social equality.

Three great Maharashtrian leaders of thought, Lokahitavadi Gopalrao Deshmukh, the protesting social reformer, M. G. Ranade, the non-violent social reformer, and Veer Savarkar, the radical social reformer, recognised the greatness of Dayanand Saraswati. These three leaders were above the narrow-minded social policy sponsored by Vishnushastri Chiplunkar.

In the meanwhile, Jotirao, with Ramchandra Hari Shinde and Krishnarao Bhalekar, formed a company called Toona Commercial and Contracting Company' and undertook to supply stones for the building of the right bank of the Khadakwasala canal. The contract proved very profitable.

At the annual meeting of the Satya-Shodhak Samaj in September 1875, Jotirao transferred, as was his policy and should be the policy of a real leader in order to create confidence in his young followers, presidentship of the Samaj to Dr. V. R. Gholay and Treasurership to Ramsheth Uravane. That year they had elected one Elaiya Soloman member of the Managing Committee. The Satya-Shodhak Samaj had 232 members on its roll. The annual function was a great success.

At this time people of Ahmedabad suffered on account of great floods and the Samaj collected money and sent it to Ahmedabad. Jotirao asked the Bombay Satya-Shodhak Samaj also to send funds to Ahmedabad.

Members of the Samaj held prayers on Sunday evenings. Once every fortnight on a Saturday there were lectures arranged to train workers in the art of public speaking. The Prince of Wales visited Poona in November 1875. On that occasion Dhondiram Namdeo Kumbhar and Krishnarao Bhalekar sang songs in praise of the Prince of Waleat a meeting of the Samaj.

The Samaj distributed gratis to Indian princes and influential men copies of Jotirao's two books *Slavery* and *Priestcraft Exposed*, which were donated by their author. It also sent its constitution and rules of procedure to them.

Raghavendrarao Ramchandrarao, Translator in the Bombay High Court, was gratefully thanked for giving his opinion that the marriages performed by the Samaj were legally valid. That opinion was conveyed to every branch of the Samaj in Maharashtra.

The Samaj had declared two prizes for an essay on 'What should be done to improve Indian agriculture' with special reference to the British Agricultural System. This shows the way the Samaj worked and reflected the mind of its leader.

A peon was employed by the Samaj to see that no Shudra children loafed in the streets witnessing tricks and other per formances of street entertainers. Jotirao made speeches and gave model lessons at schools encouraging teachers to adopt better methods of teaching to keep up the interest of the children. The Samaj petitioned the Principal of the Engineering College to admit a few non-Brahmin poor students free. It succeeded in its demand.

In May 1876 a special elocution competiiion was held on the utility or otherwise of idol-worship and the caste system. The winners were given prizes. The leaders of the Samaj began to spread education in rural areas. They established a school at Hadapsar. a village near Poona, which developed into a stronghold of the Satya-Shodhak Samaj. K. M. Chatfield, Director of Public Instruction, was thanked for issuing orders to Government schools to admit five per cent of the students from the poor classes free. The Samaj also thanked the *Satya Dipika, Subodha Patrika* and *Dnyanprakash* for their co-operation and for giving accurate reports in their journals of the work of the Samaj. Hari Raoji Chiplunkar was highly praised by the Samaj for the aid he gave to the Samaj for the spread of education. It hoped that the example set by him would be followed by the Indian Princes. Its membership rose from 232 to 316.

The Samaj obtained premises for its office. Ramchandra Mansaram Dhaware Naik, a Poona contractor, allowed the use of his building at a monthly rent of Rs. 10. A Brahmin donor, Hari Ganesh Patwardhan, alias Annasaheb Sanglikar, was praised for his generous donation and the interest he took in the welfare of the lower castes. Jaya Karadi Lingu and Tuka-ram Tatya Padval were gratefully thanked for their donations to the Samaj for the cause of education.

A condolence resolution was passed on the death of Jaya Pallappa Lingu, a generous and devoted member of the Samaj. A committee consisting of Gangaram Bhau Mhaske, Jotirao. Rajanna Lingu. Laxman Hari Shinde and Vinayakrao Bhandar-kar, was appointed to find ways and means to establish a Boarding House for the poor students from the mofussil area. A press was purchased by Vyanku Baloji Kalewar and Ramayya Vyankayya Aiyyavaru and handed over to the Poona Satya-Shodhak Samaj, but owing to some differences it was decided to send it back to the Bombay workers of the Satya-Shodhak Samaj.

The annual report of the Samaj for the year 1876 made a

fervent appeal to the lower castes for funds and to educated persons to assist the Samaj in promoting education among the lower castes. It warned them that if they failed to grasp enthusiastically their educational opportunities during the British regime, they would be marring the future of their children.

CHAPTER XI

Poona Reactionaries

JOTIRAO HAD expressed his opinion that as there was no Municipal member interested in the lower castes, no attention was paid to provide any amenities to the poor classes. Their grievances were not attended to. Because the officer in charge of water supply was a Brahmin in the Poona Municipality, he amply provided Brahmin localities with water and cared little or not at all for the localities of the poor classes. Water supply, light and sanitation arrangements were provided mainly for the higher classes. Jotirao was selected by Government to work on the Municipal Committee. The Poona Municipality was established under the Municipality Act 1850, from June 1, 1857, but it actually functioned from May 1858. All members were of Government choice. The elective principle established by Ripon under the Local Self-Government Act of 1882, came into operation from 1883. Jotirao worked from 1876 to 1882 as a member of the Poona Municipality. A member was then called a commissioner.

The report on the work of the Satya-Shodhak Samaj for the year 1876 was passed at the annual meeting of the Samaj, and it was issued to the Press in March 1877. It attracted the attention of some leading journals and magazines in Maharashtra.

In its review of the work done by the Satya-Shodhak Samaj, the *Vividhadnyan Vistar* paid its meed of praise to the workers of the Samaj for continuous work in different fields for three years. It was pleased to note that the Satya-Shodhak Samaj had not vanished like other mushroom social institutions. An encouraging sign was that, it observed, several persons from the mofussil areas were taking a keen interest in the work of the Samaj.

The *Vividhadnyan Vistar*,[1] however, sounded a discordant note. It said that there was no greater truth than the unity of the

1. March 1877.

people. In unity lay the salvation of the nation; and religion was the only unifying force between the Shudras and the Brahmins. If those ties of religion were to be preserved, the Samaj should not attack Hinduism. No religion born of several minds was, or, for that matter, any new religion could ever be perfect. No good would be achieved by embracing another religion or by organising a new sect.

Jotirao knew that all privileged classes had argued that way for ages. For the sake of unity they said that the poor classes, the suppressed classes, should never raise protests against their exploiters. The journal found fault with the grammar of the author of the report, and said that priests were the receivers and the Shudras were the masters as they were the givers. With all the perfect knowledge of grammar possessed by the editor, he could not understand the social content of Jotirao's work, which sprang from the miserable lot and the injured dignity of the lower castes. Under the camouflage of language, religion and national unity such men wanted to suppress their voice of protest against injustice and all expressions of the urge for social justice.

Another champion of Hindu religion, tradition, culture and language came forward with great fury and fire to attack Jotirao. His name was Vishnushastri Chiplunkar. Born in a Shastri family in 1850, he had grown nostalgic about Peshwa rule. There was more heat than light in his thought. While serving as a teacher at a Government High School in Poona, Chiplunkar started, in January 1874, a magazine called *Nibandhamala* on the model of the *Spectator* and imitated the vigour and polemic of Addison and Johnson.

A writer of great power and outstanding abilities, Chiplunkar gave an impetus to patriotic feelings and directed the hearts of educated young men to patriotic work. He imbued the young, educated generation with a fiery patriotism that soon inspired numerous Maharashtrians with courage to fight for the emancipation of the motherland. Inspired by his patriotic writings, several young men devoted themselves to unselfish activities for the regeneration of the country in various fields, such as history, education, industry and literature.

But Chiplunkar's main emphasis was on the past glory of India from which he derived his inspiration. Therefore, he attacked with intense violence those who criticised Hinduism,

Hindu customs, traditions and culture. He fanatically defended the defects of Peshwa rule, and avowing that everything was all right with Hindu society, he declared that it was sheer ill luck that the Hindus had lost their independence. Those who derived inspiration and guidance from his patriotic writings later maintained that the non-Brahmins, although they were Hindus, should not insist on reading the sacred Vedas which constituted the monopoly of the Brahmins.

As Chiplunkar took it upon himself to defend Hinduism, Hindu customs and traditions, he attacked the social reformers, who welcomed the new machine age, secular education and the spirit of enquiry, preached abolition of casteist prejudices and casteism, and encouraged widow remarriage.

The social reformers preached the abolition of decrepit, inhuman, wicked practices in society and upheld the principles of social equality and equal opportunity. Chiplunkar wanted Peshwa rule back whereas the reformers had fixed their eyes on the dawn of a new era. It was their aim to base their future Swaraj on a broader foundation of social equality, scientific outlook, social justice, and above all, reason.

Chiplunkar's writings flowed with passion and patriotism and pulsated with caustic satire and biting ridicule. But, as is the characteristic of such verbose and vehement writings, his writings were divorced from reality and reason, from insight and introspection, and provided a smoke-screen for his social and political revivalism. His egoistic personality displayed whatever inadequate knowledge of history he possessed with all the aggressiveness and self-justification at his command. With all their vision, wisdom and anxiety for the uplift and welfare of their countrymen. the social reformers had. however, on their part, an irritating effect upon the minds of the younger generation as they constantly harped on the defects of Hindu society and themselves rarely practised what they preached. Chiplunkar shrewdly attacked this weaker side of the reformers, whose wise words were not matched by their deeds, and he ruthlessly disparaged them.

Burdened with the thought of India's past glory Chiplunkar could not read the times, nor was he aware of the social ills of his age. Never for a moment did he give serious thought to the emergence of different institutions which clamoured for a change in India's social, religious, political and economic life. His aim was to arouse the middle class against British rule, not to reform society or remove social injustice and social inequality. He attacked the Brahmo Samaj, the Prarthana Samaj, the Arya Samaj and lastly the Satya-Shodhak Samaj which strove more or less for social changes and, excepting the Arya Samaj, were not rousing the people against British rule.

In his journal Chiplunkar reviled the Lokahitavadi for a whole year. He described men like Ranade, as did later Tilak, the successor to his school of thought, as wicked and base. He ridiculed Swami Dayanand Saraswati, mocked at his knowledge of Sanskrit, and hurled wordy shafts at him with the violence of a fanatic. With highly satiric satisfaction, he described the scene on the occasion of Dayanand procession which the Poona orthodox had wickedly attacked.

II

Chiplunkar now attacked Jotirao. He was commenting on the Report of the Satya-Shodhak Samaj.[2] So he introduced into the discussion Jotirao's two books *Slavery* and *Priestcraft Exposed.* To him Jotirao's Marathi was a horrible thing. In a sarcastic vein he wrote that Jotirao should leave alone subjects like religion, history, philology and theology and turn his attention to the grammar of Marathi. He was reminded of Jotirao's challenge to the omniscient Parashuram and said sarcastically that when Jotirao made sure that the mighty Parashuram did not appear, he attacked the Brahmins. Jotirao wrote *Slavery*, he added, by creating an imaginary adopted son to ask him some questions, so that in the event of Jotirao's death the Brahmins and Pandyas might never boast again of their glory. And derisively describing Jotirao as a Shudra Religious Teacher, a Shudra Founder of a Religion, a Shudra World-Teacher, he added that Jotirao was merely barking at Brahmins in all his writings.

Just then, the spirited young Krishnarao Bhalekar started, in January 1877, a Marathi weekly, *Din Bandhu*, Brother of the Poor, to spread the mission of the Satya-Shodhak Samaj and to give vent to the grievances of farmers, workers and the poor

2. *Nibandhamala*, pp. 440-57.

classes. It replied to Chiplunkar, who was given to satire and rhetoric, that the editor of the *Nibandhamala* was enraged at Jotirao's exposures of the Brahmins, and so he attacked Jotirao. In his reply Chiplunkar could not refute the facts which Jotirao had quoted from scriptures and *puranas*. He sidetracked and obscured the charges against the scriptures. It was the belief of the Satya-Shodhakites that British rule was a divine dispensation. Because of that rule the Shudras got an opportunity to receive education and know what their rights were. Chiplunkar was full of hatred for the lower classes. It was surprising, the *Din Bandhu* concluded, that he should attack the classes which were exploited by his own class, ground down by poverty, and kept wallowing in ignorance.

Upon this Chiplunkar's egoism was inflamed, and he boasted: "It may be that the Chitpavans have been born of the dead corpses or they might have come from Iran, but the qualities they have displayed and are displaying will not be a whit diminished notwithstanding hundreds of volumes like *Slavery* and *Jatibheda Viveksar*. The victorious deeds of Chitpavans have resounded throughout Hindusthan during the last century and their intellect and prowess are as virile as ever." "However crafty and wicked the Brahmins might be," he proudly added, "one thing is indisputable: It is that the Brahmins hold the keys to knowledge, and without their assistance the gates of knowledge will not be thrown open to other castes."

Chiplunkar further remarked that, confined as the Satya-Shodhak Samaj was to Poona and to the neighbouring villages, that insignificant thing was not worthy of his mighty pen. lf ever, Chiplunkar concluded in a derisively prophetic vein, the Satya-Shodhak Samaj grew like the Arya Samaj, and if a marble statue was erected to Jotirao in any Satya-Shodhak Samaj as a Memorial to his spotless success, the time would come to consider the merit of his views.

From this attack it is clear that Chiplunkar took up the cudgels on behalf of his caste against a man who repudiated rituals and dogmas prescribed by Brahmins. He made a frontal attack upon Jotirao who had emerged from the dumb millions of Maharashtra and who spoke their language, drew attention of all concerned to their suffering and to their appalling poverty, and became the spearhead of the attack on orthodoxy. Chiplunkar described Jotirao as a hater of Brahmins, but he himself hated all other castes! He talked and wrote as if he had descended from a Brahmin heaven!

Moreover, Chiplunkar had a grudge against Jotirao who had described, in *Slavery*, Chiplunkar's father as a vicious Bruhaspati. This had given an added edge to his attack on Jotirao. So again the legendary fight was renewed between Waman and Bali, Chiplunkar a Waman and Jotirao a Bali! Chiplunkar's ideas about the superior power, leadership and valour of Brahmins would not allow him to go deep into the grievances, miseries, ignorance and poverty of the Shudras. Chiplunkar proudly bestowed on himself the title 'Shivaji' of the Marathi language. In his brilliant prose he incidentally referred to popular prejudices, but he never uttered a word of sympathy for those who had heroically suffered in the cause of social reform. He totally lacked sympathy for the masses and the low castes, and he lacked imagination.

There were famines and widespread agricultural unrest prevailed; there was dreadful poverty and people were going through life on insufficient food; but Chiplunkar's pen remained unconcerned and was quite satisfied with the songs of the glory of the past. He was utterly incapable of understanding the reformist role of Jotirao whom he condemned as an enemy of Hinduism.

The ridicule Chiplunkar poured on Jotirao has now turned into roses for Jotirao. Almost all thinkers of Maharashtra have appreciated Jotirao's pioneering work, sacrifice and courage, although some may not have liked the way he expressed his thought.

Chiplunkar had a mastery of language but little or no insight, whereas his peasant opponent possessed no power of language but had vision and insight. Rich diction, self-respect, religiosity and patriotism which were the virtues of Chiplunkar's brilliant and bellicose style undoubtedly inaugurated an era in the history of the Marathi language. However, the main part of Chiplunkar's hated prophesy came true. At several places statues are erected to Jotirao, notwithstanding the rude simplicity of his language, while one would with difficulty discover any erected to Chiplunkar outside Poona.

In his satiric vein Chiplunkar observed that from reports he had learnt that Jotirao was a veteran worker and had been making a noise during nearly twenty-five years for the welfare of the people. His pretence that he was ignorant of the existence of Jotirao was a transparent lie and he adopted it for the sake of rhetoric. Chiplunkar's father had been once a colleague of Jotirao when he established a committee to look after the girls' schools. A man who carried on so many public, useful activities and had made hundreds of speeches in Poona was surely not unknown to Chiplunkar. How this unkind, cutting remark, this egoistic effusion was rewarded by Jotirao the Mahatma will be seen later.

That the keys to the gates of knowledge were in the hands of Brahmins alone was Chiplunkar's another vain claim. The gates of knowledge were opened to Indians by the British and, excepting instruction in the Sanskrit language, they have done nothing to spread knowledge among the masses. Chiplunkar's utter disregard for the social changes, his hatred for the reformers who stood for the social equality and fraternity, and his burning partiality for Brahmins undid the work of the social reformers who were preparing the ground for social cohesion, equality and justice which would have led to the unity of the people. Chiplunkar thus drove a wedge into Maharashtra and as a result the non-Brahmins kept away from the national ferment set up by Chiplunkar school of thought. Chiplunkar's attack on the reformers retarded the growth of social cohesion and social revolution in Maharashtra.

Not long afterwards, Tilak, on whose shoulders fell the mantle of the leadership of the Chiplunkar school of thought, ruthlessly moved his intellectual steam-roller over the social reform movement in Maharashtra. The thinker in Agarkar made him part company with Tilak and he died soon after, without being active in his work. The followers of Jotirao kept themselves aloof from Poona politicians. Many years later, the lower classes in Maharashtra joined the Indian National Congress when Mahatma Gandhi's appeal to farmers and Untouchables was projected through the Congress in 1930.

III

In order to educate the members of the Satya-Shodhak Samaj,

Jotirao held at the Samaj debates and discussions on different topics. He invited experts to deliver lectures on science, on eclipse, the importance of education, poverty of India and such other subjects.

The Satya-Shodhak Samaj announced two prizes in April 1877, one in an essay competition and the other in an elocution competition. The announcement was made over the signature of the Samaj Secretary, Jotirao Phooley. The essay was to be on an imaginary topic. Queen Victoria was supposed to be touring India. She came to a certain village where a Mahar and a Mang kept down their bundles of taggots, met her and narrated to her their miserable conditions under Peshwa rule and their disabilities under British rule.

They narrated to her the agonies, hardships and oppressions they had to undergo under Hinduism and their sufferings under her rule while they remained part and parcel of Hinduism. A few days later, Jotirao himself wrote a booklet on this topic and published it under the caption *Kaifiyat*.

The topic for the elocution competition was: 'What were the causes of repeated famines and why Shudras were the first to fall victims to them and die of hunger; and what remedies should be adopted to remove the causes?'

If any candidate taking part in the essay competition referred to political issues, his essay would not be considered for the prize; if any candidate referred to politics in his speech he would be disqualified.

The topic for the elocution competition was famine because in 1876-77, the Deccan had been in the grip of acute famine followed by a plague of vermin which added to the miseries of the people. The occurrence of famine had been pretty frequent since 1860. In 1875 there had been serious agrarian riots in the districts of Ahmedabad, Poona, Satara and Sholapur. Strained relations between the agriculturists and money-lenders led to these riots. Jotirao was terribly worried about these events as the peasants and poor classes were largely affected by them. He had often shed a clear light in his writings and speeches on the frauds committed by money-lenders in obtaining from ignorant peasants bonds for larger amounts than were actually paid or due from them. He had been crying himself hoarse about this since 1869. The Government appointed a Commission of Inquiry and their report led to the Deccan Agriculturists' Relief Act, 1879.

The object of the Act was to relieve the agricultural classes from indebtedness and to improve the relations between the agriculturists and money-lenders by providing some safeguards against money-lenders committing frauds in their accounts and making false documents.

The *Din Bandhu* had supported the Act and said it would prevent money-lenders from depriving poor and ignorant cultivators of their lands and their property. The existing wretched condition of the peasants, it affirmed, was attributable to the excessive greed of the Sowkars and Brahmin priests. If there were fewer transactions between the two, the farmers would be self-reliant and industrious and would endeavour to live within their means. Their illiteracy and ignorance had resulted in the impoverishment of the cultivators.

Again, in its issue of November 23, 1879, the *Din Bandhu* said that the newspapers conducted by Brahmins protested against the Deccan Agriculturists' Relief Act because Brahmin money-lenders were losers under the operation of the Act. Appealing to Government to pay no heed to their protests, it asked Government to appoint a commission to inquire into the working of the Act if it wished to ascertain the results. The pious learned Dr. Wilson attributed the riots to the instigation of educated Brahmins while the Brahmins attributed it to the revenue policy of the Government in increasing the assessment on land and its aggressive system of collecting it. Since ill-timed rain or failure of rain was the curse on Maharashtra that repeatedly played havoc, during this famine also wealthy farmers were reduced to poverty and they sought jobs and service. Lakhs of people died from hunger.

Jotirao played a prominent part in relieving the distress. He wrote article after article in the *Din Bandhu* urging Government to give the people work and food. As Jotirao was an active leader he was deeply moved at the terrific death rate of innocent children. At Dhankawadi Camp he opened an orphanage called Victoria Balashram, where two thousand children from the age of two to twelve were fed with bread in the morning and again in the evening. He was helped in this work by Seth Uravane, Hari Raoji Chiplunkar and Shinappa, the Chief Officer of the Poona Municipality. Government, too, distributed for some months bread to famine-stricken people in Poona.

On May 17, 1877, Jotirao, Secretary of the Satya-Shodhak Samaj, made a frantic and fervent public appeal to the members of the Samaj in Poona, Bombay and in other places for speedy help. In his appeal he said that a large number of poor, famine-stricken people from neighbouring talukas had flocked to the Victoria Balashram in Poona. For want of food they had been reduced to a skeleton and were also in rags. Their hardships, he concluded, were indescribable.[3] This work was discontinued at the end of May 1879.[4]

There was another essay competition organised by Jotirao. The subject was why the Shudras who produced rulers like Shivaji, Princes like Shinde, Holkar and Gaikwad had become shameless enough to take up the jobs of looking after the clothes not only of the Brahmins but also of their wives, and why a Brahmin, however poverty-stricken, thought it below his dignity to do such a thing. This was in February 1878.

The contract which Jotirao's Poona Commercial and Contracting Company had undertaken was being executed. It seems from an announcement made about the essay competition, that Ramsheth Bapusheth Uravane had joined them as Shinde had accepted a job. The contract work continued till the middle of 1879. By then Bhalekar, who was very busy with the publication of the *Din Bandhu*, had left the company.

Jotirao was a very active member of the Poona Municipality. While discussing, in October 1878, the budget for the year 1879-80, he made a suggestion that instead of appointing one clerk on a monthly salary of Rs. 50, two clerks on the salary of Rs. 30 and Rs. 20 should be appointed. The suggestion was accepted. A few days later, he was also appointed a member of the subcommittee to scrutinize the Accounts for the years 1875-76 and 1877-78.

IV

About this time the *Din Bandhu* harshly criticized the Prarthana

3. The *Dnyanprakash*, 24 May 1877.
4. The *Dnyanprakash*, 2 June 1879.

Samaj. According to it the Prarthana Samaj was a Brahmin institution used to hoodwink the poor classes. It said that the leaders of the Prarthana Samaj had no interest in the promotion of education among the poor classes, nor did they utter a word for the rights of the poor classes. The *Subodha Patrika*,[5] the mouthpiece of the Prarthana Samaj, observed that its followers approved of the aims and objects of the Satya-Shodhak Samaj and wished it success, but the charge that it was a Brahmin body was unjustifiable and unjust. It was a fact that a majority of the members of the Prarthana Samaj were Brahmins, but it did not mean that they were running the Samaj to raise the prestige and power of Brahmins as alleged by the *Din Bandhu*. If, the *Subodha Patrika* concluded, the Shudras joined it in large numbers, they would be able to dominate it.

It is very interesting to note that both the Satya-Shodhak Samaj and the Prarthana Samaj said prayers in congregation. Yet, the *Din Bandhu* was scornful of the Prarthana Samaj, saying that since they kept their eyes closed like herons they were religious hypocrites! Opinionated as they were, they regarded with suspicion any institution conducted by Brahmins, however broad-minded and liberal they were. The Prarthana Samaj leaders danced before their God with jingling bells worn on their ankles. Such things must have irritated Jotirao and he pooh-poohed them. Jotirao was a believer in the Lord of the Universe, and beyond that his religion prescribed no such ways to propitiating God.

The carping criticism of Brahmins by the *Din Bandhu* was, it seems, creating displeasure in non-Brahmin circles. The *Kalpataru*,[6] Sholapur, edited by a Shimpi, mildly expressed its disapproval of it and said that such criticism was injurious. A follower of the Bhakti cult, the editor of the *Kalpataru* must have taken fright at the biting articles against Brahmins in the *Din Bandhu*.

As almost all his partners left him on some ground or other, Jotirao pressed Gyanoba Sasane to come and work with him. The Poona Commercial and Contracting Company went in for a new trade. For nearly four months Gyanoba did purchasing

5. The *Subodha Patrika*, 22 December 1878 and 12 January 1879.
6. The *Kalpataru*, 21 November 1879.

at the vegetable markets in Poona. The company sent vegetables to the Bombay market, but the enterprise proved unprofitable. Jotirao, therefore, had to close the company and reluctantly terminated the services of Gyanoba Sasane who had left Government service on Jotirao's asking and joined him. In appreciation of Sasane's faithful services, he granted him a certificate to the effect that although Gyanoba had not attended any school, he could write a very good Modi-Marathi hand and was punctual and diligent. Poor Gyanoba preserved the certificate as a memento of his master.

The Din Bandhu, started with eight subscribers by Bhalekar, had few subscribers during the famine years, but made a great noise. It observed: "Regeneration of India will be effected by imparting technical education to the lower classes and by destroying the rigid caste system which has done so much to bring about the ruin of the country."

Jotirao took a deep interest in the proceedings of the Municipality. In April 1879 he was appointed to recommend a place for dumping the refuse of the City. He was watchful of the rights of the members of the Municipality. He and his friend Dr. Gholay were criticized in September 1879 along with the majority of the members who turned down a proposal to erect suitable rooms for the use of the Poona Native General Library on the site of Budhawarvada. This had been burnt down during the revolt of Wasudeo Balwant Phadke.

The *Dnyanprakash* said that it did little credit to the hearts of those who supported the resolution. Rao Bahadur Khanderao Vishvanath Raste moved and Rao Bahadur Viziarangam Arya Mudliar supported the resolution. The permission was refused on sanitary grounds. If they had permitted it, one member said, the Municipality and the Government would have been guilty of deliberately dishonouring the name and prestige of the Peshwa who had built Budhwarwada.

The Managing Committee of the Poona Municipality spent some money without the sanction of the General Meeting. Jotirao supported a resolution moved by Hari Raoji Chiplunkar sanctioning the money but asking the Managing Committee not to spend money without the previous sanction of the General Committee.

Just at this moment Poona was passing through a patriotic

wave caused by the revolt of Wasudeo Balwant Phadke. Born on November 4, 1845, Phadkc worked as a clerk for some time in the Military Finance Office in Poona'. He resolved to overthrow British rule and took physical military training under Lahuji Mang, who was also the teacher of Jotirao in 1847 in military exercises, and had assisted Jotirao in collecting Mahar Mang children for his school. Phadke rose in armed revolt against British rule. This revolt rocked Maharashtra to its roots from March to May 1879. The news of the revolt thrilled the pages of Indian and English newspapers. Once again Phadke proved that the memory of their military, political hegemony all over India was tenaciously retained by the Maratha people. Phadke failed, and his trial took place in Poona from October 22 to November 7, 1879. He was sentenced to transportation for life and he died in Aden Jail on February 17, 1883.

It is claimed by some that Jotirao had secretly supplied bread to the soldiers of Phadke. In his last book *Sarvajanik Satya Dharma Pustaka*, Jotirao refers slightingly to Phadke as a robber, or a rebel, and therefore was not likely to applaud Phadke's mission of overthrowing British rule. Vishnushastri Chiplunkar described Phadke as a robber, Ranade called him a mad patriot, and many other persons and journals did the same thing. Phadke's acquaintance with Jotirao and their common bonds with Lahuji Bawa Mang, under whom they had taken military training, might have moved Jotirao to show sympathy for the hardships of Phadke's fighting men and their valour. Had Jotirao actively helped him, he would not have referred to him in his book in 1889 in the terms he used. Jotirao was not by nature a politician, to disown shrewdly Phadke after his failure for fear of being implicated in his trial.

Jotirao wrote many articles in the *Din Bandhu* on a variety of subjects, and then his lieutenants propagated those subjects in their villages and towns About the close of 1879 and early in 1880, he wrote on the necessity of compulsory free primary education and demanded it as early as possible. England under its Education Act of 1870 provided schools and made in 1880[7] primary education compulsory upto the age of 10. Almost all progressive changes in Britain had their repercussions on India.

7. Somervell. D. C., *Modern Britain*, 1870-1939, p. 5.

Jotirao, who had been demanding primary education for the masses, got an opportunity to urge the Government to give their active consideration to it. Success never turned his head; hardships and failures did not daunt him. Incidentally, it is interesting to note that Scotland declared free primary education in 1890, and in 1892 Ireland followed suit.

After the completion of the canal work, the farmers were found most reluctant to make use of the canal water for their fields. Any innovation was anathema to them. Jotirao had written articles and made speeches making suggestions to Government to provide the farmers with better seed, implements and manure. Jotirao had not vainly lauded the attempts by Government at irrigation work. Superstition and ignorance came in the way of the peasants using modern methods of agriculture. So with a view to setting an example to them, Jotirao purchased a plot of 200 acres of land and cultivated it himself by new methods, using the canal water and growing potatoes, oranges, cauliflowers and sugar-cane. Some part of the land at the Manjari forest near Poona was known as Phooley Mango Grove. Then other farmers followed their leader, and gradually the way was paved for better agriculture in Poona District.

CHAPTER XII

Labour and Liquor

JOTIRAO'S FREQUENT visits to Bombay made him conscious of the hardships of millhands. They were harnessed to work from sunrise to sunset, with a brief spell for eating. His chief lieutenant Narayanrao Lokhande, who had taken charge of the *Din Bandhu* since May 1880, was devoting his time to the study of the problems of millhands. He was born in 1848 in a poor Mali family at Thana. After receiving high school education in Thana, he came to Bombay and stayed at Byculla, where he made fiiends with a Khoja merchant named Fazalbhai Nashi. After serving in a railway locomotive office and then in a post office, as a clerk, he got a job of storekeeper in a cotton mill at Mandvi, Bombay. Here he studied the various difficulties and hardships the Mill workers had to undergo. A young leader of the Satya-Shodhak Samaj, he determined to fight for the improvement of the condition of millhands.

The first Cotton Mill called the Spinning and Weaving Company was established on July 7, 1854[1] by Cowasji Davar, at Tardeo, Bombay, with support from a cosmopolitan band of co-partners. He was the son of a Parsi Merchant and was thirty-nine. A few weeks later, Maneckjee Petit followed his example. This idea of a mill industry was first mooted[2] in 1850 by Dr. Bhau Daji Lad in Bombay, but no definite plans emerged. Since then the mill industry had grown; but there was no organization to represent their grievances, although Sorabjee Shapoorji Bengalee, a Parsi scholar and social reformer, tried to talk to the Millowners and evoke their sympathies for the millhands. A few progressive individuals supported his stand.

A commission consisting exclusively of leading millowners was appointed in March 1875, but the commission was found not in favour of imposing any legal restrictions on the infant industry

1. Mehta, S. D., *The Cotton Mills in India*, 1854-1954, p.1.
2. Ibid., p. 7.

and made light of the complaint that young children were made to do full-time work and the hard, long hours to which women were subjected. About this time there were forty-one mills in Bombay, five at Calcutta, two at Madras, two at Kanpur, one each at Hyderabad, Indore and Nagpur; in all there were then 53 mills in India.

So prompted by Jotirao, Lokhande, born fighter that he was. gave himself up to voicing the grievances of the dumb millhands as soon as he became editor of the *Din Bandhu*. His was a conciliatory approach, and the millowners had no objection to the workers being organized. Lokhande was a man of great action, who championed mainly the cause of the millhands, and Krishnarao Bhalekar, a man of unflagging energy, worked for the welfare of the agriculturists. Jotirao's two chief colleagues were thus working in two different fields.

Hard labour, observed the *Din Bandhu*,[3] about fourteen hours a day was exacted from the millhands in Bombay. The millowners said that most of the operatives were not employed on any fixed pay but worked by contract; so it was in the interests of the operatives to work in mill incessantly. The operatives had to work in a closed place in one position. The millowners said that the workers were allowed to go out by turns into the open air. But as a matter of fact, the *Din Bandhu* continued: "They were fined four annas each for leaving their work for so short a period. So there was an actual prohibition against taking rest from the fatiguing work. The statement of the commission appointed by Government in 1875 to the effect that the children employed in the mills, though they spent the whole of their time there, did their work in a leisurely way, was not proved." This was a labour problem which concerned the poor, and the *Din Bandhu* had to fight alone for its solution. Men like Chiplunkar were interested in Addison and Johnson and had nothing to say about the miseries of workers and peasants.

There was a Gujarati journal called *Rast Goftar*, socially progressive but politically conservative. It sympathised with the aspirations of the workers. It was, however, true that Lokhande edited probably the first[4] paper devoted mainly to labour problems.

3. 18 January 1879.
4. Mehta, S. D., The Cotton Mills in India, 1854 to 1954, p. 131.

Lokhande and Jotirao addressed several workers' meetings in Bombay, and Lokhande organised the workers who were then almost all Marathi-speaking.

That is why Lokhande has been hailed as the founder of organized labour in India. He founded the Millhands' Association early in the year 1880. It was the first organization of mill workers, and he was its elected President. The millowners raised no objection to the creation of the workers' organization. They conceded the right of the employees to organize themselves. When Government appointed another commission called the Factory Commission, to examine the conditions under which workers were labouring, Lokhande convened a conference. He was elected by it to make representations to the Factory Commission.

There was one Deccan Social Reform Association founded by Poona Brahmins. Its President was Prof. Kero Laxman Chhatre. The first annual gathering met on October 14, 1880. Its managing committee had met early in March 1880 and considered the proposals that came up before it for the celebration of *holi* festival by holding wrestling bouts, performing plays and other activities of a similar nature. Frankly, there was no question of Jotirao's joining such a worthless institution with a big name. Nothing was heard of the Association later.

On July 25, 1880, Ganesh Wasudeo Joshi, *alias* Sarvajanik Kaka, died. A real Public Uncle, he had launched several activities for the uplift and welfare of the Indian people. He was a man of boundless energy, and the governing passion of his life was service of the people. It was he who fought out a case on behalf of a poor Brahmin lady in which some Brahmins were convicted. He was a lover of Swadeshi, and his self-respect and fearlessness were his leading characteristics.

A condolence meeting was held under the presidentship of Rao Bahadur Lokahitavadi Gopalrao Deshmukh to mourn the death of this eminent Indian. A resolution was passed appreciating his self-sacrificing and patriotic services. The second resolution was moved by Sirdar T. N. Rajamachikar and seconded by Vaman Shivram Apte, who a few days later, became Superintendent of the New School established by Chiplunkar. The resolution expressed most loyal sympathy for the Government in the prevailing crisis, and hoped that the prestige of British arms would soon be restored, as a heavy disaster to the Indian army, on the other side of Kandahar, had taken place.

Jotirao Phooley moved the third resolution and was seconded by Vinayak Bapuji Bhandarkar. The resolution said that the Poona Sarvajanik Sabha be asked to convey the foregoing resolution to His Excellency the Governor, with a request that he might communicate it to Her Most Gracious Majesty the Queen Empress of India and to His Excellency the Viceroy. Jotirao[5] made a few appropriate remarks. It is not known whether these remarks were concerning the death of Sarvajanik Kaka or concerning the debacle at Kandahar.

Jotirao's active work continued in the Poona Municipality. In June 1880 Hari Raoji Chiplunkar moved a resolution recommending that the managing committee of the Municipality be appointed yearly, before the commencement of each official year, by the members collectively.[6] There were half-yearly changes, and members had no adequate time to apply themselves to work. Jotirao supported the resolution. There were some amendments, but these failed. The original proposition was carried out. The point in the main proposition was that the managing committee should be responsible to the General Committee. Defender that he was of the people's rights, Jotirao always fought against any proposal trying to invest power in a group of persons that was likely to develop into a clique.

Two months later there was a proposal before the Municipal Committee for building a new vegetable Market in Vetal Peth. Hari Raoji Chiplunkar moved an amendment, and Jotirao seconded it to the effect that the amount for erecting the shed should be sanctioned; but no shop should be charged a rent of more than annas four a monh. While a member on the Municipal Committee, Jotirao either looked after the interests of the poor people or defended the rights of the Municipal members against the Government.

Jotirao's disinterestedness and fearlessness was again seen when he opposed the spending of money over the decoration of the city to celebrate the visit of the Governor-General, Lord Lytton. By promulgating the Vernacular Press Act, Lord Lytton had

3. The *Dnyanprakash*, 9 August 1879.
6. Mangudkar, Dr. M. P., *Poona Municipality Centenary Volume* (Marathi), p.504.

aroused hostile opposition to the Government. He had grown unpopular. The President of the Poona Municipality sent a circular-letter on November 30, 1880, to the members, requesting their sanction for an expenditure of Rs. 1,000 to decorate the city on the occasion of the Viceroy's visit.

Out of thirty-six members, Jotirao was the only member who had the courage to vote against the proposition. He said that instead of spending money on the decoration and Address to be given to the Viceroy, the money saved should be spent on the education of the poor citizens.[7] The governing principle of Jotirao's life was the welfare of the poor classes. The Viceroy visited Poona, and he was honoured. But by thus displaying courage Jotirao established the right of the member of the Municipality to turn down a proposal put up by so important an officer as the Collector and to oppose even the proposal for honouring the Viceroy!

II

A few days after this incident, Jotirao again clashed with the Government. To cope up with the situation arising out of the growing illicit liquor business, Government was thinking of increasing liquor shops in Poona. In the year 1880 Government therefore permitted some new liquor shops to be opened. So their number increased. Jotirao, who was against the evil of drink, protested against this policy of Government and wrote to Plunkett, the Chairman of the Managing Committee of the Municipality, on July 18, 1880, that "The Poona Municipality has at a great cost kept a large sanitary establishment and is also maintaining a department, especially with a view to preserving the health of the inhabitants. But the existence of a large number of liquor shops in the heart of the city which were altogether unknown to it a few years ago, and which are sowing over the land the seeds of every kind of mortal disease is not calculated to ensure this object."

"I think it will be readily admitted by all that these liquor shops are not only injurious to the morality of the inhabitants

7. Mangudkar, Dr. M. P., *Poona Municipality Centenary Volume* (Marathi), pp. 505-06.

but highly injurious to their health. Since the opening of these liquor shops, drunkenness has increased to such an extent that many families have been utterly ruined, and it has now become almost an established vice in the city.

"With a view to checking in some degree at least the spread of this evil I would beg to propose that the Municipality should tax liquor shops in proportion to the mischief done by them. I am informed that in no other Municipality are liquor shops subject to local Municipal taxation, notwithstanding the levy of the imperial taxes on them. If necessary, inquiries may be instituted. I shall, therefore, thank you to lay this proposition of mine before the next general meeting."

The news of this letter made a stir in the city. Commenting on the views expressed by Jotirao and supporting his stand, the *Dnyanprakash* observed: "The subject to which Mr. Phooley has for the first time, we believe, drawn the prominent attention of the Municipality is very important and Mr. Phooley undoubtedly deserves the best thanks for having done so. His letter was placed before the Managing Committee at their first weekly meeting after its receipt, when the following resolution was recorded.

"To be submitted for the consideration of the President as to whether the subject should be brought before the General Committee. Spirits are not taxed in the orders of the Government of India on which Government Resolution No.3004 of 22nd October, 1877, was passed.

"The committee beg to express a hope that it may be possible in future contracts to reduce the number of liquor shops in Poona City."

The original letter, continued the *Dnyanprakash,* together with a resolution of the Managing Committee was sent for orders to Richey, President of the Municipality, who on the 27th July forwarded it for report to Henry Dickenson, the Abkari Inspector. Dickenson submitted the following report on the 30th July: "In reply, the undersigned begs respectfully to submit a statement which shows that from 1873-74 to 1876-77 there were but four shops in the city. The increase of six shops making the number ten took place from 1877-78.

"The reason why the increase of six shops was allowed by the Collector was with a view to discouraging smuggling (which was extensively carried on previous to the increase in the localities) where the new shops have been established. The liquor so smuggled into Poona was of a very impure nature and consequently injurious to health."

The sale increased from 15,697 gallons in 1874 to 22,912 gallons in 1879.

It would appear that, the *Dnyanprakash* went on, Richey was convinced from Dickenson's report of the truth of the principal statement made in Phooley's letter that the vice of drinking was making rapid progress in the City of Poona, for he recorded a minute on the correspondence in which he openly expressed his belief that the increased facilities for obtaining liquor granted to the people were calculated to lead many to form a taste for drinking liquor who would not otherwise form it. Consumption of European liquor increased, and the number of liquor shops also increased.

Richey sent on August 8, 1880, this reference to the Police Superintendent. He replied on August 27: "that the prevailing impression is that drinking has made rapid strides in the city of Poona, but is only noticeable because the vice has crept in amongst the well-to-do people who possibly never drank before and who even now do not indulge in the use of the country manufactured spirits."

"Every kind of vice," the Police Officer further observed in a practical manner, "has a tendency to increase if not checked; the vice of drinking is no exception to this rule. The means proposed however by Jotirao Govindrao Phooley is one not in the smallest way calculated to remedy the evil, if such evil is admitted to exist. The reduction of the liquor shops in the city would in no way decrease the consumption. What would necessarily be consumed by a legitimate sale through shops being established in convenient places, would be consumed by impure liquor being either smuggled into the city, or by persons going to the shops standing and there taking at once a large quantity to avoid going to the place a second time on account of the distance. This is likely to tell on the health of the people more than anything else, and I would therefore advocate an increase rather than decrease in the number of shops."

Richey returned the entire correspondence to the Municipality with an endorsement that the evils complained of were not traceable to the increased number of shops.

The *Dnyanprakash*[8] finally remarked that the point at is this was not whether the increased number of liquor shops led to increased consumption and the spread of vice; but whether any measures ought to be taken to check the spread. The Managing Committee, it reminded, in their resolution on Phooley's letter expressed a hope that in future contracts care would be taken to lessen the number of liquor shops.

According to the British rulers, the problem was whether addiction to pure liquor was not less injurious and less dangerous to health than to impure, illicit liquor. Jotirao wanted to check the spread of the evil. It cannot be said that he subscribed to the utopia of prohibition. The extensive list of names of wine and spirits both in the classics and in the modern languages of India leave little reason to doubt that the cultivation of wine had been practised at the time of the Vedas.

Jotirao, however, was not the first person to raise his voice against the evil of drink. In 1852 the people of Satara had sent a memorial to Government appealing to it to close down distilleries and liquor shops. C. W. Bell, a Government official, had submitted a Report in 1869 on the excise policy of the Government of Bombay. In it, he had said that in the latter part of Peshwa rule the drink habit was growing and the revenue from it was increasing, and there was rigorous punishment for the offenders against it.[9]

III

Towards the close of July 1882, Hari Raoji and Jotirao moved a no-confidence motion against a municipal official named Narso Ramchandra who was responsible for spending extravagantly on the purchase of metal sheets for the use of the Municipality. But the proposition was merely recorded as it was felt that there was not sufficient evidence to merit an inquiry.

Although it was the confirmed view of Jotirao that no religious book contained unadulterated truth from beginning to

8. 27 September 1880.
9. Bakhale, P. S., in *Mouj Silver Jubilee Number*, 15 August 1947, p. 107.

end, he never criticised Christianity as he attacked Brahminism. His colleagues began to criticise Christians and attack their religion. It seems that whatever little influence Christian missionaries had on Jotirao, it began to wane about this time. There was a controversy over it in the *Dnyanodaya*. The *Dnyanodaya* commented that everyone took pride in the superiority of his own religion. Jotirao's colleagues criticised, too, the Government. His young colleagues, Bhalekar and Lokhande, were against the exploitation of Indian peasants and workers as it was carried on by the British, and particularly Bhalekar in his ballads and poems criticised the British Government. If the other patriotic leaders of their times had openly opposed the exploitation of the poor classes by money-lenders and priests, these leaders would have bolstered them up.

Jotirao's energetic leadership and activities now began spreading all over Maharashtra. He was invited to deliver speeches at some places in the Phalton State. His voice breathed the grievances, and sorrows of the people. In the past generations no one from amongst the lower castes had made such a thundering and stirring appeal against social inequality and injustice, discrimination and privilege. Jotirao made desperate efforts to shake the villagers out of their inertia and apathy through the local men whom he wanted to mould into social workers by giving them the concept of a new life. It was his aim to better their lot and change the pattern of rural life. A primary school in every village, a farmer following the methods of modern agriculture, a village freed from the clutches of unclean habits, debts and drinks, and liberated from the clutches of priest-craft and casteist prejudices. These were the things he visualised. He brought the people hope and solace and offered a healing touch to those who suffered distress.

As Jotirao's movement began to get a footing in society, all the property holders, privileged classes and priestly class began to shower curses on him. He visited also Sawantwadi, a small Maratha State, and there made stirring speeches on the importance of education and equality. He was the first eminent leader to make a tour of Maharashtra with a view to rousing the common man from his age-long slumber, superstition and bondage. N. C. Kelkar, biographer of Tilak and a leader of a judicious affable mind, was right when he observed that before the birth of the New English School[10] in 1880 at which Tilak started his career, the non-Brahmin movement had been already started.

Allegedly and on the face of it, the Satya-Shodhak Samaj movement looked a non-Brahmin movement. However, it was not in the main a non-Brahmin movement in Jotirao's day. Since the Brahmins held the levers of administrative and economic as well as social and religious power, and the non-Brahmin majority suffered a number of disabilities, the revolt against them naturally gained a non-Brahmin complexion. Besides, it aimed at punching holes in the barrier between the urban and rural parts of the country. The rural part was unaware of the vast changes taking place in the rest of the country and in the outer world. This movement dealt with all aspects of rural life by furnishing the villagers with news and knowledge, and by striving to remove the webs of ignorance and prejudices.

By now Vishnushastri Chiplunkar, who was serving in the Government High School as an assistant teacher, returned in May 1879 to Poona on leave from Ratnagiri, after his father's death. He resigned from Government service and opened a new school with the object of educating the younger generation with the assistance of B. G. Tilak. G. G. Agarkar later joined the school as promised. In January 1881 the trio launched two newspapers, the *Kesari*, a Marathi weekly, and the *Mahratta*, an English weekly, to educate the people on public affairs. The first editor of the *Kesari* was G. G. Agarkar and the first editor of the Mahratta was B. G. Tilak. Shortly afterwards, the mind of Chiplunkar was distracted from his school. He had to manage his Chitrashala, Kitabkhana and his *Nibandhmala*. By nature he was reticent and industrious, but now he looked washed-out, distracted and indifferent to school affairs.

Those fearless champions of the people's cause criticised the native rulers as well as the British rulers. At this time the affairs of the Kolhapur State engaged the minds of these young editors. Since 1877 the adopted Prince Shivajirao had been showing signs of suspected insanity. It was rumoured that the Dewan, Madhavrao Barve, supported by the Maharani, was concocting plans to depose him or to remove him from the *gadi*

10. Kelkar, N. C., *Biography of Lokamanya Tilak*, (Marathi) p. 73.

By administering dangerous drugs to him. Meeting after meeting was held at Kolhapur and Poona, demanding that the Prince should be placed under a new guardianship.

The *Kesari* and *Mahratta* published a series of articles depicting Mr. Barve as the villain of the piece. Barve sued the editors and publishers of the *Kesari* and *Mahratta* and also the editor of the *Dnyanprakash* for defamation. One of the two men who came forward to stand security for Tilak was Ramsheth Uravane. He did it at the instance of Jotirao Phooley, his colleague and leader who was interested in this case, as, according to Jotirao, they were on the side of truth and justice.

IV

While the case was being fought out at the law court in Bombay, Chiplunkar was suddenly taken seriously ill. He was then barely thirty-two. When he was at death's door, he felt an intolerable heat in his stomach. So he ate some slices of watermelon. When Dr. Vishram Gholay was called in by his uncle, Chiplunkar sighed: "Uncle, run to my arms! I am dying, Give me a drop of water, a drop of water." And looking at Dr. Gholay he thundered at him: "I won't take your medicine. I shall not be poisoned![11] Take care you will have to answer. This is Kolhapur Maharaj's case". Dr. Gholay refused to prescribe for him and said he would advise the next day a country physician to do so.

Chiplunkar died on the early morning of March 17, 1882. He had lost touch with the river of change and lived in back-water complacently, self-satisfied, ostracized. Greatness never comes from narrowness of mind. Nor does greatness come from mere learning, if it does not ensure justice or compassion. Much of the patriotic effusion from the verbose and bellicose writings of Chiplunkar has settled down. His brilliant essays on Johnson, the English language, Moropant and Elocution now belong to history. His mordant criticism of the Lokahitavadi, Dayanand and Jotirao, has been left as ashes, and the three men Swami Dayanand, the Lokahitavadi and Jotirao emerged as truer and

11. Chiplunkar, L. K., *Biography of Vishnushastri Chiplunkar* (Marathi), pp. 256-57.

holier and mightier personages, several times greater than the patriotic writer Chiplunkar.

The anxiety caused by the Kolhapur case weighed despite himself on Chiplunkar's mind. There were persistent rumours that Chiplunkar had ended his life by taking poison, as he had developed a fear of the consequences of the Kolhapur case. The police intervened and told all those concerned that unless they produced a medical certificate to the effect that Chiplunkar had died a natural death, they would not allow them to cremate the dead body. A doctor-friend of Chiplunkar's who had administered medicine to him flatly refused to issue the necessary certificate. Prof. Keronana, a leading man in the city, and several others, sought the help of Dr. Gholay. Jotirao felt pity for his dead critic, and he returned good for evil. He prevailed upon Dr. Gholay, his colleague to issue the necessary certificate, and Dr. Gholay did so.[12]

The funeral procession swept along to the burning place. The processionists had to be content with just one funeral oration as they again feared interference by the police at any moment.

The Barve defamation suit continued. The eminent men on whose security and approval Tilak and Agarkar had published the so-called original documents, withdrew their support. Tilak and Agarkar each tendered an unconditional apology to Barve that he did not accept. The jury found them guilty; the judge sentenced them to four months' imprisonment.

Chiplunkar's valiant colleagues Tilak and Agarkar were released on October 26, 1882, after 101 days of jail life. Jotirao and his two lieutenants Narayan Meghaji Lokhande and Damodar Savalaram Yande were prominent among those who hailed the young leaders as heroes and honoured them in Bombay and in Poona publicly and fearlessly. This honour done to Tilak and Agarkar had sprung partly from Jotirao's honest pride in Shivaji's dynasty and partly from the rightful and heroic conduct Tilak and Agarkar showed in facing danger for the vindication of truth.

Damodarpant Yande tells us that Jotirao had taken a four-wheeled horse carriage to the gate of the jail to receive the

12. Patil, P. S., *Mahatma Jotiba Phooley* (Marathi Biography, 1938), p. 43.

young patriotic editors. It is said that early in 1883 Agarkar had gratefully acknowledged in the *Kesari* a debt of gratitude to Jotirao for the help he had rendered in their time of need and the great interest he had taken in according a magnificent welcome to them on their release.

In the last week of July 1882, one Tukaram Nathu Naik serving in Poona Municipality had applied for permission to retire from Municipal service. Sane said that Naik's good services should be gratefully acknowledged. Jotirao made a proposition that a watch worth Rs. 200 should be presented to him for good services. But the proposition failed. Jotirao was keenly interested in setting a good precedent in appreciating the services of a faithful servant.

The *Din Bandhu* engaged in this heroic reception to two patriots, who had fought for the descendent of Shivaji, turned its attention to the tomb of Shivaji which had fallen into a dilapidated condition. Jotirao and Lokhande addressed meetings in Poona and in Bombay, appealing to the people to collect funds for properly repairing the tomb—*samadhi*.

Jotirao had sung the glory of Shivaji when most leaders had forgotten his exploits. Shivaji put Maharashtra on the map of India, and a self-respecting India on the map of the world. Jotirao visited Raigad and he removed the weeds over the octagonal base of the samadhi and thoroughly cleansed it.

After this, James Douglas scathingly lashed at the Mahrattas in *A Book of Bombay*,[13] saying that "no man now cares for Seevaji over all those wide domains, which once owned him Lord and Master—not one man now contributes a Rupee to keep or repair the tomb and temple of the founder of the Mahratta Empire." Nations that live and survive never forget their heroic liberators. People who never look to their noble liberators and saviours can hardly hand over the torch to and do justice to posterity.

A very big meeting was held early in 1885 under the presidentship of Shri Guru Maharaj Chafalkar Swami, and the preceptor of the Raja of Satara, at Hirabag in Poona, which Jotirao addressed along with other patriotic leaders of Poona. Sinclair, the then Collector of Thana repaired the *samadhi* at

13. P. 433.

his own expense. Government also made certain repairs and placed a railing round the *samadhi* at a cost of Rs. 25 and sanctioned an annual grant of Rs. 4 towards the upkeep of the *samadhi*.

This cooled down, it seems, the enthusiasm of Jotirao, the supporters and the movement lagged behind. It was later taken up by Tilak and others. In June 1895 they gave an organised shape to it by collecting funds to repair properly the tomb of Chhatrapati Shivaji Maharaj at Raigad, to erect a temple there worthy of him, to make permanent arrangements for its maintenance there and to provide for the regular performance of the festival. They achieved the object for which Jotirao had moved early in 1880.

CHAPTER XIII

Thoughts on Mass Education

THE Indian Education Commission appointed by the Government of India in 1882 was touring all over India. It was popularly known as the Hunter Commission after its President Sir William Hunter. In every British Indian Province, a Provincial Committee was set up to help the Commission by giving it detailed information on the educational conditions. The Commission studied the problem in every province and examined witnesses. Memorials were addressed to the Commission and one of these was from Jotirao.

The filtration theory of educational policy had failed in the face of the caste system and could not yield the results expected by its early advocates. The missionaries condemned the Government secular schools as godless. It only produced a small urban class, and education did not filter down to the lower classes.

In Poona the statement submitted to the Education Commission by V. S. Apte, Superintendent of the New English School, asked for the transfer of Primary and Secondary Education to popular control. It also said that the missionary schools did not represent indigenous enterprise, nor were their objects purely educative. So grant-in-aid should not be paid to missionary schools if they insisted on the teaching of the Bible in their schools.

M. M. Kunte, a leading public figure in Poona, described in his evidence before the Commission, as said already, that the question of admission of Mahars and Dehers into Government Schools was not real. It was a groundless agitation caused by sentimental English officials and unpractical native reformers.

From these statements and others it may be safely concluded that the objectives of many of the educational institutions were to raise an intellectual aristocracy that had no concern with the masses. Intellectual elevation of some of the best men removed them from the sphere of general usefulness. College education did not quicken sympathy for the masses. Was it worth imparting it at a high pressure, asked those who favoured mass education. All were in favour of education to begin at the top. Except Jotirao there was no spokesman who could frankly say that the Government had neglected the educational interests of the lower classes. The country could not rise unless its millions were lifted into a higher moral atmosphere and given a feeling of social responsibility.

In his memorial dated the 19th October 1882, Jotirao styled himself "merchant and cultivator and Municipal Commissioner." He gave a detailed account of the schools he had established, the period of his service as a teacher and his experience in the field of education.

Jotirao quoted some pertinent extracts from the introduction to his book *Slavery* and restated his view that though revenue and cess were collected from the farmers the Government spent profusely on the education of the higher classes believing in the Utopian idea that they would endeavour to spread it among the lower classes. The Universities educated many children of wealthy men, and advanced the material prospects of some of them. But. they had made no contribution to the great work of regenerating their fellowmen.

"How have they," observed Jotirao, "begun to act upon the masses? Have any of them formed classes at their own homes or elsewhere, for the instruction of their less fortunate or less wise countrymen?" "Upon what grounds," he asked, "is it asserted that the best way to advance the moral and intellectual welfare of the people is to raise the standard of instruction among the higher classes? To show the growth of the national happiness, it would only be necessary to refer to the number of pupils at colleges and lists of academic degrees. Each wrangler would be accounted a national benefactor, and the existence of deans and proctors would be associated, like the game-laws and the ten-pound franchise, with the best interests of the constitution."

"One of the most glaring tendencies ot the Government system of high class education," Jotirao stated, "has been the virtual monopoly of all higher officers under them by Brahmins. If the welfare of the *ryot* is at heart, if it is the duty of government ment to check a host of abuses, it behoves them to narrow this monopoly day by day so as to allow a sprinkling of the other castes to get into the public services. Perhaps some might be inclined to say that it is not feasible in the present state of education. Our reply is that if Government look a little less after higher education and more after the education of the masses, the former being able to take care of itself, there would be no difficulty in training up a body of men every way qualified and perhaps far better in morals and manner."

Jotirao then stated that primary education was utterly neglected in the Bombay Presidency. Primary schools were not provided with proper requirements. "Government collected", he went on, "special cess for educational purposes, and it is to be regretted that this fund is not spent for the purposes for which it is collected. Nearly nine-tenths of the villages in this Presidency, or nearly 10 lakhs of children, it is said, are without any provision whatever for primary education. A good deal of the poverty, their want of self-reliance, their entire dependence upon the learned and intelligent classes, is attributable to this deplorable state of education among the peasantry."

The cultivating and other poor classes, Jotirao observed, did not avail themselves of the primary education. A few of the latter classes were found in primary and secondary schools, but they could not continue long in school because they were extremely poor; they required their children to tend cattle and to look after their fields; and they received no inducements in the forms of scholarships and prizes.

"I think," Jotirao pleaded sincerely, "primary education of the masses should be made compulsory up to a certain age, say at least 12 years. Muhammedans also hold aloof from these schools as they somehow evince no liking for Marathi or English. There are a few Muhammedan primary schools where their own language is taught. The Mahars, Mangs and other lower classes are practically excluded from all schools owing to caste prejudices, as they are not allowed to sit by the side of the children of the higher castes. Consequently special schools for these have been opened by Government. But they exist only in large towns. In the whole of Poona and for a population exceeding over 5,000 people there is only one school in which the attendance is under 30 boys. This state of matters is not at all creditable to the educational authorities. I beg to urge that Mahars, Mangs and other classes, where their number is large enough, should have separate schools for them, as they are not allowed to attend the other schools owing to caste prejudices."

"In the present state of education," Jotirao opined, "payment by results is not suitable for the promotion of education among the poor and ignorant people as no taste has yet been created among them for education. I do not think any teacher would undertake to open schools on his own account among these pupils as he would not be able to make a living by it. Government schools and special inducements as noted above are essential until such a taste is created among them."

Jotirao further said that the primary education imparted in Government schools must be placed on a satisfactory, sound basis, must be practical and useful in the future life of the children. Both the teaching machinery employed and the course of instruction then followed required a thorough remodelling. He was in favour of bettering the service conditions of teachers and recommended an increase in the salaries and status of the primary teachers, and also the appointment of trained teachers.

"The teachers now employed," Jotirao continued, "in primary schools are almost all Brahmins; a few of them are from Normal Training College, the rest being all untrained men. Their salaries are very low, seldom exceeding Rs. 10, and their attainments also very meagre. But as a rule they are all impractical men, and the boys who learn under them generally imbibe inactive habits and try to obtain service, to the avoidance of their hereditary or other hardy or independent profession. I think teachers for primary schools should be trained, as far as possible, but of the cultivating classes, who will be able to mix freely with them and understand their wants and wishes much better than a Brahmin teacher, who generally holds himself aloof under religious prejudices.

"These would," he proceeded, "moreover, exercise a more beneficial influence over the masses than teachers of other classes, and who do not feel ashamed to hold the handle of plough or carpenter's adze when required, and who will be able to mix themselves readily with the lower orders of society. The course of training for them ought to include besides the ordinary subjects, any elementary knowledge of agriculture and sanitation. The untrained teachers should, except when thoroughly efficient, be replaced by efficient trained teachers. To secure a better class of teachers and to improve their position better salaries should be given. Their salaries should not be less than Rs. 12 and in larger villages should be at least Rs.15 or so. Associating them in the village polity as auditors of village accounts on registrars of deed or village postmasters or stamp vendors would improve their status and thus exert a beneficial influence over the people among whom they live. The school masters of village schools who pass a large number of boys should also get some special allowance other than the pay as an encouragement to them."

II

Jotirao had peculiar ideas about village education. "The course of instruction," he said, "should consist of reading *Modi* and *Balbodh* and accounts, and rudimentary knowledge of general history and general geography, and grammar; also an elementary knowledge of agriculture and a few simple lessons on morals and sanitation. The studies in the village schools might be fewer than those in large villages or towns, but not the less practical. In connection with lessons in agriculture, a small model farm, would be a decided advantage, and if really efficiently managed would be productive of the greatest good to the country. The text-books in use both in the primary and in the Anglo-Vernacular schools require revision and recasting inasmuch as they are not practical or progressive in their scope. Lessons on technical education and morality, sanitation and agriculture, and some useful arts, should be interspersed among them in progressive series. The fees in the primary schools should be annas 1 to 2 for the children of cess payers and non-cess payers."

As regards the supervising agency over the primary schools, Jotirao said that it was defective and inadequate. "The Deputy Inspector's visit once a year," he remarked, "can hardly be of any appreciable benefit. All those schools might at least be inspected quarterly if not oftener. I would also suggest the advisability of visiting these schools at other times and without any intimation being given. No reliance can be placed on the district or village officers, owing to the multifarious duties devolving on them, as they seldom find time to visit them and when they do, their examination is necessarily very superficial and imperfect. European Inspectors' supervision is also occasionally very desirable, as it will tend to exercise a very efficient control over the teachers generally."

The number of primary schools should be increased—

"(1) by utilizing such of the indigenous schools as shall be or are conducted by trained and certified teachers by giving them liberal grant-in-aid;

(2) by making over one half of the local cess fund for primary education alone;

(3) by compelling, under a statutory enactment, municipalities to maintain all the primary schools within their respective limits;

(4) by an adequate grant from the provincial or imperial funds, the Municipalities in large towns should be asked to contribute the whole share of the expenses incurred on primary schools within the municipal area. But in no case ought the management of the same to be entirely made over to them. They should be under the supervision of the Educational Department.

"The municipalities should also give grant-in-aid to such secondary and private English schools as shall be conducted according to the rules of the Educational Department when their funds permit, such grant-in-aid being regulated by the number of boys passed every year. These contributions from municipal funds may be made compulsory by statutory enactment.

"The administration of the funds for primary education should ordinarily be in the hands of the Director of Public Instruction. But if educated and intelligent men are appointed on the local or district committees, these funds may be safely entrusted to them under the guidance of the Collector, or the Director of Public Instruction. At present the Local Boards consisting of ignorant and uneducated men, such as *Patils, Inamdars, Sirdars* and others, would not be capable of exercising any intelligent control over the funds."

Giving his views on the indigenous primary schools, Jotirao further said that they were conducted on the old village system by teachers generally earning from the dregs of Brahmanical society. Their qualifications hardly were beyond reading and writing Marathi very indifferently and casting accounts up to the rule of three. They set up schools as the last resort for getting a livelihood. No arrangements existed in the country to train up teachers for indigenous schools. Grant-in-aid should be paid to such schools if trained, certified or competent teachers were employed.

As regards higher education, he observed that it was amply provided for whereas that of the masses was neglected. But for all that no well-wisher of this country would desire that Government should at that stage withdraw its aid from higher education. It would be injurious to the spread of education. Boys from the middle and lower classes among whom higher education had made no perceptible progress would be compelled to take recourse to inefficient and sectarian schools, and so such a withdrawal of aid from higher education would be a great hardship and the cause of education would suffer. So Jotirao said it was his view that for a long time to come the entire educational machinery, both ministerial and executive, should be in the hands of Government.

Private high schools could not be a means of gaining a livelihood; nor would they succeed half so well in their results or their efforts be permanent or stable. Private schools, such as those of Vishnushastri Chiplunkar and Bhave with adequate grants-in-aid, might be rendered very effective, but they could never supersede the necessity of high schools.

The missionary schools did not succeed half so well in their results, nor did they attract half the number of students which the high schools attracted. The superiority of Government schools was mainly owing to richly paid staff of teachers and professors, which it was not possible for a private school to maintain.

Describing the education given in high schools as impractical, unsuitable for the requirements of ordinary life, Jotirao said: "It is only good to turn out so many clerks and schoolmasters. The Matriculation Examination unduly engrosses the attention of the teachers and pupils, and the course of studies prescribed has no practical element in it, so as to fit the pupil for his future careeer in independent life." "Although the number of students present," he further observed, "for the Entrance

Examination is not at all large when the diffusion of knowledge in the country is taken into consideration, it looks large when the requirements of Government services are concerned. Were the education universal and within easy reach of all, the number would have been larger still, and it should be so, and I hope it will be so hereafter."

"The higher education," he continued, "be arranged so as to be within easy reach of all, and the books of the subjects for Matriculation should be published in the Government Gazette as is done in Madras and Bengal. Such a course will encourage private students and secure a large diffusion of knowledge in the country."

"It is a boon to the people," he said, paying glowing tribute to Bombay University, "that Bombay University recognises private students in the case of those presenting for the entrance examination. I hope the university authorities will be pleased to extend the same boon to higher education. If private studies were recognised by the university in granting the degrees of B.A., M.A. and others, many young men will devote their time to private studies. Their doing so will still further tend to the diffusion of knowledge. It is found in many instances quite impossible to prosecute studies at the colleges for various reasons. If private studies be recognised by the university, much good will be effected to the country at large and a good deal of the drain on the public purse on account of higher education will be lessened."

Concerning the system of Government scholarships, Jotirao said that it should be so arranged that some of the scholarships should be awarded to those classes among whom education had made no progress. The system of awarding students scholarships by competition, he added, although abstractedly equitable, did not tend to the spread of education among the poor classes.

The educated natives, by nature of the course of training, which was not technical or practical, found great difficulty in betaking themselves to other manual or remunerative employments as all could not be employed in Government service. Hence the cry that the market was. overstocked with educated natives who did not find any remunerative employment.

"The present number of educated men," Jotirao expressed a hope, "is very small in relation to the country at large, and we trust that the day may not be far distant when we shall have the present number multiplied a hundred-fold, and all betaking themselves to useful and remunerative employments, and not be looking for service."

"In conclusion," Jotirao ended, "I beg to request the Educa¬tion Commission to be kind enough to sanction measures for female primary education on a more liberal scale."

In his unpublished book *Cultivator's Whipcord* Jotirao observed that as the Hunter Commission had not taken the evidence of the farmers and had depended upon the evidences of Parsis, Christians, and Brahmins, and as they had accepted addresses presented by these communities, he said it could not be hoped that the Hunter Committee's Report would be beneficial to the illiterate and ignorant farmers.

III

On October 30, 1882, a proposal for starting a veterinary college came up for discussion before the General Committee of the Poona Municipality. Jotirao proposed that the Madras Municipality which was running such a college should be contacted and consulted as to the expenditure. Jotirao's proposal was carried. There was another resolution under which it was proposed that the number of scholarship to primary students should be raised by the Municipality. Jotirao supported an amendment which sought to postpone the decision on the issue until the proposal for transfer of Primary Schools was decided one way or other by Government. But the original proposition was carried.

A proposal for erecting a new building for the market came up, on December 4, 1882, before the General Committee of the Municipality for discussion. The officers and members concerned were in a hurry to get the proposal through as a new committee was going to be formed soon in conformity with the new Local Self-Government Act. Hari Raoji Chiplunkar and Jotirao were of the opinion that such a big amount as Rs. 3,25,000 should not be spent on a building, the original idea being to have a building worth Rs.1,00,000. Instead, Jotirao said, that the money should be spent on the education of

1. *Education Commission*, Bombay, Vol. II, pp. 140-45.

poor citizens. Three other amendments were moved, but it was resolved by a majority vote that a building worth Rs. 2,00,000 should be built with 200 shops. The place for the market was also fixed by choosing the garden belonging to Khasgiwale and Chamaya.

The *Kesari* vehemently opposed this proposal and said it was very costly for Poonaites to have such a market, Yet, the construction work began soon after, and one of the biggest markets in India was built by 1885.

Just then, Lord Ripon, who was the first Catholic to become the Viceroy of India, inaugurated a new era by passing much beneficent legislations and especially by repealing the obnoxious Vernacular Press Act and by promoting Local Self-Government. According to that Act, new elections were held on March 28, 1883 and it is surprising why Jotirao did not contest the election from Peth Junaganj. Perhaps the delimitation of the Wards must have been made in such a way that the election of the saviour of the lower classes would be an impossibility. Shortly before this, the *Sarvajanik Sabha Journal* had expressed its disapproval of some people's tendency to use the word Swaraj for Local Self-Government, for there was a vast difference, it observed, between the two.

The *Din Bandhu*[2] again had a clash with missionaries when it criticised carpingly the Rev. Tukaram Nathuji. This was a new facet of the Satya-Shodhak movement. The *Dnyanodaya* expressed its displeasure over this trend in the *Din Bandhu*.

2. 5October 1882.

CHAPTER XIV

A Tale of Indian Peasants

EARLY IN 1883 Jotirao was working on his book *Cultivator's Whipcord* which he was writing in the interests of the Shudra community. He read out to different persons, during his travels, parts of that manuscript as they were completed. He read some sections of the book in Poona, Thana, Junnar, Otur, Hadapsar, Vangani, and at the other places, to eager social workers and important persons who testified to the authenticity of the facts mentioned in the proposed book.

The Israeli Dharmadeep,[1] a Marathi Weekly conducted by the Bombay Israelites, gives an account of a speech made by Jotirao Phooley at Byculla in Bombay on December 10, 1882, on the condition of peasants. "It was," it observed "a very interesting speech. He must have toiled much and spent a lot of money to collect the information. It seems his main object is to impress upon the higher classes that they should gave a better treatment to the lower classes and improve their status. If they unite in doing public work, the people and the country will be much benefited. A worthy man should be given a worthy position."

After completing the book, Jotirao read it at a meeting in Bombay, in April 1883. About this time he went to Baroda and read it out to Sayajirao Gaikwad, the young Maharaja of Baroda, whom he had met at Poona when the Maharaja had first come to Poona after his installation in the *gadi* in 1881. The young Maharaja, who had been well-groomed as a ruler by F. A. H. Elliot, his teacher, and Sir T. Madhaorao, the Diwan of Baroda, had broad sympathies. An intelligent, judicious, able young man, he had an excellent education and was gifted with a quick grasp of social problems. As he showed a genuine interest in the well-being of the lower classes, he evinced much enthusiasm for Jotirao's visit to Baroda and spent much time in listening to Jotirao reading to him parts of *Cultivator's*

1. The *Israeli Dharmadeep*, 15 December 1882.

Whipcord. The Maharaja offered him financial help and also conferred on him a dress of honour.

Jotirao completed the book by July 1883 and submitted copies of it to the Maharaja of Baroda and the Governor-General of India. On the copy of the manuscript sent to the Governor-General, he inscribed the words: "Presented to H.E. Rt. Hon'ble Sir Frederick Temple Hamilton-Temple Blackwood, Earl of Dufferin, Viceroy; signed by the author p. 89, Poona, 18th July 1883."

It is, however, clear from a letter he wrote on June 2, 1886, to Mama Parmanand, a man of eminence and political sagacity and a leading personality of his generation in Bombay, that the book was not published. He wrote to Parmanand that he would send him a copy of the manuscript of the *Cultivator's Whipcord* if he so desired, but it would take about two months to make a copy of it.

The manuscript opens with an introduction that is significant.

> For want of education intellect deteriorated.
> For want of intellect morality decayed,
> For want of morality progress stopped,
> For want of progress wealth vanished,
> For want of wealth the Shudras perished,
> All these sorrows sprang from illiteracy.

In the introduction Jotirao restated his thesis that the Kunbis, Malis and Dhangars were originally agriculturists, but because of pressure on land, the growth of population and the fragmentation of land, those who turned to gardens for livelihood were called Malis, and those who turned to tend sheep were called Dhangars i.e. the shepherds. They orginally belonged to one community and interdined, but did not intermarry.

They followed now different trades. Some dealt in hay and wood; a few followed the work of writing of deeds; some were contractors. There were Jagirdars, but most of them were illiterate and lost their estates through drinking and enjoyment.

The Indian Princes were mostly illiterate and were guided or misguided by their Brahmin ministers. This led to their downfall, moral and political. They were, as a result, helpless to effect any reform or to do good to anybody. In the daytime the Shudra Princes of Indian States gave away gifts to Brahmins, and in the night they surrendered themselves to a lewd life. The

Brahmin Princes showed interest in the welfare of Brahmins alone. The Shudra Princes were surrounded by Brahmin ministers who removed from service all able men of the Princes' caste. Jotirao depicted the Indian Princes as a worthless lot, given to a lewd life.

The first part of *Cultivator's Whipcord* described how a Brahmin priest persecuted a Shudra farmer all the year round from cradle to cremation, from pregnancy to pilgrimage, and how all this exploitation was done under the cloak of religion and its unending rites and rituals. Such of the Brahmins as could not take to higher education were, by leading a saintly life, living on the ignorance of the poor, illiterate masses.

The farmer had no money to send his children to school. The British officers who mostly were given to merrymaking, did not pay close attention to the grievances of the agriculturists. The British officers relied upon the guidance of Brahmins who worked under them. The farmers did not have sufficient food and clothes for their families. It was the most costly Government, run by high-salaried officers and burdened with heavy pensions.

Buddhism had exposed the designs of the Brahmanical religion and tried to save the poor classes from its clutches. Shankaracharya incorporated the Turks into the Maratha Community [Rajputs?] and got the Buddhists destroyed by their sword. He also asked the Brahmins to give up beef and wine.

The Brahmins did not admit the children of farmers to their Sanskrit Pathashalas. Bajirao II patronised the Brahmin Pandits; he did not care for the children of the poor peasants who were the chief source of his income. The Brahmin clerks and officers in Government courts who ran the administration and dispensed justice were corrupt. They distorted the farmers' applications, evidences and documents, and managed to decide cases in favour of those who gave them the highest bribe!

According to Jotirao, the causes of the utter poverty of the peasants were various. In the pre-British period, the rulers and princes had maintained armies. Vast number of people were engaged in the service of the army. So there was not heavy pressure on land. After the downfall of the Peshwa, the Maratha army was disbanded. The advent of British rule brought peace in the land. Consequently there was vast unemployment.

Pressure on land grew as the military men returned home, and the population, too, increased in peaceful times. The fragmentation of land among the members of the family went at an unabated rate. On fragmented land, the farmers found it difficult to live and rear their bullocks. The forest department gulped down the village grazing-grounds, there being no land for sheep and goats to graze. Thus the farmer had no fallow land to fall back upon; the land wasted away. It lost its fertility.

Fragments of land were either sold or rented to other farmers who owned bullocks and ploughs. These poor landless peasants did their utmost to obtain small jobs under the weavers, carpenters, and blacksmiths, for earning their livelihood. But these traders also had almost run out of their work as they could not compete with the British machine-made goods such as cutlery, needles, pack-needles, sewing-machines, threads, locks and keys, iron-plates, tar, bellows, different kinds of carts, and cloth brought to India without any customs duty. The result was a terrible slackness in indigenous trades. The weavers, blacksmiths, and carpenters eked out a miserable living. They often sold their raw materials to new money-lenders and ran away. They lived stealthily, subsisted on the husk of wheat and rice, and on mango-stones. When hunger was unbearable, they drowned their sorrow in a cheap drink of toddy. They could not call their soul their own. The British workers lived on fine wines, cakes and biscuits and possessed adequate warm clothes, while the Indian workers were reduced to utter penury.

II

The Brahmins, observed Jotirao, were responsible for the injunctions in Hinduism which banned foreign voyages and travels beyond Attuck. This narrowed the vision of the Hindus, broke their contacts with the outer world and they considered themselves mere nobodies. The Brahmin objectives were fulfilled. They got slaves to serve them and to work on their farms and to weave cloth. However, the Brahmins of Jotirao's day realised their blunders, and pretending to rectify these blunders, they shouted: 'Let us reform our customs!' But this was a white-wash.

Brahmins who were appointed teachers in villages were not

trained. They were illiterate and they cared more for their ideas of purity than for the art of teaching. They were selfish and illiterate. They told the children of farmers that the Brahmin teachers would have to beg at their doors with an almanac in their hands if the farmers' children were educated and secured jobs in Government offices. The Brahmins shrewdly flattered the British officers and presented them with addresses which were also signed foolishly by some rich but ignorant Shudras. The British officers in turn recommended these Brahmin officers for the titles 'Raobahadur' or 'Raosaheb'. From this Jotirao drew his conclusion that the country could recover from any havoc wrought by a swarm of locusts or by famine, but it would not recover from the havoc caused by Brahmin servants who actually ran the British offices over which merry-making Europeans presided. The Khots were ruining the illiterate cultivators in Konkan.

Jotirao wrote at the end of the second part of his unpublished book that whatever he had written about the Brahmin servants in Government offices could be verified by the several decisions in different courts in which Brahmin servants and officers had been convicted.

In the third part of his manuscript, Jotirao observed that wisdom and heroism were not hereditary qualities since two sons born of the same parents were not of the same quality — one might be a fool whereas the other might be wise and brave. According to him, the quality of the child depended upon the condition of mind and body of the parents at the time of their union. The quality that dominated them at that particular time asserted itself in the child. Besides, the surrounding atmosphere had something to do with the child's growth. That was why great generals and kings had often sprung from farmers, shoe-makers and shepherds.

Jotirao opined that Pralhad and others were cowards and chose not to fight courageously on behalf of their countrymen. The Brahmins absorbed them in their religion and made them Kulkarnis. They were called Deshastha Brahmins. In colour, customs and worship of deities the Deshastha Brahmins were akin to the Shudras. Because of this, he observed, no marriage took place between the Deshasthas and the Konkanasthas, i.e. the Chitpavans, nor did they even dine together. The Peshwas who were Chitpavans tried to establish marriage relationship between the two castes.

Then Jotirao described how the Portuguese forcibly converted the Brahmins, Shudras and Atishudras to Christianity and made them happy; how the Muslims forcibly converted the harassed Shudras and Atishudras to Islam and freed them from the Brahmin religion and made them happy. All the while Jotirao suggested that these men embraced Christianity or Islam because they were suppressed, harassed and ground down under poverty.

But the most vital idea he suggested in this chapter was the importance of a Republic. He stated that because the Shudras abandoned the system of a Republic, they had been reduced to slavery which was a deserving punishment for their sin. He pointed out that the Greeks had preserved their republics, and he praised the Spartan heroes, describing how they routed the vast armies of Iran. The Romans drew inspiration from the Greek Republics and resisted Hanibal! Jotirao condemned Julius Caesar for having neglected the ideal of a Republic and for having usurped power himself. He hailed Brutus as a noble patriot for having killed Julius Caesar who had deviated from the ideal of a Republic and formed coteries of flatterers. Brutus, Jotirao opined, saved the people from the chains of a monarchy!

Jotirao observed that the Muslims had destroyed the Iranian Kingdoms, came to India and conquered it. But they gave themselves up to enjoyment and the British easily conquered India. Jotirao did not consider the conquest of India by the British a very heroic achievement, as one-tenth of the population of India was Brahmin and the Brahmins had dominated the religious and political fields by keeping the other nine-tenths of Indians away from the fields of education, knowledge, and power. When the British realised the importance of the leadership of Brahmins and the weakness of the Shudras, they shrewdly utilised the Brahmin community to run the Government, the Brahmins being in charge of the lower state affairs and they in the higher. They both thus enjoyed themselves by imposing increasing taxes such as a local cess and a tax on the poor man's salt.

As regards the irrigation, Jotirao complained that water was not supplied to the farmers in time; if supplied in time it was not adequate. There was partiality and jobbery in the dealings of the Department. He was of the opinion that Municipal taxes also were troublesome from the points of view of the small trading men such as green-grocers, and small vendors. What was worse was that the agents grabbed the profit, and the poor green-grocers were deprived of their dues. He sincerely praised a Brahmin officer named Vishvanath Daji who was very popular with the masses and was highly respected for his impartial work, spotless career and noble mind.

As a result of heavy taxation, the farmers and the poor workers were reduced to utter poverty. Nearly four crores of people did not get even one full meal daily. Hardly a day passed when starving people were not found on the roads.

Jotirao made an appeal to Government to fix a reasonable assessment on land and to free the farmer from ignorance and superstition, so that he might not join any Brahmin revolt and perish in that rebellion. The British workers produced cheap articles because they worked on machines. The British merchants purchased in India raw material such as cotton and hides and made huge profits over them by turning them into useful goods.

Consequently, the Indian artisans and workers were reduced to penury in an increasing number. The report of the native officers that the farmers lavished their money on marriage functions was a wicked lie. The result of such reports was that there was no customs duty on British goods. The English money-lenders had derived a huge amount of interest for years and if the Government had sympathy for the poor Indian farmers they should stop giving interest of five crores of rupees each year to British money-lenders and should declare the Indian farmers free from their debts. The Government would be praised for its just and kind act. It was no use depriving small money-lenders of their interest.

There should be no high-salaried officers; the cost of administration should be lowered. The Government should not spend Indian revenue on its war affairs. William Wedderburn should make efforts to stop the payment of interest of the British money-lenders. New Banks would not be able to solve the problems of the poor Indian agriculturists. The farmer must be relieved from his debts; he must get adequate food, and must be placed in a position to send his children to school.

III

Although the farmer and his whole family toiled hard, their monthly income was Rs.31 while a European or native officer spent freely on enjoyment and drinks Rs.15 or more a month. The big salaries of Collectors and other officers indicated the unjust policy of the British Government.

The income of an English soldier in India was ten times higher than the income of an honest, hardworking farmer who, with all the members of his family, toiled from sunrise to sunset on the farm. The poor farmer worked barefoot with a piece of cloth around his loins, a little cloth purse stuck in his waist band, containing pieces of betelnut, betel-leaves and tobacco, a tattered turban on his head, his body bare to the waist in the hot sun, an old melodious song on his tongue and the wooden plough in his hand. When the farmer went to court he wore *Khadi* short breeches, a waistcoat, torn shoes. For his meals he had husks of jowar or nachni, sweet potatoes, carrots, fish curry if possible but a lump of chutney all the year round! Jotirao compares this condition to that of the British soldier. The soldier wore a very fine uniform consisting of shorts, shirt, cap, socks, boots and belt, put a gun on his shoulder, and happily marched on the parade grounds.

From the point of view of sanitary arrangements, the farmer's house was sticky, covered with wet cow-dung, often having a dirty smell oozing from the cow-pen close by; the earthen pots in the kitchen, old quilts and mats in the rooms, and a depleted corn-bin tilted in some corner.

As regards the fate of Atishudras, Jotirao observed, Henry Fawcett should come to India with W. E. Gladstone, Prime Minister of Britain, and look into the condition of the Atishudras and stay with them for a week or two. If they did so, Jotirao was sure that rather than talk idly about their condition they would run to America! Henry Fawcett was a dauntless British politician and economist who championed the cause of India and always fought to save the Indian system of finance from being exploited by British statesmen in the interest of their own country.

Because there was not a common holy book on the Hindu religion, like the Bible for the Christians and the Koran for the

Muslims, the Shudras did not know what religion meant. They ignorantly drank the water made dirty by the toe of the Brahmin priest and worshipped metal-images, cows, cobras, tulsi plants and spirits. He insisted that Government should provide for compulsory free education of the farmer's children. The existing Marathi and English schools in villages should be closed. First, the teachers from the Shudra class should be recruited and trained. Then special boarding schools should be opened for the peasant children. The children should be compelled to attend schools upto a certain age. These new Shudra class teachers should be appointed to teach in these village schools. The pupils should be provided with books, slates and clothes. The Brahmin teachers were not taking an active interest in teaching the peasant children. They had no heart in it. They were hacks.

Concerning the children of artisans, labourers, carpenters, blacksmiths, coppersmiths, chamars and also the children of the criminal tribes, Jotirao said that different kinds of schools should be opened and pupils should be instructed in their trades in those schools, so that children of the low castes might not turn out to be wicked men. They would improve their lot like the workers in Europe and America. If they did not send their children to these schools, compulsory attendance should be enforced.

Those Brahmin agitators who wanted, Jotirao said, Parsis, Mussalmans and other Hindus to unite were not speaking the truth. It was mere white-wash. Unless they expressed their readiness to solve the problem of the Mahars and Mangs he would not trust their protestations. Only those Shudras who were ignorant would be deceived by their speeches and writings.

Jotirao paid glowing tributes to Dr.Benjamin Franklin and Thomas Paine for their great work in the uplift of their countrymen.

As Brahmins kept their knowledge confined to the Vedas, Military and Scientific education did not grow in India. So they did not know the use of the telescope and how, with the help of it guns, were directed to the target in battles.

Jotirao also noticed that the Brahmin Indian Princes generally never helped the cause of the Shudras and Atishudras, whereas the non-Brahmin princes were duped by the Brahmins. When the poor and beggars were treated partially by the Brahmins, there was no question of gifts, being distributed by Brahmins among the non-Brahmins. Jotirao's point can be substantiated by citing a case. Rao Saheb V. N. Mandlik, a well-known leader in the Bombay Presidency, celebrated his 61st birthday in Bombay and gave away money equal to his weight to Brahmins only. This casteist angle of charity was criticised at that time by the *Subodha Patrika*.[2]

If the Brahmins really wanted to uplift the country and desired unity they should denounce their religion which taught the tenets of highness and lowness, and should abolish the caste-system which bred inequality. There would be no real unity unless social equality was established. If the Brahmins succeeded for a time in winning over. half-educated Shudras to their side in their struggle for the uplift of the country, the Shudras would be sooner awakened to reality and they would ultimately come to grief.

There should be, continued Jotirao, Government directives to watch the conduct of the farmers. They should neither rob anybody of his money nor lead an immoral life. They should be men of right conduct. Those Shudras who lived immorally must be punished. They should not have more than one wife. They should not perform the marriages of their children at an early age.

Brahmins should be given posts in Government offices in proportion to their population. Till the time the Shudras were educated and were qualified to serve in public offices, Muslims, British or Hindus other than Brahmins suould be appointed. As the number of educated men from the Shudra farmers would grow, they should be provided with the posts of Mamlatdars, and other similar posts, so that there should be an increase in Government income and everywhere the friends of farmers would be established.

IV

One of the most important suggestions Jotirao made was the necessity of a watch on the Marwaris and tradesmen who sold spoiled goods and used false measures. This was as important

2. The *Subodha Patrika*, 15 September 1878.

as the law passed to regulate the transactions between the farmers and the money-lenders. The drunkard village police officer, Patil, should be watched.

The farmers should be educated and until they knew how to use modern implements for agriculture, the Europeans in India and the Muslims should be prohibited under a law from eating beef and instead they should be compelled to accept goat and sheep meat only. At the most they should import cows and oxen for these purposes. Unless.a law was enacted to restrict beef-eating, the condition of the farmers would not improve. This done, they would be able to have a good supply of bullocks and agriculture would improve.

The Government should build dams across valleys at important places with the help of the army, black and white, and with the help of the reserved police force. A very useful suggest on indeed! Whenever unseasonal rain fell it should be absorbed in fields, and then the water should be channelised to the rivers. The dry leaves, the bones and manures of all kinds would not be washed away. The army would enjoy fresh air and would be kept active and healthy. Moreover the army would increase the wealth of the nation. The additional police forces, too, would be utilised. Tanks should be built on hills, dams should be built across rivers, and bones, ashes and cow-dung should not be allowed to be washed away. The river water should be stored in wells for watering gardens and fields. The land where the water fell was washed away by the current; it should be carefully buttressed.

Those farmers who would be able to sink wells without the guidance or help of the Government should be given suitable prizes and the mud settled in tanks, lakes and rivers should be furnished to farmers gratis. The grazing grounds should be returned to the villagers, wood for fuel, foliage and dry leaves should be given to them, but trees should not be cut down. A law should be passed prohibiting the cutting down of trees.

New fine breeds of sheep and goats should be imported and given to the farmers, so that they would be useful for wool, and the droppings would be useful too. Farmers should be provided with guns, to protect their farms. If pigs and such other wild animals did damage to crops, the loss should be made good to the farmers through the salaries of the police officers. If this is done, the farmers would get sufficient time to take rest and sleep at night. In every *Shravan*, the fifth month of the Hindu year, there should be exhibitions for agriculturists, and in *Ashwin*, the seventh month of the Hindu year, farmers should be awarded prizes for producing the best crops and for the art of proper ploughing.

The low class singers and actors should not be permitted to sing obscene songs or perform obscence *tamashas*. The activities of Joginis, Murlis, Kolhatanis, Kasbinis should be watched carefully and they should be kept in separate places. This done, the farmers' young generation would grow healthy and strong.

Farmers should be provided with books on farming and agriculture. High-salaried posts in the Judiciary, Police, Army and Revenue Departments consumed much of the revenue, whereas the farmers did not get even ordinary food. The salaries and wages of low class workers should be raised. The local cess must be utilised for the education of the farmers' children. If money from the royal fund was utilised for the education of the Brahmins, and the young Brahmins some day defeated the Government, that would be a deserving reward for the neglect of the farmers from whose toils the revenue came.

Thus one can have in Jotirao's *Cultivator's Whipcord* a glimpse of the Indian farmers in the closing decade of the nineteenth century. Jotirao desired to put science at the service of agriculture, and to develop the idea of scientific breeding of farm-yard cattle. He knew the importance of fodder and fire wood, manures and fertiliser. He wanted to put the land to the fullest use. He was worried about the diminishing yields of crops and about soil conservation, so he appealed to Government to adopt both protective and productive works. He gave a moving account of an Indian farmer who was engaged in a desperate struggle for a bare living, and was illiterate, ignorant and unemployed for a third part of the year. His cattle were even more starved than he was, and were utterly ill-bred and ill-used. His farm was filled with primitive implements and the land was parched for want of water.

Jotirao prayed that peasants should not be left to the mercy of rains which are irregular and undependable. What was wrong with Indian agriculture is seen in his book. Dams and barrages across the valleys and rivers which were the ideals of Jotirao's dreams are realised today by a Free India, but the methods and implements of agriculture are much the same. Much protection is guaranteed by law against money-lenders, and landlords and landlordism are almost abolished. Yet the yield per acre is much Iower than the yield in progressive countries, and the vast farming population of India lives on the borderline of starvation. The day these teeming millions go to sleep on a full stomach will be a great day for India.

In the end, Jotirao expressed gratitude to the Scotch Mission in Poona and the Government institutions for imparting him sound knowledge of the rights of Man and to the pious Europeans for giving him financial aid in his work, and, above all, to British rule under which he could express his views freely and fearlessly. He prayed that God might open the eyes of the peasants to the realities of life.

V

Jotirao's followers were now making gradual progress in social matters. His colleague, disciple Ramayya Vyankayya Aiyyavaru founded an institution for women in Kamathi Pura, Bombay, where the Telugu community resided. The Telugu leaders were Fulmali by caste and their community had moved to Telangana during the famine of 1296. Every Saturday women in the locality would hold a meeting at the house of Ramayya Vyankayya Aiyyavaru. This was a step forward. Women from Eulmnli Samaj and other such Lower class communities coming together to discuss things was certainly a great advance in those days.

The social reform movement was gaining ground in southern India also. The Shánkaracharya and his followers had excommunicated a Munsif of Rajmahendry for having participated in the remarriage of a widow. He filed a suit against his opponents and the Shankaracharya. The Lower Court decided the case in favour of the defendants. But the High Court granted the Munsif's appeal and fined the defendants Rs. 200 or simple imprisonment for twenty days.[3] Progress in religious thought and social ideas had left the religious Heads behind. Without progressive thought and action the religious Heads were passing

3. The *Kesari*, 3 May, 1883.

their days in idle ease. Their office had lost its charm and power.

About this time a fund was collected to bring European lady doctors to India for attending Indian women and children. One Parsi millionaire contributed a lakh of rupees. Men of progressive views appealed to Government to appoint women clerks. They suggested that their service would be cheaper. But the authorities turned down the appeal saying that the time had not come for such an innovation in India.[4] A graduate Hindu girl of Calcutta[5] was a student of the Medical College at this time, and a lady from Madras was practising as a lawyer at Vizagapattam.

In an appendix to his unpublished *Cultivator's Whipcord* and later on in *Satsar*, a booklet consisting of his advice to his disciples, Jotirao expressed his joy at the defeat and discomfiture of the Hindu reformers who could not retain Pandita Ramabai in Arya Dharma. To those who sang the glory of Hinduism he asked why Max Muller himself was not embracing *Veda-Dharma* if he was convinced of its glory and greatness.

Pandita Ramabai was the daughter of a Chitpavan Brahmin, who was a great Sanskritist and master of Vedic lore and of Vedantism. Under her father's guidance she and her brother had studied Sanskrit literature and had attained a mastery of the Vedas and other Hindu scriptures. Eight months after the death of her parents in Karnatak, in July 1874, her sister too died. She and her brother travelled about two thousand miles all over India for six years, crossing rivers, hills and mountain ranges. In her travels she used to read the *Bhagwat* and was then a devotee of Vishnu. During her travels, she suffered a lot and they both lost their faith in the religion that went by the name of Hinduism. They came to believe in one God. She emerged as an outstanding Sanskrit Pandita at Calcutta, where she made stimulating speeches.

Having refused marriage offers that came from men of learning in different parts of India, the Pandita married Babu Bipin Biharidas, a Shudra who was a lawyer and a Brahmo. After the unfortunate death of her brother in May 1880 and that of

4. *The Indu Prakash*, 9 July 1883.
5. *The Indu Prakash*, 30 July 1883.

her husband in February 1882, she returned to Bombay. Deciding to devote her life to the uplift and emancipation of women, she established an institution called Arya Mahila Ashram. By nature she was an ambitious woman, a woman of great moral force possessed phenomenal energy and great organising ability. She was on friendly terms with the leaders of the Prarthana Samaj. She went to England to study at the instance of some Christian Missionaries. There she studied and became a lecturer of Sanskrit at a college. Reportedly, she also wanted to be a woman doctor.

A month before her conversion, Ramabai wrote that she had no idea of embracing Christianity as all religions possessed some sort of defects or embarrassing practices. Her letter was circulated by her reformer friends in Bombay, who believed her implicitly when she said that she had no idea of embracing Christianity or entering a European family or adopting the habits and manners of the West. But she suddenly made a *volte-face* and embraced Christianity.[6]

The *Subodha Patrika*, spokesman of the *Prarthana Samaj*, felt embarrassed and criticised the Pandita. The *Indu Prakash*[7] said she had borne out the suspicion it entertained about her. "It is the tragedy of a lady blessed with beauty, youth and learning. Oh, it is your luck that you took so much time to become a holy personage! You are a learned lady but a feeble woman," added the *Indu Prakash*!

There was a controversy over this conversion of Pandita Ramabai between the *Subodha Patrika* and the *Indian Spectator* of Malbari.

"We have no wish," observed Malbari, "to defend this eccentric young lady to the prejudice of her countrymen. But we are far from persuaded that her conversion is the result of the sudden freak. Ramabai's conduct has been anything but fair."[8]

Malbari criticised the leaders of the Prarthana Samaj as mere talkative admirers and added that they could have prevented what had happened. The provision they had made for Ramabai might have "been inadequate or conditions attached to it must have been galling to a high-spirited and self-willed woman,"

6. The *Indu Prakash*, 28 October 1883.
7. The *Indu Prakash*, 22 October 1883.
8. The *Indian Spectator*, 18 November 1883.

he continued. Malbari reminded the Samajists of their having circulated her letter with gusto and remarked that when they circulated it they did not know that the poor woman was deceiving herself![9]

When a liberal-minded Parsi took such a view of Ramabai's conversion, Jotirao, who never supported the idea of conversion, utilised the incidents in order to have a dig at the Brahmins. He said that when Ramabai had not studied other religions she made brilliant speeches in Poona in exposition of Hinduism! Poor lady, ignorant of the position to which Hinduism had assigned woman and Shudra, but in England she must have realised the true position of Hinduism. This was Jotirao's interpretation of it.

The stand taken by Jotirao against conversion was in keeping with the great tradition and traits of the great men India has produced. Later, Mahatma Gandhi and Gurudeo Tagore took the same stand, let alone the great stalwarts like Vivekanand, Lajpat Rai, Tilak, and Savarkar. A convert embracing a foreign faith and then developing a desire for converting the women of her home country to Christianity cannot rise in the estimation of posterity. Her soul had lost its glory and grandeur. She had neither the heart of a saint nor the heart of a national liberator. After assuming the name Mary, she had lost the altruistic force of her life and mission. If Gandhi and Tagore had embraced Christianity for the sake of their mission, would India have placed them on the pedestal of the Mahatmas and Gurudeos?

Jotirao personally had a dislike of conversions. He once dissuaded a Mahar peon of his school from embracing Christianity. He took him to his friend Jagannath Sadashiv, who helped the peon, and Jotirao got his salary increased. Jotirao and Rajaramshastri Bhagwat were, however, the two social reformers who maintained a good opinion of the Pandita even after her conversion to Christianity. In her dislike of the Hindu religion, Ramabai went to the length of prohibiting her daughter from studying the Sanskrit language. Jotirao and Bhagwat, these two social reformers, did not live to see Ramabai's real work which ended in the proselytism of Hindu women and children to Christianity.

9. The *Indian Spectator*, 28 October 1883.

The *Dnyanodaya*[10] observed that the overtures made by the leaders of the Prarthana Samaj in Bombay and Poona on the eve of Pandita Ramabai's departure to London, to win over a person like Ramabai to their side, were inconsistent with their words and spoiled the good opinion she had formed of the Samaj. The nature of the gestures made towards her is not known, but her good relations with the Prarthana Samaj leaders, till the day of her conversion, prove that she held them in high esteem.

10. 18 October 1883.

CHAPTER XV

Agitation

JOTIRAO'S YOUNG colleague Narayan Meghaji Lokhande was valiantly fighting for the amelioration of the lot of the millhands. The Indian labour movement in its early stages was a branch or an offshoot of the Satya-Shodhak Samaj. The Act of 1881 was passed, but its application to the mills was not rigidly enforced. The millowners were alarmed. Mead King, Inspector of Textile Factories in Manchester, was deputed to Bombay to supervise and report on the working of the Act in Bombay. Accordingly, he made a report. It recommended that children below eight should not be employed in a factory, and that women and children should not be allowed to work either before six in the morning or after six in the evening. During the period of work they should have recess. Sorabjee Shapoorji Bengalee moved in the matter, and Lokhande agitated for a better deal for the workers.

As a result, a new Commission was appointed in May 1884, under the presidentship of W. B. Mulloch, Collector of Bombay. N. B. Jeejebhoy, Muncherji N. Banaji, Sorabjee S. Bengali, Munchrrjee Murzban, Dr. Thomas Blaney and G. Cotton were the members of the Commission. A Doctors' Committee was also set up to inquire into the sanitary conditions in the mills. Lokhande gave evidence, and thirty-five other witnesses were examined. The report[1] of the Commission was published. The minimum age for the employment of children was raised from seven to nine, the maximum from twelve to fourteen years. A child was expected to work between seven in the morning and five in the evening, with an hour's interval for meals and rest. The report further recommended four holidays in a month to children and women. It was of the opinion that rules regarding sanitary conditions, too, should find a place in the legislation.

1. Mehta, S. D., *The Cotton Mills in India from 1854 to 1954,* p. 127.

Jotirao was keenly interested in this agitation. Whenever he went to Bombay he met Lokhande and gave an impetus to the working class agitation which aimed at improving the conditions of life. The Satya-Shodhak Samaj voiced the grievances of both the peasants and the millhands. The whole movement laid a certain emphasis on economic betterment and social justice. Another of its aims was to put a stop to the exploitation that was going on through religious rituals and social customs.

Jotirao helped his young colleagues to found, in May 1884, an institution called the Din Bandhu Sarvajanik Sabha. Its main founder and leader was Krishnarao Bhalekar. They met every Sunday to discuss social problems, and non-Brahmin leaders addressed the meetings at Dr. Sadoba Gavade's residence.

Modelled as it was on the Sarvajanik Sabha, the Din Bandhu Sarvajanik Sabha represented to Government the public grievances of the people, made every effort to diffuse knowledge among them, and to abolish evil customs and traditions. No religious subject was to be discussed at its meetings. Membership subscription was half an anna a month. To strive to remove the grievances of the people, it believed, was to worship God.

The *Din Mitra*,[2] after stating the aims and objects of the Din Bandhu Sarvajanik Sabha, observed: "The establishment of British rule in India has been a very great blessing to this country. We now enjoy many privileges which were unknown to our ancestors. Although we are living under a foreign Government, yet it is the best Government India has ever had." But the information, it thought, which was obtained before the enactment of the laws through the Press, the various public associations and the high Officials, was not correct. "Therefore we who belong to the poor agriculturist, mercantile, artisan and other ignorant classes have established the Din Bandhu Sarvajanik Sabha."

"The object of establishing this Sabha is to represent in a right royal and constitutional manner our common but real difficulties and grievances to our benign Government. Whenever Government in making new enactment express a desire to acquaint themselves with the actual grievances of the people, the Sabha undertakes to make a proper and an unvarnished representation

2. July 1888.

of the state and opinions of the people belonging to these classes."

Jotirao's friend Govande died on April 8, 1884. Govande worked nobly for the welfare of the society, and Jotirao's mind must have been filled with reminiscences. Govande had genuine sympathy for the cause of the downtrodden and showed an insight into social and political problems. A Brahmin of broader sympathies, deep thought and courageous conduct, he supported all social, educational and public activities in Poona. Govande worked as a leader of the Sarvajanik Sabha in later life, but he never lost sympathy for the cause of the downtrodden. Maharashtra owes much to Govande, and yet Maharashtrian historians have not cared to note his great services to Maharashtra.

The new institution gave a fillip to the activities of the workers of the Satya-Shodhak Samaj in villages. They invited their leader Jotirao to make speeches at villages and to explain his social philosophy. He was invited by Bhau Kondaji Patil to make speeches at Otur, a village in the Poona District; That village being an important centre, hundreds of villagers flocked to hear their leader. Several of them had never before attended a meeting. Jotirao spoke their language, knew their mind and their grievances, and understood how the godless Brahmins exploited them in the name of God. He made stirring speeches explaining the stand of the Satya-Shodhak Samaj at several villages like Junnar.

Afterwards, in a song Jotirao described graphically the atmosphere created by his work. At "Otur, Bhau Kondaji went wild, the Junnar money-lender was terrified. The Brahmins had a glimpse of Phooley and ran with holy howls and begging bowls. In the newspapers they raised a hue and cry and called out the name of Shankaracharya. Everywhere in Junnar the reading of holy books began and thus they tried to deceive the ignorant minds. 'Oh Kashibai, Yamunabai, hungry I pine away and die.' Some Shindia ran to succour and said to the Brahmin, 'Take something for your hunger!' "

A friend of the editor of the *Dnyanodaya*[3] described this Junnar atmosphere very vividly. In his article dated the 18th

3. 24 July 1884.

July 1884, he observed that a furious dispute had arisen between the non-Brahmins of Junnar and the villages around it, and the Brahmins. The Salis, Malis, Telis, Tambolis and such other castes from about a hundred villages around Junnar had been struggling resolutely over the previous ten years to liberate themselves from Brahmin thraldom, and their unjust and exorbitant religious fees for rites and rituals.

For that purpose, in May 1884, Jotirao Phooley and N. M. Lokhande, Proprietor of the *Din Bandhu*, and other influential men, addressed two or three huge meetings at Junnar. These were attended by about three thousand men of Sali, Mali, Sonar and other Hindu communities. According to the prevailing standards, it was a mammoth meeting. Phooley and some others made powerful speeches. Besides the Marathas, Muslims and Christians too attended these meetings. They were received with due courtesy at the meeting place. Brahmins were conspicuous by their absence. But their lackeys were identified and compelled to stand aside. They were treated as Untouchables.

All the speakers exposed the hypocrisy, cunning and evil deeds of Brahmins and explained how their actions and conduct were unjust. The facts stated were mostly true, for which the Brahmin priests must have hung their heads in shame. The lackeys were enraged at the speeches, but they fluttered in helplessness and banged their doors. Although much of what the Satya-Shodhak leaders said was correct, said the writer of the article in the *Dnyanodaya*, they exaggerated some points.

Jotirao said that the Brahmins had abandoned their religious duties. They had learnt the English language, a foreign language, and throwing away their titles such as Pandits, Shastris, and Vaidiks, they had obtained degrees such as Bachelor of Arts and Master of Arts. They filled almost all Government offices. Wherever one might go, to Court, Police Office, Education Department or Revenue Department one would see only Brahmins. They did not allow men from other castes to enter these departments or stick to their jobs! Jotirao added that those Brahmins who were converted to Christianity hated the Mahars, Mangs and Shudras and suppressed them. The Christian missionaries excluded the converts from rising to respectable posts in the official hierarchy. The writer of the article expressed his doubts as to the correctness of Jotirao's arguments regarding the Brahmin

Christians. Jotirao might have attacked the Christian missionaries, he thought, without proper knowledge of the situation.

After these meetings, the writer in the *Dnyanodaya* observed, Phooley unveiled an image of the god Maruti at a place in Junnar. He performed marriage ceremonies at several places in the neighbouring villages, but village priests were not admitted. They therefore lodged complaints with the police and with the Courts, but nobody paid much heed to them. They were obliged to sit at home in a helpless condition. The arguments put forward by the non-Brahmin leaders were much on the lines of Christian missionary views. Needless to say how the Vedas, the scriptures and the *puranas* would come in their way if the Marathas organised an independent religious cult. Nobody would be able to say where the new reforms would lead them. The writer in the *Dnyanodaya* said that it was not known under what scriptural authorities they performed their religious functions. According to Hindu scriptures, he went on, the world was controlled by God. God was governed by the mantras. The mantras were influenced by the Brahmins, and the Brahmins were the gods of the Hindus!

Considering, the writer observed, the Vedas, scriptures and *puranas* and the Bible, Jotirao recommended the Mahars and Mangs to go over to Christianity and to improve their lot. People would be pleased if on some other occasion he made that point clear. He was surprised that Phooley should have asked only the Mahar and Mang castes to embrace Christianity. According to the *Jatibhed Vivekasar*, all the castes formed one community and therefore the writer in the *Dnyanodaya* asked whether there was any necessity for the Mahar and Mang people to embrace Christianity, or whether it would not be right for all other castes to do so. Jotirao would have been convinced of it, had he read the said book. From the speeches, the writer concluded, it followed that Hinduism was unable to improve the lot of its adherents.

Two points in the article summarised above are doubtful. In what context had Jotirao expressed, if at all he did so, any suggestion that the Mahar and Mang should be converted to Christianity? Jotirao called them his own people and said that the Mahars, Mang, Malis, Dhangars, Salis and others belonged to one Shudra caste. He never favoured conversion of the lower castes to any other religion. Whenever he gloated over the conversion of Brahmins, he did so to provoke the Brahmins and to show how the terrestrial gods of India were falling a victim to a foreign religion.

The other point is about the unveiling of an image of Maruti in a temple at the hands of Jotirao. It is not known whether this is a fact. Jotirao believed in God, but he said God was not visible or was not pleased with this or that gift. Moreover, he was not an idol-worshipper.

II

The editor of the *Dnyanodaya* published an extract on the same subject from the *Arunodaya*, a Marathi weekly from Thana. Its editor was a Brahmin. He said that all over the country there were disputes and confusion over the religious questions, and one could not understand what would be their result. In former times Brahmins were held in high respect, but in his day people were ready to harass them. He was not sorry about this; on the contrary, he was glad. For ages the Brahmins had been hailed as leaders of this nation, and their conduct in those times deserved that honour.

However, their conduct had become in his day so debased that they surpassed others in perpetrating vile deeds. People had, therefore, lost respect for them. Although their conduct had been debased in his day, they had not lost their intellect which they had developed over centuries. The pot would not be filled unless it went down into a well. It was likely that by their great intellect the Brahmins would make efforts to win back their glory. They enjoyed supremacy in religious and political matters. It was natural that they should have lost their position and authority in the field of religion because they themselves had acted against the tenets of their religion, and they had grown debased. They deserved disgrace and dishonour as they had ruined the Kingdom of Shivaji and handed it over to foreigners.

The various charges levelled against the Brahmins were justified. Yet it was very strange, continued the editor of the *Arunodaya*, that people were trying to be Brahmins. Those who were eager to pull down Brahmins from their high pedestal, would have been held in high respect had they made any efforts to win back their power and prestige. But their actions belied their protestation. For winning back power, unity was necessary. Those who harassed Brahmins were not themselves uniting. But far from it. If they were convinced that the Brahmins were responsible for the downfall of their power and position, the Brahmins should be drowned in the sea, and they themselves should win back their power. In doing so, nobody would hinder their path. They should annihilate one brother out of ten if he was coming in their way, but they should bring glory to their predecessors. If that happened, the editor of the *Arunodaya* concluded, Brahmins would ultimately come down in the world.

The *Dnyanodaya* commented on both articles. Much work of reform, it said, was being done in Junnar Taluka among the Hindus called the Shudras. The main object of the reform was to oust Brahmin priests from all kinds of religious functions and to get these performed by Shudras themselves. Brahmin priests were boycotted. It was a courageous step and those who had given a bold lead in this respect indeed deserved praise. The Brahmin priests who were deprived of their means of livelihood were not unduly perturbed.

It was a fact, observed the *Dnyanodaya*, that the Shudras were responsible for the prestige of the Brahmins. Brahmins did not hold Brahmin priests in such high respect. Brahmins, who got Brahmin priests to perform the religious rites and functions, treated them as their servants, perhaps respectable servants but men to do all their bidding, at most, on the basis of equality. But this was not the case with the Shudras. They regarded the Brahmin priests as their superiors, as demi-gods and obeyed them in a servile manner. They prostrated themselves before them, and drank water made holy by Brahmin toes to purify themselves. The Shudras asked the Brahmin priests often whether a particular thing was auspicious, whether it would be beneficial to them. They worshipped the priests as their saviours and guides, prostrated themselves before them, and raised their importance. If the Shudras gave up venerating the Brahmin, his position would be low, at least in the field of religion and gradually it would vanish. It was taught to them for generations that their religious and spiritual welfare was based on the worship of Brahmins.

In spite of this belief they had rejected the Brahmin priests and were performing their own religious functions without Brahmins. This was no mean achievement or an ordinary change. To effect such a radical change required supreme courage. Brahmins lacked this. Neither did the learned and wise members of the Prarthana Samaj possess this sort of courage, the *Dnyanodaya* added.

How was this great change effected? It was the outcome of various factors, several institutions and great efforts made by a number of leading personalities. The missionary schools and religious propaganda in that part of the presidency played no mean part in it. The Satya-Shodhak Samaj founded by Joti Govindrao Phooley was openly opposed to Brahmins. His followers and the *Din Bandhu* under his guidance did much in that direction. But above all the Brahmins overbearing conduct and their harassing attitude led to the revolt.

Referring to the article in the *Arunodaya*, the *Dnyanodaya* further observed that the editor of the *Arunodaya* was right to some extent when he said that the Shudras should make efforts to win back their position and glory and should not imitate the Brahmins in putting on the sacred thread or in observing such other useless customs. It was true that the pot went down into the well to be filled, but, he concluded, the pot had holes and was likely to be empty when it came up.

The non-Brahmins mustered strong under Jotirao's flag. They resolved to give effect to his teachings. One of them, Balaji Kesaji Patil, performed the marriage ceremony of his son in conformity with the rites prescribed by the Satya-Shodhak Samaj. The Brahmins took objections to it. Without a Brahmin priest, they said, a marriage could not be solemnised. Every party now threw a challenge to the other. The Brahmins from far and near held a meeting at Otur and protested against the encroachment upon their rights. A marriage could not be performed without the officiating priest. So they urged the village priests, Waman Jagannath and Shankar Bapuji, to proceed legally against Balaji Keshavji for damages. Accordingly, they did.

A similar case had been fought out in 1878 in the High Court of Bombay. Dinanath Abaji and other village priests had filed a suit against Sadashiv Hari Madhave and others. It was the contention of the village priest that Madhave had employed another priest to perform ceremonies at his residence sidetracking the priest's right to perform them. He claimed the fee which would probably be payable to him if he had been employed to perform such ceremonies.

The question was whether the village priest, even if not employed to perform a ceremony, should be paid a fee similar in amount to that which the man paid to the priest actually employed. M. G. Ranade, who was then the First Class Subordinate Judge at Poona, decided the case in favour of the plaintiffs. His verdict was that the plaintiffs were entitled to perform the ceremonies irrespective of the host's wishes, as well as to receive the fees. Although such rights were denied by the courts of Bengal and the North-West Frontier Provinces, Ranade, the social reformer and judge, meant that according to the law he interpreted, a village or city priest alone was entitled to perform the ceremonies irrespective of the host's wishes, and the plaintiffs should be paid their dues even if they had not acted as priests. The District Judge, Poona, varied the decree in appeal stating that the plaintiffs were entitled to perform for the defendants the ceremonies they had mentioned in their plaint, and to receive the fees customary, or if not employed, to receive on each occasion a fee equal in amount to that paid by the defendants, or any of them, to the person or persons employed by them instead of plaintiffs.

Sir M. R. Westropp, Kt., Chief Justice of the Bombay High Court, quoted a case decided by a Judge when the High Court was not in existence and approved of the variation made by the District Judge by his decree in that of the Subordinate Judge. "We affirm," said the Chief Justice, "the decree with costs, and are somewhat surprised that the plaintiffs should have thought it worth their while to appeal against it in consequence of the slight variation made by the District Judge."

The stalwart Rao Bahadur V. N. Mandlik appeared for the priests in the High Court. It speaks much for his views, just as it did for Ranade's.

If Ranade's decree had been carried out, the village artisans to whom *inams* were assigned to secure their presence for the performance of duties, would have insisted on similar rights as against the inhabitants. The potmaker would insist that pots made by him alone should be purchased! Later the Madras High Court denied such rights, although the Dinanath Abaji's case, discussed above, was cited in the Madras Court.

III

Now a similar case arose out of the marriage of the son of Balaji Kesaji Patil. The Brahmin priests of Otur filed a suit and the Poona Brahmins supported them solidly. As might be expected, Balaji ran to Jotirao for guidance. In those days the majority of the lawyers were Brahmins, and it was difficult for them to secure the counsel of a non-Brahmin lawyer. Jotirao, a responsible leader who always stood by his principles, tried to secure legal guidance from Polsani Lingu, who was a lawyer in Poona. In the Lower Court the Subordinate Judge was a Brahmin, and he decided the case in favour of the Brahmin priests by awarding the plaintiffs' claim. Patil appealed to the First Class Subordinate Judge at Poona. Khan Bahadur M. N. Nanavati was Subordinate Judge. The contention of the plaintiffs was that they were hereditary priests of the village of Otur, in the Poona District, and complained that at the marriages of the daughters of the defendants their services were not employed, although as priests they had a right to officiate on such occasions and were ready and willing to conduct the ceremonies. They claimed damages, no fees having been paid to them, from the defendant.

The defendant Balaji, a non-Brahmin, denied that the plaintiffs had a right to the office of priest, and alleged that he had employed his own caste men to perform the religious ceremonies, as did his ancestors. The First Class Subordinate Judge at Poona with appellate powers reversed the decree of Lower Court in November 1887. It was a great shock to Brahmins. At Junnar and Poona they held meetings and decided to fight the case in the Bombay High Court.

The Brahmin priests accordingly preferred a second appeal. It was a fight between two groups, the traditionists and the reformists. Poona was divided between two groups, Brahmin and non-Brahmin, Poona East and Poona West, and men with *pugrees* (headgears) and men with *phetas* (turbans). Few leaders took up such responsibilities upon themselves as stemmed from their teachings. Jotirao had consulted even European barristers and was leaving nothing to chance as the fate of the movement he had launched was dependent upon the success he would achieve in this case.

From this discussion and description the vigour and extent of Jotirao's influence can be judged. Junnar Taluka was the stronghold of this Indian Martin Luther. It jostled against Brahmin supremacy for liberty. This was fighting without a war!

IV

Sometime later, there was again agrarian unrest at Junnar. The agriculturists sent a memorial to the Government that they should be given protection against money-lenders and landlords who were mostly Brahmins.

Commenting on this memorial, a reporter from Poona observed in *Native Opinion*,[4] Bombay: "The painfully interesting piece of information this week is a petition to Mr. Winter by the Kunbis, Malis and other cultivators of the Junnar Taluka against the Brahmin clerks in Government service of that place. The complaints are as follows: The Brahmins deceive the Kunbis and take bribes from them in several ways. The Brahmins form the majority of clerks in Government offices. The Brahmin priests screw out money from the Kunbis by officiating at their marriages against their will. The Kunbis of Junnar are reduced to utter poverty by the troubles of Bhats, and are unable to give them anything."

"The complaints, if true," proceeds the reporter, "are of a very grave nature indeed; but taking into consideration the fact that the average gains of Bhats in such villages hardly exceed Rs. 20 a year, one must look elsewhere for the cause of the appalling indigence of the cultivators. The disease of Brahmin-hating which is so common with any European officer, has affected some half-educated non-Brahmins who try to sow these bitter seeds of dissension." This reporter, a shrewd

4. 11 July 1884.

economist, attributed the appalling poverty of the cultivators to English capitalists, Indian Railways which deprived the Kunbis of their coolie-charges, and to the excessive Government demands on the cultivators.

The farmers refused to cultivate the land for a year, and they appealed to Government to redress their grievances against the money-lenders and landlords. Jotirao led this agitation. The boycott on the land was lifted when the Government officers, the landlords and money lenders arrived at a settlement with Jotirao, the leader of the peasants. In those days leaders from the Brahmin community seldom protected the interests of the peasants. Since the landlords and money-lenders were mostly Brahmins and Marwaris, their organisations and journals in the Presidency always viewed their grievances, though they managed to explain them, mixing their sympathy for the peasants with their support for the rights of the landlords and money-lenders.

The *Indu Prakash*[5] an Anglo-Vernacular weekly, describing this agricultural unrest, said that "the condition of our agricultural population is such as to cause the utmost anxiety to all thinking people. Government have become fully alive to the gravity of the situation and the efforts of many benevolent people are directed to devising means to remedy the evil."

The *Indu Prakash* was of the opinion that the insatiable cupidity and dishonesty of the money-lenders was not the sole cause of it. "We admit," it proceeded, "that the *ryot* is no less to blame than the Sowkar. We have on several occasions maintained in these columns that the poverty of the cultivating class is the result of many complex causes. It was the fashion to keep all odium on head of the money-lender and to deliver the unoffending *ryot* from the clutches of the money-lending wolf was the professed object with which Hon'ble Mr. Hople had his Relief Act passed." It added that it was pointed out by the Native Press that the heaviness of assessments and their inexorable collection were in no small measure responsible for the royts' misery.

Criticising the proposed Insolvency Act by Hart-Davies, it further said: "A measure like the Act proposed by Hart-Davies means the wholesale spoliation of the sowkars, and encouragement

5. 22 July 1884.

to the *ryots* to free themselves from their honest engagements. What a premium will be set upon fraud and dishonesty and how people will be cheated out of their money under the aegis of such an Act will be dear to those who have watched the operation of the insolvency law in Bombay. It has been found that the *ryot*, cannot live without the sowkar, nor the sowkar without the *ryot*, and the proposed Insolvency Act will, instead of doing good to either, only destroy the harmony that exists, or at all events that existed before the Deccan Agriculturists' Relief Act between the village cultivators and the village money-lenders and will entirely unsettle the society in the village."

"All such measures of relief," it suspected, "as the Deccan Agriculturists' Relief Act and the proposed Insolvency Act have an element of socialism latent in them which is obscured from view by their philanthropic object. But even the philanthropy that prompts them is only a euphemism for the phrase 'Robbing Peter to Pay Paul' for so long as the debtor does not meet his engagements by honest exertion, any enforced relief given to him by law is so much a deduction from the gains of the Sowkar. The provisions of such measures lose sight of what Herbert Spencer calls the 'political momentum' of legal enactments. To us it seems, any legislative interference with private contract is highly injurious. Our *ryot* population is poor, but their poverty will be increased by teaching them that they might incur debts and not pay them."

"The only way," it concluded, "to help them out of their poverty is, we think, to instil into them a sense of self-help and honest work. In order that they may not be crushed by their present loads the utmost that can be done for them is to afford them facilities to pay their debts, such as by giving them longer time to pay, by ensuring a lighter rate of interest, and by preventing them from being over-reached by their creditors or altogether deprived of the means of living. The portion of the Deccan Agriculturists' Relief Act which serves these ends is, we think, so far beneficial and unobjectionable. But when a debtor can overhaul all previous accounts or get himself relieved of all liabilities by a statutory discharge, he can scarcely be expected to cherish any self-reliance or honesty."

This was the outlook of the progressives of Jotirao's day. So he had no truck with them and asked the cultivators not to truckle to their exploiters. The article in the *Indu Prakash* was written to defend the *Sowkar* who was made to look like an honest man quietly earning his modest income in a village. The Sarvajanik Sabha was no better as an exponent of this doctrine than the *Indu Prakash*. Both were under the protective wings of Ranade the economist.

Jotirao did not spare the foibles and faults of the peasants. He could perceive both the internal and the external causes that led to the poverty and misery of the cultivators whom he called the Shudras. A foreign Government which, though not motivated by altruistic aims, made an attempt to examine the conditions of the agricultural classes, was opposed by the leaders of those days; even Tilak and Gokhale, who came later, were not exceptions to it. The editorial in the *Indu Prakash* raised an alarm as the measures proposed for the improvement of the poor cultivators appeared to it dreadfully socialistic! Socialism, which aimed at ending the exploitation of the peasants and workers, rivetted the pointed attention of all the thinking world on the abject poverty of the labouring classes, and declared that man had a right to food, shelter and clothes, was bound to be a red rag to the representatives of the privileged classes. So Jotirao had no faith in their leadership.

V

Jotirao's movement was now well established. He wanted to extend it to the States of benevolent Maratha princes. With the march of education, energetic and brilliant youths from the lower castes were also appearing on the horizon of Maharashtra. Ramchandra Vithoba Dhamnaskar was one of these brilliant men. He came of a Maratha family named Jadhav. That family possessed the rights of the *khot* of the village Dhamanse which is about ten miles to the north-east of Ratnagiri. His grandfather served during Peshwa rule at the historic fort of Ratnagiri. His father had risen to the post of a Munsiff and died in 1860 at Ahmednagar. Of his five children, Ramchandra was born at Bhalavali in Rajapur Taluka in 1848. After his father's death the family removed to Ratnagiri. The mother sold all her belongings and maintained the family. A brilliant student, a favourite of Dr. R. G. Bhandarkar at Ratnagiri High

School, a teacher at nineteen, Dhamnaskar soon rose from clerkship to be a Mamlatdar.

Risen as he had from poverty, Ramchandrapant Dhamnaskar had genuine sympathies for the poor classes. His generosity ever flowed to needy students of the poor classes. While he was a Mamlatdar at Satara, he came in contact with the social philosophy of the Satya-Shodhak Samaj, and became a member of it and a staunch admirer of Jotirao. In 1884 Ramchandrarao was appointed an Assistant Sarsubhe in the Baroda State through the good offices of Mama Parmanand who introduced him to Kazi Sahabuddin, the then Dewan of Baroda. In those days the young Maharaja of Baroda was on the lookout for able, energetic and intelligent men who would be useful for running the administration of his State. A few years later, Dhamnaskar rose to be the Dewan of Baroda.

Meantime, Jotirao wrote an open letter in the *Din Bandhu* to Sayajirao, the Maharaja of Baroda. The letter was in verse and consisted of fifteen stanzas. In these poems he asked Sayajirao to take pity on the Shudras: "The Brahmins, by keeping them from education, have enfeebled them and reduced them to dire straits. It is not right to ruin women for one's own enjoyment; it is a disgrace for men to dance in a *tamasha*. To listen to the songs of a prostitute is to stain one's mind. No use blaming others for the vice which springs from oneself. Bestow not food grains on idle Brahmins by spending State revenue. The farmers who toil in the field have to go half-starved."

"Annual grants flow to Brahmins from the revenue and the farmers who contribute to the exchequer toil endlessly in the field. The bullocks of the farmers which live on the leaves of banana trees die of hunger. The Brahmins get gifts of corn, and are feasted all the year round, but the farmers do not get even a square meal a day. They give gifts to Brahmins with reverence while the Kunbis do not get remission of their debts. Dancers and priests are presented with dresses of honour, why not give such presents to farmers for their achievements in the field? Liquor is taxed and vice is given prominence, the consequences are not anticipated. Illiterate are the farmers, why don't you become their saviour?

"The chief minister has seen the miseries of the poor, you

are a great and merciful donor, so I have addressed this letter to Your Highness. That time and tide wait for none is known to all. Wealth does not always remain in one's possession. Only the soldiers know the importance of drinking water from a bottle; the resident of Kashi does not respect the Ganga. Jotirao prays Sayajirao to make hay while the sun shines."

After this poetic letter, an interview was arranged through Ramchandrarao Dhamnaskar who had a high regard for Jotirao, and Jotirao was invited to Baroda in December 1884. Jotirao's was an eminently likable personality. His fearlessness and frankness, his tireless mission for the uplift of the common man, his championship of the underdog, his selflessness and his spotless character impressed the young Maharaja of Baroda.

Jotirao made a few speeches at important places in Baroda. He was asked on two or three occasions to have his say at special meetings attended by Sayajirao and his party. The Maharaja listened to him attentively. This was the second visit of Jotirao to Baroda. At the time of his first visit, he had read the *Cultivator's Whipcord* to His Highness. Ramchandrarao Dhamnaskar thus began to play a very important role in the life of Jotirao, his leader and philosopher! Some days later the Maharaja abandoned the practice of distributing *khichadi*, (a mixture of rice and pulse) to Brahmins. It might not be the direct result of Jotirao's preaching, but without doubt his suggestions attracted the Maharaja's pointed attention to this practice.

CHAPTER XVI

Congress and the Lower Classes

JOTIRAO WAS happy that the movement he had ushered in was gathering force. The leaders of the Satya-Shodhak Samaj decided to go in procession in Poona on the first day of the Hindu year in April 1885. This was no mean venture to give expression to their thoughts in Poona, the Rome of Hindu orthodoxy, challenging its supremacy over and hegemony in religious and social fields.

Some workers of the Satya-Shodhak Samaj and men of some importance were invited to Poona to participate in the celebrations. Green, yellow and red turbans were wound around a pole nine inches thick and eight feet long. From its upper end fluttered yellow and green flags. That pole was held by two volunteers in a bullock cart. A band led the processionists. Next came the Mahars with their music and drums. They were followed by country tomtom-beaters. Next came a batch of trumpet and drum-beaters. The cart carrying the flag followed them, and the processionists and workers, of the Satya-Shodhak Samaj and its leaders walked behind the cart.

Among those who participated in the procession were Jotirao, Ramayya Vyankayya Aiyyavaru, M. G. Ranade, Krishnarao Bhalekar, Taravade, Dr. Sadoba Gavade, L. K. Ghorpade, Deorao K. Thosar, H. N. Navalkar and others. The procession started at four o'clock from Vithoba temple at Bhavani Peit and wended its way through important localities reaching Dr. Sadoba Gavade's house, its destination, at nine at night. There Aiyyavaru, Ranade and Jotirao made speeches. Ranade, who had the vision to see the significance of the movement inaugurated by Jotirao for the awakening of self-respect and self-reliance in the lower classes, took part in it.

The second annual conference of Marathi writers was held at the Sarvajanik Hall in Poona on May 24, 1885, under the presidentship of Krishnashastri Rajwade. About 300 writers attended the conference. Some letters from writers who could not attend it were read out to the conference. Of the forty-three letters, the first letter read was from Jotirao.

On receiving M. G. Ranade's invitation to attend the conference, Jotirao wrote a letter to Ranade. Acknowledging his letter dated the 13th May 1885, Jotirao said: "I was very glad to receive your invitation. But oh, dear brother, our institutions and books have nothing to do with the authors who have not the courage or guts to grant willingly or openly human rights, and from the prevailing tendencies it is presumed that they would never bring themselves to grant these rights to those who have been deprived of them. The teachings and message of their books are poles apart from the message of the books written by us."

"Their forefathers have taken vengeance on the Shudras and Atishudras and have condemned them in their fake writings as their slaves. Their old, decayed manuscripts bear testimony to this. The miseries and sufferings through which the Shudras and Atishudras had to go for ages and have to experience now in their life cannot be imagined by the wiseacres who make useless casual speeches at such meetings.

"This is all known to the Sarvajanik Sabha and its organisers; yet for a few temporary advantages for themselves and their children, they have drawn a veil over their eyes. And as soon as they got pensions, they turned against the British Government, assumed again the pride of caste, became arrant idol-worshippers, assumed a look of perfect purity, and began to condemn Shudras and Atishudras as insignificant and low. They considered it a pollution to touch paper money made by the British Government who gave them pension. Is this the way the Brahmins are going to uplift this unfortunate country?

"We Shudras will not now believe any more in the professions of our exploiters. In a word, we will not gain anything by mixing with them. We must think for ourselves and rely on ourselves. If these men of note aim at bringing about real unity among all sections, they should find out how lasting brotherhood and mutual love be established among all mankind. They should find such basic principles and declare them to the world through their books. It is not right to draw a veil over the real situation. This is all that I can say. Please send this short letter for the consideration of your conference. This is the first salutation from a simple old man.

Yours sincerely,

Jotirao G. Phooley."[1]

The *Dnyanodaya* noted that the Brahmin editors in Maharashtra violently attacked this letter of Jotirao. It opined that though the letter was provocative, it was indeed thought-provoking.

Why Jotirao did not co-operate with the Marathi writers was very clear. Their ambitions, the world of imagination, novels, dramas and poetry hardly reflected the problems of the vast mass of people and their abject poverty. The early Marathi plays mostly dealt with *puranic* themes and whatever social plays did was to reflect the problem of the higher classes. The writers boasted of their culture of which nine-tenths of their countrymen possessed not a whit! At present conditions in India are not much better.

In the month of *Shravana*, the fifth month of the Hindu year, Jotirao's followers had clashes with the Poona orthodox. It was the time of *Shravani*, the ceremony of renewing sacred threads. It was Jotirao's thesis that the Shudras and Atishudras were Kshatrias. This was later proved beyond doubt by the eminent scholar and sociologist Dr. Babasaheb Ambedkar. It was the view of Dr. Ambedkar that because the Kshatriyas had violent conflicts with the Brahmins they refused to perform the thread ceremonies of the Kshatriyas. So the Kshatriyas were degraded to the fourth *Varna* (class) which did not exist previously, and this fourth class was called Shudras. The Brahmin arrogance in Southern India went one step further. They regarded Hindu society as divided between two groups, Brahmins and Shudras; the Kshatriya and Vaishya castes, they thought, were wiped out from the face of Maharashtra!

This arrogance had led the Brahmins to boycott the coronation of Chhatrapati Shivaji whom they afterwards fondly described as protector of Brahmins and cows! So when the followers of Jotirao performed the ceremony of renewing the sacred threads

1. The *Dnyanodaya*, 11 June 1885.

in spite of the Brahmins, it angered the Brahmins. It is very strange that they mocked at Brahmin customs and yet they performed these mock-heroics. It is not known whether Jotirao liked this or not. The deepest respect in which a Brahmin was held during the days of the *Shrutis* was paid to "him not because of his thread but because of his selfless, pious work and his knowledge.

In the rainy season of 1885, Sayajirao Gaikwad stayed for two months in Poona when he attended some school functions. Jotirao and his followers organised a function in honour of the Maharaja. M. G. Ranade and Dr. Bhandarkar were invited to attend this function. Earlier, Ranade had made some speeches in Poona in honour of the Maharaja. Jotirao and others made speeches explaining the ideology of the Satya-Shodhak Samaj. Ranade, while speaking on this occasion on the subject of Marathas and Maharashtra, delivered a "very important speech. He said that although the caste system existed it had not hampered the progress of the nation, and that the conditions of the farmer were better than those prevailing thirty years earlier. The *Dnyanprakash* paid glowing tributes to Ranade for his speech; and describing Jotirao's views as obstinate and one-sided, blamed him.

II

Within a month of these attacks, Jotirao issued a booklet replying both to Ranade and to the *Dnyanprakash*. The booklet was entitled *A Warning*. He had written it in June 1885, but after Ranade's speech in September, he immediately wrote a preface and published it. In the preface he vehemently condemned Ranade for his 'misguiding' speech before the Maharaja. He described Ranade as a man of Shankaracharya's ability, but dubbed him a bashful person and added that he bluffed before the Gaikwad. Education imparted to Brahmins at the cost of the local cess had not improved the outlook and attitude of the Brahmins. It was true that the harassment of the lower classes by the Brahmins had slightly abated. Ranade was ashamed to admit it frankly. But the slight improvement in the condition of the farmers was due to missionary education which helped to some extent to remove the ignorance of the lower classes.

Brahmin families did not know what it was to carry on their heads baskets of refuse in the hot sun. They lived idly on the toil of others, and the money they grabbed they put into the purses of prostitutes.

Jotirao gave a vivid picture of the harrowing sufferings the farmers had to undergo under the rule of Bajirao II. That rule treated the poor subjects as if they were as worthless as bugs or blades of grass. According to that rule, to govern meant to torture, to murder and to loot! If they survived they were to slave for them. Therefore, the poor subjects of his day prayed that the British raj should last for ever! Under Peshwa rule, the farmers had grown lethargic and poor because their life and money and stocks of grains were always in danger. But now they could be safe; their corn, too, was safe as there was justice in the land, and all were equal before the law. Travelling was safe; wealth was safe. There were bridges, tanks, canals, roads, schools, dispensaries and travellers' bungalows for the use and convenience of the people. The Brahmin rule wasted the revenue; it did not use money for the welfare of the people. Money was lavished on feasts for Brahmins, on their dress and on the gifts given to them.

Farmers' children died from hunger. The farmer ate his bread with salt, pepper or onion, wore a torn turban, put on a rough blanket on his shoulder, and walked bare-foot, whereas the Brahmins had hearty feasts till they developed nausea for food. Owing to pressure of work the wife of the farmer often could not wash her only sari, her chief garment. When she could find time she went to the river or rivulet; she unwound half her sari and washed it with anguish and shame. She then wore the washed wet part of the sari and washed the other half, waiting till it dried. Then the mending business followed with needle in hand. The patching went on till at last the sari was shortened; the countless patches disfigured the shape, and the original colour of the sari was beyond recognition! Jotirao has cited a story of a Brahmin money-lender. It is a harrowing tale; how the Brahmins, Marwaris and other money-lenders deprived the farmer of his land and house and reduced them to beggary with honeyed words and false documents; all a heartless, fraudulent business!

Jotirao published a new booklet called *Satsar*—the Essence

of Truth — in June 1885. He desired to continue it as a journal if there was a good response. In the first book there are references to the conversion of Pandita Ramabai. Jotirao seemed to hold her in high respect. He said, in order to tease the Brahmins who were drunkards, that they should denounce her. The missionaries had simply sprinkled water over her head and had done nothing else. They who were drunkards and full of vices had no right to condemn her, he added.

Writing about the Prarthana Samaj and the Brahmo Samaj in the *Satsar*, Jotirao said that as long as they did not mix with the Shudras and Atishudras and assimilate them, they had better stop talking about Shudras joining their institutions. The argument that the Brahmins assimilated Vyas and Vashistha was deceptive. Because their fathers were Brahmins, they were incorporated into the Brahmin caste. Those children who were born of a Brahmin woman and a Shudra husband were not incorporated in the Brahmin fold. Somebody asked him how crores of non-Brahmins came to be under the domination of the Brahmins: his reply was a counter question. He asked how a small minority of Muslims or a small number of the British made their rule prevail over the Hindus! When the Brahmins reduced the lower castes to beggary in the name of religion, the non-Brahmins had no reason to get angry with the benevolent Christians and Muslims. This was a reply to another question. It was easy for the Brahmins to deal with missionaries and to quarrel with them; but it was not possible for them to quarrel with the Muslims on principles of religion, this was his frank opinion.

The education of woman, Jotirao went on, and the creation of all social institutions like Brahmo Samaj and Prarthana Samaj were the outcome of English education. The Brahmins incorporated in their religious books so many definitions of religion that they camouflaged its real meaning, and ultimately for the Shudras religion meant to slave for the Brahmins! Asked what religion he belonged to, Jotirao replied that the religion of Brahmin cheated God and imposed slavery on the Shudras. It was no religion at all. The Brahmins should not shed crocodile tears for the welfare of the Shudras. They might, he retorted pungently, embrace Islam, or any other good religion. About a thousand copies of this booklet were distributed among his followers at important centres.

This last portion was part of a dialogue between a Brahmin and Jotirao. He always talked to Brahmins in this tone and vein. Although his best friends were Brahmins, his blood boiled when he saw the terrible miseries and untold privations of the poor people. His love for them turned into hatred for the Brahmins, who had mixed religion and ideas of God with politics and the laws of social construction! He seldom used the word Hindu or Hinduism, but when Lord Ripon gave India Local Self-Government, he said the Viceroy made a mistake in assuming that Brahmins alone were Hindus.

Jotirao never favoured conversion. The ceremony which a member at the time of his initiation into the Satya-Shodhak Samaj performed was a Hindu affair. The Samaj ceremony of renewal of the sacred threads consisted entirely of Hindu religious rites; the marriage ceremony was purely a Hindu affair. Only the Brahmin priests, who proudly considered themselves gods on earth and therefore could not bring themselves to believe that man to man the Shudras were socially and religiously their equals, were kept away from the ceremony. Whenever a Hindu expressed a desire to go over to any other religion, Jotirao dissuaded him from doing so. Those who lived and worked with him proudly narrated such recollections about him.

Jotirao published the second number of the *Satsar* in October 1885. It contained twenty-two pages and its price was one anna. It was solely devoted to the cause of Indian women. In it he stated that all the religious works were written by men, and they selfishly condemned Indian women to a low status for centuries. It added that it was very cruel on the part of the authors of those religious books to condemn their very mothers who gave birth to them. It was the beneficent British Government that gave them opportunity for educating themselves, and women were learning in his day how to read and write, though their number was sparse. After this number, the *Satsar* was discontinued.

III

During the early part of the year, Jotirao was engaged on one or two booklets. He issued a pamphlet called the *Asprushyanchi Kaifiyat*.[2] It is a statement regarding the conditions of the Untouchables. In it a *Mahar* and a *Mang* are imagined as stopping the carriage of Queen Victoria, who is passing through their village while on her tour of India. They entreat her loyally and fervently ask her to visit their localities and see whether there is any change in their conditions under her rule. She visits. They tell her that they were treated mercilessly during Peshwa rule. They were regarded as sub-human beings. In those days they were buried alive, and were forced to labour without any remuneration. Under British rule, their life was safe; but they could not yet walk freely in the streets. They could not go to the market freely; their abject poverty could not allow them to send their children to school. Their economic condition was the same as before. They had no means of livelihood. They had no access to water-courses. They appealed to Queen Victoria to remove their poverty and misery and bestow on them all human rights. Queen Victoria said that her Government would look into their grievances.

Jotirao made another important contribution to the solution of the problem of untouchability. It was he who created leaders from amongst the untouchable classes. He used to visit localities of Untouchables and encourage the energetic and intelligent men from among them to be active in society, to do some social work, to write and to speak.

One of such men selected by him was Gopal Baba Walangkar. He was one of the pupils of Jotirao. He was a writer, a preacher and a good speaker. On his return from military service, he started propaganda for the abolition of untouchability. He wrote many articles in the *Din Bandhu* and *Sudharak*, and visited several places in Maharashtra, awakening the Mahar-Mangs to their pitiful conditions. Jotirao made provision for his tours and household affairs. Like his master's, it was Walangkar's confirmed belief that untouchability was man-made, not god-made. He wrote a booklet in 1888 and challenged Hindu leaders to prove that untouchability was god-made. He strove to convince Hindus of their inhuman behaviour towards their co-religionists. He had started some institutions to promote the

2. The Untouchables' Case.

interests of Untouchables. Later, at the social conference of 1895, he made a stirring appeal to caste Hindus to throw open schools, travellers' bungalows, public water-courses, public services and trades to their countrymen and co-religionists whom they had condemned as Untouchables.

Jotirao composed several poems called *Akhandas*. In one of them he sings the glory of Mohammed. He praises Mohammed for his bravery and energy and for the status of equality he bestowed on his followers. Mohammed fought single-handed for truth. He said there was no high and low in society; all were equal. He sank all differences. There was one God. He opposed idol-worship. Islam liberated the Dasyus, i.e. the Shudras from the thraldom of the Brahmin Aryas. Because there were disunity and differences in Hindu society, Muslims took advantage of this situation.

In other poems Jotirao the poet describes how the god Ganpati with an animal's head and human body keeps Untouchables at arm's length and bestows sweetmeats on Brahmins. In the name of the Ganpati festival funds are squandered. Marwaris squeeze the poor and then build temples for their personal fame. They harass the world in the name of God, and go to hell definitely. True worshippers of God toil and support their family. Education to the illiterate and food to the crippled is worship of God. Ramdas had shrewdly become a devotee of Rama, had met Shivaji and used his influence for the benefit of Brahmins.

When Dr. Santuji Ramji Lad and others had gone to Poona to take out the flag procession, Jotirao had showed them the poems he had composed to be sung at the time of marriage celebrations. The main feature of those poems was that the bridegroom and bride would repeat alternately two poems each and the guests would sing the last stanza blessing the couple. The old practice was that the Brahmin priest used to say mantras which neither he nor the bridegroom understood, nor did the bride or those who attended the marriage ceremony. Here, according to Jotirao's new poems, the bridegroom knew what kind of promises he was making, how the dignity of women was to be maintained and the bride knew what her duties were.

In the month of September 1885, Jotirao went to Bombay. This time also he made speeches in different labour localities.

A few days before this, he had delivered a series of speeches at Wangani. The theme was his social philosophy. People thronged to hear their fiery and fearless leader, who wanted to deliver them from Brahmin thraldom as he used to put it. Then he went to Thana where Dr. Santuji Lad had organised, in consultation with Jotirao and others, the annual celebrations of Satya-Shodhak Samaj. Satya-Shodhakites, workers and leaders, came to pay homage to their great leader. The celebrations were performed with boundless enthusiasm, and the speeches made on various subjects by the leaders were on the right lines.

Lokhande was authorised to publish essays under the series *Satyashodhak Nibandhamala.* Afterwards he published some essays attacking the hypocrisy in Brahminism. Their titles used to be Satya-Shodhak Nibandhamala or the true knowledge of Hinduism. Again in December 1885, Jotirao went to Baroda. It cannot be said whether this trip was specially undertaken to attend the marriage ceremony of the young Maharaja or for some other work. When he had met the Maharaja at Poona, he had introduced some of his lieutenants to him and given him an idea of his work and programme.

IV

The year 1885 is a landmark in the history of modern India. It witnessed the birth of the Indian National Congress, the first attempt at the political, emotional and patriotic integration of modern India. A force was released which rose against British power in India and was first of its kind in Asia. It became along with other factors responsible for the liquidation of British power in India.

Jotirao had no faith in the leaders of the Congress. He said that it could not be truly national until its leaders showed genuine interest in the welfare of the Mahars, Mangs and farmers, and respected their human personality. They were putting the cart before the horse. The Congress was at that time the idea of a few enlightened, educated and patriotic men who desired Government to appoint Indians at least to a few administrative posts. Nobody said that they wanted to end their Indian Empire. During its early stage, they sang the British anthem and even flew the Union Jack at the annual sessions. Jotirao and his followers, who were enormously impressed with the blessings of peace, education, irrigation and railways which British rule had bestowed on India, and with its law which regarded all men as equal, wished that God should continue British rule in India for ever, although Jotirao himself believed that it would not be permanent.

In those days British rule was regarded by many as a Godsend. Ranade, one of the founders of the Indian National Congress, and its early leaders like Pherozeshah Mehta, believed in the divine dispensation of British rule, and the British statesmen who supported the Congress movement regarded it as a safety valve for the wrath and revolt of the Indian people. Even Tilak told the British Court in England that he never advocated violent emancipation of India. "If it means acquisition of greater rights I do, but if emancipation means complete freedom from British rule I do not."

Jotirao had his grievances against British rule. He wanted it not to neglect the Mahars and Mangs, the Indian peasants and the labouring classes. His contention that Congress would not be national unless it took an interest in the lower classes was not unjustified. Later Tilak influenced the middle classes, Gandhi, the lower classes and Dr. Babasaheb Ambedkar, the lowest classes. Jotirao said that the Brahmins agitated in the name of Hinduism through the Sarvajanik Sabha and the Congress, for more rights, but enjoyed these rights themselves. They did not extend such rights to all other Hindu classes which they regarded as inferior, sub-human and depressed. It was difficult for the Congress leaders, he thought, to wield India—a people of so many divergent views, customs and modes of living—into a nation. Indians hugged casteist prejudices and ideas of highness and lowness. He, therefore, warned the Shudras that they would loose on all fronts if they joined the Congress. They would alienate the British rulers who were raising their status and giving them human rights, while the Congress, dominated as it was by Brahmins, would never think in terms of social equality and grant them the rights to education, food and shelter.

The Congress was for many years an urban upper class movement inspired by nationalist sentiment. In the circumstances it was obvious that if the demands of its leaders were conceded it would establish an oligarchy of a limited class. That seems to be the lurking fear in Jotirao's mind.

In a song sung in honour of Laxman Jagannath Vaidya, Dewan of Baroda, Jotirao wishes him success and expresses a wish that the uplift of the country be the aim. To that end Jotiba wants unity between the Mahar-Mangs and the Brahmins and wishes them to dine together. The Brahmins eat meat and drink wine with the British, but display their pollution phobia to others and hate the Mangs. In dispensing justice, they receive bribes. They kiss even Muslim concubines, but ill-treat the Mahars. Such are the perverse Brahmins; they should be boycotted.

The National Congress, Jotirao says, should be formed of men of all religions. The caste system is dearly loved by Brahmins because it is beneficial to them, and harmful to others. According to it, Brahmins are superior by birth. They designed it to exploit the Shudras. There should not be such discrimination observed between Brahmins and Mohamedans, Christians and Mangs. One should be above religion, country, and caste; all people should be united in the worship of one God.

Jotirao's arrowing artides appeared in the *Din Bandhu*. The articles provoked criticism and added to the tension created by two authors, R. B. Gunjikar and Rajaramshastri Bhagwat. Gunjikar had harshly criticised the Chitpavan Brahmins in his book *Sarswatimandal*. Rajaramshastri gave a spirited reply to Gunjikar in his booklet *Tit For Tat*. Referring to these books and Jotirao's articles in the *Din Bandhu*, the editor of the *Indu Prakash*[3] said that such writings created bitterness among different sections of society and led to factions.

Jotirao's mission and his books had attracted the attention of Bombay leaders like Narayanrao Parmanand, alias Mama Parmananda. Risen from poverty to a high position in public life of the Presidency, Mama was political *Rishi*,[4] Guide and Philosopher to eminent worthies like Ranade, Telang, Wedderburn and Motilal Ghose. Parmanand wanted to help H. A. Acworth and Shankar Tukaram Shaligram who were compiling a book on Marathi ballads. They wanted some information and some points clarified.

3. 3 November 1884.
4. A saint.

Parmanand, therefore, wrote to Jotirao as the latter had written a ballad on Shivaji. In his reply dated the 2nd June 1886, Jotirao said that he had not come across the ballads on how Shivaji, with Gopinathpant's help finished Afzulkhan, how Tanaji captured Fort Sinhagad and other similar topics. English and European authors wrote history without examining the facts with regard to the Shudras, relying on the authority of Brahmin authors and on the information of Brahmin Officers. Some educated youth of Brahmin caste were composing ballads and were slowly introducing them to the public. He had come across such ballads, but he had not preserved them as he considered them fake. Jotirao felt that the role of Dadoba Konddeo and the Brahmins had been overestimated.

Jotirao was not the only leader who doubted the authenticity of the history written by Brahmins. The non-Brahmin leaders think that the Brahmin authors record and represent history in such a way that it appears from their writings that non-Brahmin leaders were not by themselves able to achieve anything great. Several factors contribute to the success of a great man. Credit might be due to the men around him, but it should not be stressed that Shivaji had Ramdas as his Guru and Guide, when one was a mighty man who ushered in a new epoch in India, and the other was important only from the point of view of Maharashtra.

The market affair in Poona again assumed a dangerous complexion. The new building was ready by 1885. It was named after Lord Reay. Although the building was ready, merchants were not willing to occupy the shops. The officers also feared that people would not come to the market for purchase of vegetables. The vegetable-sellers were whipped to go to the new Reay Market, where rents were high. The *Kesari* had all along opposed the idea of a new market. Instead of spending lakhs of rupees on a building for which the need was not urgent, the Municipality, Jotirao urged, should spend the money on the education of the poor masses. The money had come from them. Jotirao said that the poor would not be able to pay such high rents. He intervened on behalf of the poor vendors. He met the officers and members and requested them to consider the problem from the viewpoint of the poor. It was Jotirao's opinion that tax should not be levied on the green-grocers.

Jotirao said that the green-grocers were so poor that every day they took a loan of eight annas or a rupee from money-lenders and did their business of selling vegetables on that basis, moving in different localities in the hot sun. It was difficult for them to earn their livelihood. Those who worked then in offices and the leisure classes in Poona were mostly Brahmins. They were the customers of these vegetable grocers. It was their rule in life to live frugally and sparingly. They would not purchase vegetables at exorbitant prices. So the poor vegetable sellers would be heavily burdened if taxed. But the officers and members of the Municipality remained stubbornly opposed to Jotirao's views on this subject.

Jotirao was against the idea of a new market, and now that the name of Lord Reay, Governor of Bombay, was given to it, English circles in Poona were highly displeased with him. Jotirao's opponents were happy that on some account at least he got on the opposite side of the British Government. Jotirao was concerned with the welfare of the poor classes. Whenever he saw that a certain measure would be detrimental to their interests, he fearlessly opposed it. So he opposed the scheme of the big market. It was a freak of destiny that years later this very market was renamed Phooley Market.

Those members who were malicious, enjoyed the situation which they had created by ordering baskets of excretion or refuse to be carried past Jotirao's house. Jotirao said indignantly in reply to them: "Let that Municipality be infested with the vermin of Brahmins. Don't utter its name before me."

Jotirao did not make a grievance out of this harassment. He bore it calmly. A Muslim Tamboli happened to see Jotirao in the matter of a similar complaint against the Municipality. To whom could a poor man go? To Jotirao, of course, their spokesman, leader and liberator. During Jotirao's talk with the poor man it transpired that the Depot to which the carriages of night-soil moved was mischievously shifted to a place in the neighbourhood of Jotirao's house. The poor man was enraged at this outrage and he wrote a letter to the *Din Bandhu* about the heinous deeds of Jotirao's enemies. This has been the way of the world, the way of the leisured casses, the so-called cultured classes, to mete out punishment to the spokesmen of the poor. Law has always been upheld to the disadvantage of the poor!

When the news of this harassment ol their leader by the Poona Brahmins spread through the *Din Bandhu* to different villages and towns, the devotion of the disciples and the admiration of the supporters of Jotirao grew, and the evil deed perpetrated by his enemies became indelibly impressed on their minds.

CHAPTER XVII

Acclaimed as Mahatma

As several marriages under the auspices of the Satya-Shodhak Samaj took place at different villages in Maharashtra, the tension between the Brahmins and the Satya-Shodhak followers increased. In March 1887 Narayan Meghaji Lokhande, editor of the *Din Bandhu*, visited his ancestral place, Kanersar, a village in the Khed Taluka of Poona District, for the purpose of attending a marriage ceremony of one of his relatives. A Brahmin told him that Bhau Kondaji Patil, the noted leader of the Satya-Shodhak Samaj at Junnar, had surrendered to the Brahmins. Lokhande scoffed at the idea and told the Brahmins that he knew Bhau Kondaji better than they. The main intention in doing this was to make these leaders nervous and to arouse the followers' suspicion of their leaders. But the trick did not work.

At Talawane in Junnar Taluka, another follower of Satya-Shodhak Samaj performed his own marriage according to the ceremony prescribed by the Samaj. His name was Gunaji Bapuji Patil-Shinde. On the eve of the marriage, the Brahmins instigated his kinsmen and tried to raise an objection to his marrying under the auspices of the Samaj. But the valiant Bhau Kondaji Patil performed the marriage ceremony with the help of the police to the discomfiture of the Brahmins.

The Satya-Shodhak Samaj advocated not only marriages without a Brahmin priest, but also other religious functions without them. Money on gifts and *dakshina*, clothes and feasts was saved. Money thus saved was utilised for the education of poor students.

In June 1887 the movement assumed a still graver look. Jotirao, on invitation from his followers, went to Dhamdhere's Talegao, a village in Poona District. There, under the aegis of the Samaj, he performed the marriage ceremony of a barber despite the opposition sponsored by the Brahmins of the place. The man who had bearded the Poona Brahmins in their dens cared not three straws for jackasses. The Brahmin priests and their supporters bribed some Kunbis to work against Jotirao, but their opposition fizzled out, as the overwhelming non-Brahmin population was under the influence of the Samaj. They determinedly went through the function.

Consequently the barbers of Talegaon refused to shave the Brahmins. But the Brahmins said that they had boycotted the barbers! They barbered one another and with kit-bags hung on their shoulders wandered about in the city[1] The Brahmins cut off their noses, but spat at the barbers. Guided by their leaders in other villages non-Brahmins took sides with the barbers, and the fight spread over a wider field. At last the Brahmins went on bended knees to the non-Brahmins. The *Kulkarni*, the village accountant, however, swore that he was the true son of a Brahmin and he would repay the insult some day and wreck vengeance on the non-Brahmins. But the compromise did not work; and marriages under the auspices of the Samaj were performed as before.

It was not, however, the first time the Brahmins had taken up the razor. In 1860 a barber in Poona had the opening ceremony of his newly-built house performed by some Brahmin priests. Brahmins excommunicated the Brahmin priests who had performed the ceremony at the barber's house. Consequently the barbers boycotted the Brahmins who were harassing the Brahmin priests. In June 1875 the Poona Brahmins shaved one another as the rates of shaving were raised by the barbers of Poona.

The *Native Opinion*[1] wrote a very sarcastic note on this funny incident. It said that the profession the Brahmins had selected was in harmony with the spirit of the times. Brahmins were the *gurus*, preceptors, of all castes. Formerly they had two weapons: One was the power of the curse and the other was the sword. In the *Satya age* they had lost the first, and the second was seized by the British. There was a proverb that if one had no job one should go barbering. Rightly they had done so. They had combined now the duties of a priest and a barber in themselves, so that their income would be doubled! They should go on preaching this new trade at different places of pilgrimages all over

1. 11 July 1875.

India. To what a pitiable state, the Native Opinion wrote, the Brahmins had been reduced!

Jotirao made his will in July 1887. In it he said that his deceased brother Rajaram and he earned money and lived independently for a number of years. Since he had no child, he and his wife had brought up Yashwant from his birth, performed the ceremony of naming him on the twelfth day, and regarded him as their son. His nephew Ganpat Rajaram Phooley had no right to his property. His son Yashwant was appointed to look after his estate. He and his heirs should enjoy its fruits. He was about thirteen, and was at school. If he did not prosecute his studies after his matriculation examination and try to obtain some degrees or turn out to be a vagabond, he should be cut off with only a small part of the property.

In that case his wife Savitribai should select another suitable and clever Shudra boy, preferably a Mali, Kunbi or Dhangar, in consultation with the majority of the members of the Satya-Shodhak Samaj and should appoint him to look after the property and inherit it. Yashwant should be authorised to perform whatever obsequies were needed in conformity with the rites laid down by the Satya-Shodhak Samaj. He should devote his life to explaining to the Shudras and Atishudras their human rights and liberating them from Brahmin thraldom. He should do everything in his power to help the British Government, as it was his belief that this Government was the saviour of the Shudras.

In Jotirao's Will it was stated that they should bury him in salt according to the tradition and customs of his family, and not cremate him. No Brahmin or any followers of Brahmins should be allowed to touch his dead body or cast his shadow over it.

From the Will it seems that Jotirao owned one house, and that he shared another with his brother, both houses being in Poona. He had claims to ancestral property in Khanawadi.

Jotirao looked after his son's education attentively. He gave him every facility and opportunity to build up his career. He wished him to be a fighter for the emancipation of the Shudras. Although he was a strict disciplinarian and a man of kindly disposition, the boy must have found it difficult to come up to his expectation. He possessed the gifts of a teacher, and so Yashwant must have acquired much knowledge from him. At home Jotirao was called Tatyasaheb. A handsome, grave personality, he was a terror to wrong-doers. His enemies always hired some anti-social element in the street to harass him. These hirelings sometimes honoured him at meetings with garlands full of poisonous reptiles, dead or alive. Because he had assumed the role of a preacher superior to Brahmins, ignorant people with ill-will asked him provocative questions just to drag him into violent controversises. But he did not lose his temper, and forgave them, preventing his followers from doing any harm to them. He said the men who garlanded him with reptiles hidden in flowers gave him an opportunity to show that even dangerous creatures became harmless in his presence.

Once on his way to the locality of the Untouchables, he found a little snotty-nosed boy weeping bitterly for food. His parents had gone out for work. He lifted the boy, cleaned him and purchased something for him to eat. A gentleman who recognised Jotirao asked him how he could bear to fondle a dirty, snotty boy. Jotirao replied that owing to the poverty of the boy's parents he was in that condition. People like his acquaintance did not provide such children with water, soap and clothes, and so they were dirty. It was not their fault. It was the responsibility of society. The boy's body wanted washing, but the mind of the questioner needed cleaning, Jotirao calmly added. The man understood the quip and went his way.

One day Jotirao was returning home from his shop. It was noon. A beggar was standing near his house, stooping and collecting grains. The piece of cloth that held the grains had given way, and the grains were scattered here and there. Jotirao asked him what he was doing. The beggar said: "The kind woman there gave me grain, but unfortunately my old cloth could not bear the weight. It gave way." He asked the beggar not to worry about the tattered cloth and gave him the folded cloth which he wore over his shoulders. The beggar blessed him and said: "That goddess gave me such an ample quantity of grain and you have given me such a fine piece of cloth. You both are godlike persons." The goddess he referred to was Savitribai, the wife of Jotirao.

Jotirao was once going to Alandi where the great saint philosopher Dnyaneshwar eternally rests. Thousands of people make a pilgrimage to it every year. Jotirao, not an idol-worshipper, went to Alandi during the days of pilgrimage. He and his party met a group of pilgrims on the road. They recognised Jotirao and one of them asked him why he was visiting Alandi when he was not a worshipper of Dnyaneshwar. He replied that he was going there to convince the ignorant masses that God was everywhere.

While they were thus talking, they saw a man at some distance falling on the road. An old man from the group of pilgrims exclaimed: "Old man, why are you making a pilgrimage at this age? You should now go to heaven!" Jotirao and his men ran up to the poor man. He took the man's head on his lap like a mother and sent his men to bring water. He sprinkled water over his head and the man soon recovered. The man drank the water, and ate the bread which he offered him. He felt refreshed and gratefully sang the glory of Jotirao. Thereupon Jotirao said that he had done nothing extraordinary for him. He had done his duty by the old man as a fellow traveller. He said he was also going to be an old man one day like him. In his old age he would require looking after and nursing. One never lost anything by doing a good turn, he added.

Jotirao was on intimate terms with the family of his friend Govande. Govande's wife Saraswatibai was a great friend of his wife Savitribai. Often these two friends Savitribai and Saraswatibai attended social functions together, had long chats and stayed at each other's house for hours at a time. Once Savitribai, who had gone to attend a marriage ceremony with her friend Saraswatibai, returned late in the evening. Jotirao did not see his friend's wife in company with his wife. He got angry with his wife for coming home late; but when he heard the voice of Saraswatibai Govande, he changed his tone and talked to her as if nothing had happened[2]. Such was the respect he had for Govande and his wife.

Although his chief lieutenants Lokhande and Bhalekar were staunch adherents of his cause, able leaders and brilliant speakers, he sometimes differed from them, and this difference of opinion at times verged on open clashes. Jotirao used the appellations Shudras and Atishudras for the lower classes. They both described these as lower class Hindus. They were more accommodating and more resilient than other leaders. When the Bombay Satya-Shodhak leaders sent the

2. Govande, Dr. V. B., *Trimurti Darshan* (Marathi), p. 142.

machinery of a Press for the use of the Samaj, Jotirao neither conducted the Press nor thought it proper to hand it over to his young colleague Bhalekar. Bold, energetic, ambitious, and fearless, Bhalerao, it seems, must have been hurt by the rigid attitude of his leader towards him. So was Lokhande, energetic, independent, intelligent and above all a great organiser. Jotirao did not allow sufficient latitude to these young leaders. That is the opinion one forms of him.

The Satya-Shodhak Samaj was a movement and did not have the platform of a party. The political party, which is jocularly called the madness of many for the gain of a few, was born in India with the rise of Tilak on the Indian political horizon. Indeed, it was Tilak who fostered in political workers a spirit of self-sacrifice and self-denial on which political movements are reared in their early stages. In those days there was no idea of an organised party. Even the Congress was a movement, and its leaders assembled once a year during the holidays, made speeches and returned home.

II

Some of Jotirao's lieutenants had by now surpassed Jotirao in condemning the Brahmins as a class. Jotirao had declared war on Brahmin priests. His lieutenants spoke and wrote in the *Din Bandhu* in a rough and fiery manner. They led a campaign of unbriddled ferocity and struck terror into the hearts of even good intentioned social reformers like Rajaramshastri Bhagwat, who eventually cried a halt to their ferodty. Bhagwat was a research scholar, a fearless reformer and a well-known philologist. He sounded a warning[3] to those who condemned outright Brahmins as a class. It was proper, he said, to conduct a struggle against those who harassed them, fleeced them and denounced them as inferiors; but it was not proper to denounce all Brahmins and create communal tension. Rajaramshastri was a thorough-going reformer. He later helped the non-Brahmin movement to grow and spread in Maharashtra.

The Brahmin newspapers and magazines, too, now attacked the *Din Bandhu* and the Satya-Shodhak Samaj more ferociously. One of

3. *Selected Articles of Rajaramshastri Bhagwat* (Marathi), edited by Durga Bhagwat, pp. 73-75.

them, the Vartahar, Poona, declared in its editorial dated the 12th June 1887 that the Din Bandhu was born to villify the Brahmins and therefore the Vartahar was born to put an end to the mission of the *Din Bandhu.*[4]

The year 1888 was very important in the life of Jotirao. Up to the middle of this year he was physically fit. During the previous forty years, he had made speeches, conducted several important institutions, done and promoted such work which had put a grave strain on his vitality and energy. His life was full of stress, strain and struggle. Yet he remained unrelenting at work and was as fearless as he was in his youth.

Hari Raoji Chiplunkar gave a dinner on March 2, 1888, in honour of the Duke and Duchess of Connaught at a specially built house in Poona. Rao Bahadur Hari Raoji was born at Chiplun in 1841, in Ratnagiri District, and this orphaned young boy was educated at Thana and Poona. His surname was Shinde. But because he hailed from Chiplun Taluka he was called Chiplunkar. A talented Maratha youth of nineteen, he was put in charge of the Bholagir Mongir Bava, a wealthy and influential Gosawi of Poona, who was persuaded by Jotirao to help the young, aspiring intelligent boy. Bholagir put him under the private tuition of Baba Gokhale, a teacher of repute in those days in Poona, and then put him in business, by marrying his only daughter to Hari Raoji. Fortune thus came to him with both hands full of gifts.

On Bholagir's death, Hari Raoji became the sole owner of his thriving business and vast property. He was a man of business acumen, and took a general interest in the civic life of Poona. He devoted special attention to public sanitation and the education of the backward classes. So Jotirao was greatly assisted by this youthful benefactor of Municipality, Hari Raoji had the knack of winning the confidence and friendship of English officers and often them parties on the eve of their departure from India. In 1888 he was appointed an Honorary Magistrate in Poona.

Hari Raoji was a great admirer of the Duke of Connaught and was on very cordial terms with him. So he gave a grand dinner in his honour.

4. Ibid, p. 229.

A vast amount was spent on the decorations and bunting. Rich men and noted worthies of Poona and Bombay were invited to the dinner. Close attention was paid to minute details regarding the rows of chairs; names of the worthies to sit on the rostrum were also fixed. Admission to the party was by passes. Guards and police were kept at important places at the avenue leading to the house.

The invitees gradually entered. Almost all of them were seated in their prescribed places. A few minutes to go, and the party would start. Just then a simple man came to the entrance. He had a piece of long cloth tied to his head as a head-gear, a simple home-spun short dhoti reaching to the knees, a simple garment with strings, a blanket on the left shoulder, a staff in his hand, and worn-out sandals on his feet. Who, thought the guard at the entrance, would call such a rustic to attend a grand party attended by men of wealth and distinction? So they hesitated to admit him into the hall. He showed them the pass, but they were not convinced. They would not let him in.

Jotirao began slowly to argue, and they began to answer. The argument was heard by the host. He ran to the entrance, recognised Jotirao and brought him in with a smile on his face. The invitees' curiosity was aroused as the farmer-like man was escorted by the host himself! They whispered; they wondered who it could be; and their astonishment reached its climax when the host led the man to the rostrum. He was given a prominent place on it. Then they came to know that it was Jotirao Phooley.

The party began in right earnest and with great enthusiasm. Speeches were made wishing happiness to the Royal couple. Then Jotirao was asked to say something. He rose. Those who knew him for years were sure that he would give them all a piece of his mind. Others who were Government officers and the *elite* of society in Poona and in Bombay and had not heard him before awaited with bated breath his speech.

Jotirao addressed his speech mainly to their Royal Highnesses. He said that they might be misled by the appearance of the rich clothes and diamonds glittering in the hall and think that it was a happy contented India they were seeing. This was not the case. The fact was that these rich decorated worthies with scented clothes were not the reflection of the real India Queen Victoria was ruling over. They were not the representatives of the peasants who composed the major portion of the population from the villages.

The real India, Jotirao added, was seen in villages where people were penniless and foodless, shelterless and shoeless. The majority did not even get rags to hide their shame and the common man used the kind of clothes the speaker himself was wearing, but in a tattered condition. So if he really wanted to see and represent to Her Highness, he should go to some villages nearby and see the utter poverty of the ignorant masses. He should also visit some Mahar-Mang localities and see for himself whether those localities were not worse than dunghills and unfit for human habitation. That was the real India. Concluding, he appealed to His Highness the Duke of Connaught to tell his mother, Queen Victoria, that the masses were in utter poverty and they wanted education badly.

The Duke of Connaught was surprised at the speaker's fearless and frank speech. Some worthies were displeased with him and said that Jotirao should not have been given a chance to make a speech. A few were happy that he was blunt as usual and gave a rap on the swollen heads of the audience.

The host, then, introduced Jotirao to the Duke as a prominent leader of peasants and workers. The Duke must have felt glad that he was not a revolutionary politician. The revolt of Wasudeo Balwant Phadke was fresh in the minds of the British.

In Jotirao one finds a precursor of Mahatma Gandhi. Jotirao lived among peasants and thought of their economic betterment, and motivated the peasant population with the love of independence. His staff, his half naked body, his love for the poor masses and his love of truth, are reflected in the life of Mahatma Gandhi. Socially, he was a more revolutionary man than Mahatma Gandhi. The passive resistance which was called Satyagraha by Gandhi, was practised by Jotirao when he led the peasants' and barbers' agitations. Both were truth-seekers. Jotirao's letter-heads carried at the top his motto and message 'Truth alone triumphs'. Jotirao was as harsh as truth itself. He did not allow any of his lieutenants to compromise truth.

Jotirao's colleague Ramayya Vyankayya Aiyyavaru wrote a Booklet on Christianity and dispassionately exposed its blunders as did the Christian converts like The Rev. Baba Padmanji concerning the Hindu religion. The *Din Bandhu* was pleased to remark that the booklet would serve the Hindus in their debates with the Christians on religion. Personally Jotirao had neither launched an attack on any religion except Hinduism which he called Brahminism nor refuted the charges made by Christian missionaries against the Hindu religion. But his colleagues were annoyed at the jarring notes of the propaganda Christian missionaries had launched against Hinduism.

Krishnarao Bhalekar wrote several articles in the *Din Mitra*, which was started in April 1888 by his nephew Ganpat Sakharam Patil. The *Din Mitra* was a friend to those who had no education, money, or power. Bhalekar had written a Marathi novel entitled *Baliba Patil and the Famine* of 1877 at the end of the year 1877. The *Din Mitra* was critical about Jotirao Phooley. It published a series of articles under the caption "Suggestion to those who call themselves Religious Heads." It criticised Jotirao in this series.

Dharma Gurus, Religious Heads, says the *Din Mitra*,[5] should properly guide their followers. The Satya-Shodhak sect was going the way the other religious sects had gone. Various religious rites from Hinduism were incorporated in the ceremonies of the Samaj. That they had suspended the activities of the village or city priest was the only reform they had introduced and the Brahmin priests were replaced by Satya-Shodhak Samajist priests.

The *Din Mitra* sounded a timely warning to the Samaj and its leaders against the system of priests. It also complained that there was no uniformity in the Satya-Shodhak ceremonies. The rulers for different ceremonies had not received the sanction of the people, and that was why confusion reigned everywhere. Some were of the opinion that sandal paste should be applied to the forehead in a horizontal way, some said it should be vertical, while others doubted its utility altogether. Some said they performed the *tulsi*-marriage ceremony amidst their own songs without any priest, Brahmin or non-Brahmin. Others said they all possessed the right of wearing the sacred thread. Many held that the marriage performed with the Sanskrit mantras by the Satya-Shodhak Samaj without a Brahmin priest was the true pattern of marriage. Marriage ceremonies done without Brahmin priests but amidst *puranic mantras* constituted the ideal marriage. Some said: "We

5. July 1888.

bow to You the Almighty, to great Joti who created (the Samaj). We bow to the god Kalbahiri, and to the god Mahasubhe!"

The Head of the Satya-Shodhak Samaj, the *Din Mitra* continued, should consider this and arrive at a definite formula of rites to be performed at each ceremony and avoid the prevailing confusion. Otherwise this confusion would lead them to downfall and ruin. All the leaders of the Satya-Shodhak Samaj should hold a conference either at Bombay or at other places such as Junnar or Poona and make definite rules for all ceremonies. If that was not done, who would be responsible for the unbecoming conduct of their followers? "You call me a leader, extol me to the skies, revere me, help me, and then go on begging in my name!" If somebody said that this was a false way to win popularity, the editor observed, it would be very difficult for them to reply. Those who called themselves the leaders and the followers of the Satya-Shodhak Samaj should give serious thought to this appeal. It was no use sitting idle at home. They would not like others to interfere in this matter and help. They were hypocrites.

In the next issue of the *Din Mitra* of August 1888 the articles were concluded, and it was suggested to Jotirao that suitable changes were required to be made in every institution and in every religious sect in keeping with the demands and requirements of the times.

Reformers of today are conservatives of tomorrow. In his old age Jotirao was egged on by his lieutenants to be watchful and to pay more enthusiastic attention to the doings of his followers. On May 13, 1888, the Mali community of Poona had its panchayat elected by about 1,500 people. The Fulmali Samaj in Poona numbered about four thousand men, women and children. It seems Jotirao was not interested in these elections. He did not take interest in casteist affairs.

III

While his castemen were deeply engrossed in the election of their panchayats, Jotirao was fighting out the Otur case valiantly in Bombay. He visited Bombay in the company of his lieutenant, Balaji Kusaji Patil. Jotiba consulted several lawyers and barristers and at last briefed Ghanshyam Nilkantha Nadkarni to defend their case in the High Court. It took a lot of time to arrange this defence, and Jotirao almost exhausted himself by the work. The Brahmin priests engaged Mahadeo Chimnaji Apte, a Brahmin legal luminary, to argue their case. It came up for hearing towards the end of the year.

Just then Jotirao's Bombay followers resolved to pay homage to their leader for his ceaseless struggle for the uplift of the lower classes. Jotirao had just completed his sixtieth year. He had lived the life of a saint among men and a man among saints. He was the first public man in Maharashtra who lived and worked unflaggingly for the uplift of the down trodden and the underdog, and led a matchless life full of service, struggle and sacrifice for the glory of God. The grateful leaders also decided to repay the gratitude of the great Master. All leaders from the mofussil were invited. They decided to hold a big meeting on May 11, 1888, to honour their great hero. Social worthies were requested to attend the meeting. Shri Sayajirao, Maharaja of Baroda, was also invited. He sent word through Damodar Savalaram Yande that Jotirao should be given the title of 'Booker T. Washington'.

On the noon of 11th May 1888, the poor poured into the Koliwada Hall at Mandvi. It was a unique function, organised and inspired by the common people to repay the gratitude of their liberator. The hall was decorated. The compound was gay with bunting. All the leaders from Lokhande to Lad were present. The hall was filled to capacity, and poor people thronged the compound also. There was a scene of tattered turbans, soiled caps, torn shirts, but all eyes glowed with affection and devotion, pride and gratitude. This was a unique event in the life of a modern Indian leader that he was raised to the pinnacle of glory by the poverty-stricken, hungry masses who hoped for a better tomorrow through the endless struggle and suffering of their liberator. Men of great purses might have been honoured, political leaders in a subject country might have been eulogised for their sufferings in the cause of their mother-land, but a great man in India had seldom received this type of popular appreciation.

The leaders made glowing and inspiring speeches in appreciation of Jotirao's unusually long, selfless and noble service which he had rendered to the poor for over forty years. They expressed their love and gratitude to him for fighting the battle single-handed against ignorance, orthodoxy and the privileged classes and for championing truth with unflinching courage and with inalienable fidelity to the cause of the down-trodden. Then amidst thunderous clappings they conferred upon him the title 'Mahatma'. Jotirao was overpowered by the devotion the poor classes showed for him. He said humbly that he had done his duty by them. He urged them to carry on the work and spread the mission of the Satya-Shodhak Samaj with untiring zeal. Balaji Patil, who was fighting the case in the High Court, was also honoured at this meeting. He was praised for the courageous stand he had taken and the courage he had shown in standing by the principles of the Samaj.

Jotirao was now a Mahatma. A real Mahatma. A high-souled personage. A Mahatma eulogised by the common people. The title was conferred upon him by the common people. Such examples are rare. Jotirao was the first great man in modern India to receive this highest of titles at the hands of the lower classes. A Mahatma is a patriot of humanity and such was the Mahatma in Jotirao Phooley. Later, Shishir Kumar Ghose, Swami Shraddhanand and M. K. Gandhi were the great men in modern India to receive the title of Mahatma.

Bhalekar's differences with Jotirao were widening and the *Din Mitra* conducted by the nephew of Bhalekar voiced them. In its issue of July 1888 it published the news that Jotirao and his son Yashwant Phooley had sent to the editor ten pices which they had received from some persons who had performed different functions; one was a marriage and the other was the performance of obsequies. The editor sent back the money requesting Jotirao to show the amount on the receipt side of the Satya-Shodhak Samaj and added that such money should not be spent without the sanction of the Samaj.

Yashwant was about sixteen years old at this time, and was a high school student. He had been trained to take an interest in the activities of the Samaj.

According to the practice of those days, Yashwant had passed the marriage age. It was now too late for him to get married. And who would give him his daughter in marriage when he was born out of wedlock? His mother was a Brahmin widow. He was brought up by Jotirao and his wife as their own son. Jotirao expressed his desire to Gyanoba Sasane and asked him whether he would give his daughter in marriage to Yashwant. He consented to his leader's proposal. It was a bold decision on his part. His daughter Radha was reading in Std. Ill of a primary school. Jotirao brought her to his house and put her to school and moulded her to his choice. She was about eleven.

IV

In July 1888 Jotirao had a stroke. Following the stroke he was paralysed in the right side of his body. Dr. V. R. Gholay attended his leader and Sayajirao Gaikwad and Nageshwargir Kalyangir Buva sent him immediate financial relief, which he gratefully mentioned in one of his poems. Of course Gholay did his duty by his leader and did not charge a pie for his treatment. Jotirao had now grown very weak and wore no beard.

Although the current of his energy had been half switched off, the fan of his iron will was moving undeterred. His followers were clamouring for a book which should direct them to uniform action in social and religious matters and to the path of right conduct. The critics of his own caste were driving him to desperation. They were persistent in their demand for a uniform system of religious and social rites and practices. Jotirao therefore decided to write a book on right conduct although his right hand was paralysed. He began to write with the left hand. Action was the predominant note of his life, the breath of his nostrils. He started his work and completed it towards the end of the year 1888.

From September to December 1888 Jotirao was confined to bed. During that time the correspondence that passed between Jotirao and Gyanba Sasane revealed the different facets of his mind. The first most significant thing is that he used the motto on his letterheads *'Satyamevajayate'* — Turth alone triumphs. That golden maxim earned India's traditional message. Free India has adopted this maxim as the emblem of the State. Truth-seeker that he was, Jotirao's soul was inspired by this message. Whatever he did and said, truth accompanied it.

The second point is that his wife conducted his household affairs to the end of his life as Jotirao pointed out in one of his letters that his wife did the household work and, allowed the girl Radha to prosecute her studies.

Jotirao styled Gyanoba *Satya Murti*, image of truth! The girl fiancee was to be sent to Hadapsar at her father's place, but at a pressing request from Savitribai she was detained for which Jotirao apologized. Those who want to command must first obey. Jotirao observed this rule very rigidly. Since the proposed daughter-in-law was quite intelligent and her memory was retentative, he was pleased with her. He wanted her to say 'ji', to respond respectfully to their calls, and to maintain decorum, but the bashful girl did not respond to this. In the last week of December 1888, he was again taken ill and the girl attended on him very lovingly and dutifully.

During Jotirao's illness the propaganda work of the Samaj was carried on by the *Din Mitra* in which Bhalekar wrote very pointed, fiery articles under the title 'The Shrewd Business of the Uncontaminated News papers'. It observed that every year so many journals and newspapers saw the light. But they were never contaminated by the grievances of the workers, farmers, artisans and other poor people. These never appeared to be their subjects. They were not in their pictures. Their sublime subjects were Widow Remarriage, the Congress, the Cow-protection Sabha, Rights of Brahmins, Municipal Committees, Neglect of Scriptural Injunctions, the unfulfilled dream of Peshwa Rule, Higher Education, and the Ruin caused by Agricultural Acts to the money-lenders. They would not make even a passing reference to the grievances of the crores of the ignorant, illiterate people of India. They would not raise their voice on behalf of the people and demand primary education for them. They would not stir a finger against their exploiters. They protested against the Agricultural Acts which tried to protect the rights of the peasants and said that those Acts would lead to the ruin of money-lender. But they never exposed the villainy of these the farmers of the rafters of their houses and even of their tattered shoes.

In one of its articles the *Din Mitra*, like its great philosopher Jotirao, made pungently a broadcast to all those concerned with the anniversaries to their fathers and predecessors.

"O denizens of the earth, pay careful attention to the following notice. You are sending to heaven undressed articles of provision through the agent. It has deteriorated the health of your fathers and forefathers because the food was undressed. They are suffering from indigestion and have run down in health.... If you desire that your fathers should improve in health, administer medicine to the commission agents. Some of your parents lack the knowledge of cooking and so the oilseeds and cereals are totally useless for them. You should therefore send through your agents dressed food and flour and good dishes. If, however, you insist on sending such articles through the agent, please send a fire-place, an iron plate, a spoon, a small culinary utensil, a small wooden roller, dry cow-dung and firewood."[6]

This was an attack on the abominable beliefs in Hinduism which were forms of exploitation and superstition. This was in keeping with the great message of their liberator. Brahmin believers and non believers, rationalists and religionists would not abandon this practice as it was economically ruinous to Brahmin priests, the rationalists did not oppose it either for lack of courage or their secret sympathy with the Brahmin priests!

Early in February 1889 the marriage of Yashwant took place. The bride Radha was fondly renamed Chandrabhaga. Jotirao felt great relief to see that his son was married to a girl who was clever, energetic, intelligent and came of a good family. The marriage was performed in conformity with the rules he had framed. The bride and the bridegroom both sang his poems, promising to conduct their worldly affairs with affection, loyalty and duty. They promised to work for the liberation of Indian women and the establishment of their rights. The guests and elders of the society blessed the couple in a chorus.

V

While Jotirao was confined to bed, Poona accorded a grand welcome to the Prince of Wales in the second week of November 1889. His colleagues were enthusiastic about the Prince's visit. The Indian *Spectator* gave an account of the reception which Jotibites offered him.

"There is one interesting incident," observed the *Indian Spectator,* "connected with the Prince's stay in Poona, which is worth notice.

6. November 1888.

There is in that city an association which concerns itself with the welfare of the backward and uneducated classes, and which goes by the name of the Din Bandhu Sarvajanik Sabha. The Sabha has opened a school which offers gratuitous instruction to boys belonging to those classes. At one spot by which the Prince was to pass, about 150 pupils of this school, says the *Ambalahari*, the local organ of the Sabha, stood underneath a red screen on which were the words:

"Tell Grandma we are a happy nation,
But 19 crores are without education."

"These lines", the *Indian Spectator* added, "moved the Prince, the Duke of Connaught, H.E. the Governor and others who followed, to laughter, and taken together they were droll enough to produce that effect, though it cannot be out of any want of sympathy. The statistics in second line only express the compliment of the most famous expression of Lord Dufferin used in his last speech at Calcutta, that the educated Indians formed only 'a microscopic minority'. Government, therefore, fairly lay down that the public expenditure on liberal education shall be a constantly diminishing quality without spending much more than what it saves thereby on primary education among the unlettered masses. This is the real meaning of the motto so facetiously presented to the Prince by the Din Bandhu Sabha of Poona, and it is intended as much for the information of the Royal Grand Mother on the throne of England as hint for her representatives in India, where 95 per cent of the population are unable to read and write."

The driving face behind this demonstration was undoubtedly Krishnarao P. Bhalekar. But this proves how Jotirao's teachings had dominated their thoughts. Their first and foremost demand was for compulsory primary education.

Jotibites made another significant demonstration during their master's illness. It was an attempt to awaker the Indian National Congress to its broader responsibilities. The Congress held its fifth session in Bombay in the last week of December 1889. Its president elect was William Wedderburn who had served as a member of Indian Civil Service in Bombay and was a friend of Mama Parmanand.

In his Presidential address to the Congress, William Wedderburn said that the object of the Congress movement was to revive the national life and to increase its material prosperity. He said that its methods were open and constitutional, and based solely on India's reliance upon British justice and love of fair play. The interests of the Indian services were in great measure antagonistic to the interests of the Indian tax payer whose main interest was peace, economy and reform. With a fertile soil, a glorious sun, and abundance of highly skilled labour there was no reason, he added, why India should not become a garden if the ryot were not crushed by debts. He then recalled how a practical scheme, founded on the German system of peasant Banks was submitted to the British Government to settle the old debts of the Indian farmers and to make advances to them on reasonable term, so that they might be supplied with manure and water for irrigation. But the scheme was stabbed in the back by the India Office.

Concluding his Address, William Wedderburn, President of the Congress, said: "My earnest hope is that your labours may prosper and that your deliberations may effectively promote the safety, honour, and welfare of Her Majesty and her dominion." Charles Bradlaugh said in reply to an address presented by the Congress that 'the Congress was the dawn and he saw the day'.

There is a story, perhaps an apocryphal one, that the Jotibites of Bombay raised a straw-made statue of a farmer covered with rags, his stomach and his cheeks sunken, his eyes tearful and hungry and the whole figure gave the expression of sorrow and poverty. It was a great reminder and a warning to the grand assembly focussing their attention on the fact that the farmer was the backbone of the nation and unless his case was heard, his grievances were redressed, and he was admitted to the Congress, it would not develop enough strength, vitality and courage to wrest from the British the rights it petitioned and prayed for.

CHAPTER XVIII

His Philosophy

MAHATMA JOTIRAO composed a number of poems called Akhandas in which he preaches right conduct, reason, justice, toleration. Who is a truthful man? One who is pious, blame-less and purely rational and practises truth in worldly life. He gives light like the sun, and peace like the moon. He does not strut about as a terrestrial God, like the Brahmins, nor does he inflict pain on human beings, like a serpent. Such a human being should be called a gentle man. His greatness should be sung, says Joti.

The man who has experienced truth will not harass anybody. Such a man would not be a Brahmin in thought, word and deed, displaying his superiority to the Shudras. A man cannot be virtuous because of his parentage. One who controls his anger and respects truth is the strongest man under the sun. Such a man is kind to all and by nature merciful; he controls his passions and his senses. Mud does not stick to the leaves of the lotus. Provided a Brahmin does not practise vices, he should be revered. Krishna, who was killed by a hunter, was the creation of the Brahmin imagination.

A man who has no fear of past, present or future and leads a truthful life, bears truth in his heart and loves all should be called a Buddha, a great man. No man should be proud.

God has given one a human body and reason to be able among all the creatures to struggle for the good of man. One should dedicate one's life to the service of humanity, to the cause of truth. God will be pleased with such conduct, and life's purpose would be attained. A man whose courage springs from truth, who is a sober, sympathetic, brave and truthful man and has conquered his passions, is called a virtuous man. Such a one is an ornament to humanity. He gives consideration to other man's sorrows and happiness, and treats all alike. Such a man is gentle and great.

God is one. He has provided for all. So teach the rights of men and women to all, so that all should act as brothers. The Brahmin teachers use the name of Shivaji to instigate the Shudras against the Muslims. Their love of the country is a fraud. To exploit and harass one's own countrymen is no patriotism. It is no religion either. The Bhils and Kolis are the original Kshatriyas. They were driven into the hills, and so they live on roots and fruit.

The Brahmin religious books should be read in public as do the Christians theirs, and see how the inequality, hypocrisy and injustice in them will be exposed! Christians read the Bible in public because there are no such unjust and impartial precepts in it. Christians and Mohammedans should not be regarded as inferiors or low.

No Brahmin has ever become a universally loved man. A man devoid of truth cannot be a saint. The cow eats excrement and the Brahmins call it a mother. Formerly Brahmins ate horses and cows as Yajnya sacrifice. The Antyajas are brothers to Brahmins, but they harass them and even use them as a sacrifice to Gods. Bring Bradlaugh to India, O Britishers, pull his ears, show him the wicked scriptures, the haughtiness of Brahmins. He is not aware of the harassment the Shudras have to endure. He has neither experience nor true knowledge of the situation. To hell with such learning!

That the *mantras* and japs bring about rain is nonsense; nor do they beget children. If *mantras* could produce children, no Brahmin would die childless. Without *mantras* even widows give birth to children.

The Shudras, that is, Kshatriyas, should be industrious; they should toil, maintain their families cheerfully, send their children to school and feed poor students. Old, learned men should impart education freely to others. A vicious man, a liar, a sedition-monger and a drunkard do not deserve help. Christians, Muslims, Mangs, and Brahmins should be treated like brothers. One should learn to write one's own language and effectively speak it. After forty, one should lead a dedicated life.

God's religion is one. No use discussing and debating it. Truth is the only religion in the world. Truth is action. Marathi, English and

Hindi are the three important languages. Attain proficiency in them, be a virtuous man, and make the world happy.

Man's religion is truth and truth is morality. An unclean man is the capital of the Doctor. An unclean man is criticized. Bathing brings vigour to the mind, and man takes to his work with enthusiasm. Dirty clothes bring on diseases. The human personality is sacred. Man's intellect may vary, but intelligence is not inherited. The man who has purified his mind by truth is the cleanest man. The man who does not understand the value of the mind's purity is a burden to the earth. An unblemished, industrious life brings a man health and wealth. He enjoys the fruits of his labour. An indolent man is wicked and becomes an enemy of society. An industrious, virtuous man is a great support to the poor; he makes several others happy. A vicious young man passes his old age in sorrow. A lazy man is never happy; his mind is never at peace.

A lazy man is poverty itself. Gambling ruins all. The Stock Market benefits only share brokers. That business is ruinous. Say goodbye to it from a distance. Those who pretend to be wealthy, ultimately turn out to be bankrupt, ruin others and commit suicide in the end. Be partners and start a business, but keep true accounts.

A brave man does not lose his courage and temper in distress or in disease. He maintains peace at home; he does his duty sincerely. He never cherishes thoughts of revenge. Tolerance leads to happiness and tranquillity. A wicked man's deeds bring him to ruin. He then blames God for it.

Those who abandon truth and discuss religion hotly and blindly come to blows and end in creating rivers of blood. Tolerance is the key to peace and unity.

The man who feels happy over the prosperity of others, learns and evokes virtue, and imparts knowledge to others, is a worthy man. The man who is greedy for everything, struggles for his own selfish ends, earns name and never practises self-examination or introspection is not a good man. The man who does not practise introspection but resorts to self-justification, is an utterly selfish man and disappoints the simpletons, who rely on him. Of all knowledge, Self-knowledge is the most vital. A selfish man cannot be introspective. Introspection is the real sign of intellect. Those who spend more than their income always run into debt. Selfish friends, relatives and flatterers squeeze money from them by sweet words. One should do One's duty by the household.

Courage springs from love of truth, a Dean mind and composure of heart. Courage springs from right conduct. A courageous man undergoes sufferings, overcomes dangers, protects the harassed. Wicked actions cripple the mind's strength, and wicked faces reflect worries and anxieties. Liars have no rest.

Do not trouble others. It is a sin. Be humble, be grateful, be contented. Bad conduct leads to disease and unhappiness. It is false satisfaction to believe that misery was predestined. To a drunkard's home quarrels come and from it peace runs away. He whose contentment is backed by truth and fortitude is undisturbed even though he gets into trouble.

Noble Socrates was given poison and driven to death by hatred. Yet he lost no peace of mind. Look into his works. Those who live with reason and truth for the welfare of the world, make posterity and themselves happy. Vedantists should not tolerate discriminations and prejudice. A rationalist will not take to religious practices and mutterings of mantras. That dedication is fruitless. A rationalist will not tonsure poor widows and will not worship stones and metals and trees.

Jotirao is a better poet than prose writer. His poems have a good flow. His prose is a wild fruit. It is not sweet but has medicinal properties. The prose is rough, at times suffers from grammatical errors and is occasionally obscene. Jotirao's poems reveal his wisdom and humanism.

II

Jotirao wrote a book called *Sarvajanik Satya-Dharma Pustaka* which was posthumously published. It is a book on religion.

In the preface dated April 1, 1889, to the book, which Jotirao has written for the benefit of all, he says that the Almighty.has created numerous solar systems with stars and planets and various creatures. He has written this book to teach how men and women should follow the right path and live peacefully for the glory of God and the happiness of humanity, keeping in mind the Almighty, and enjoying the fruit of the holy and veracious kingdom of God.

Although Jotirao revolted against the Brahminical scriptures, he stuck to the main theme in Hindu philosophy that insists on the kingdom of God and not on the establishment of an earthly empire.

Almost all leaders of the Satya-Shodhak Samaj have on several occasions accepted the fact that Jotirao had abandoned Hindu superstitions and customs, rigid and irrational rites, rituals, dogmas and ceremonies, and simplified the other forms of Hindu ritual.

Dr. V. R. Gholay, Hon. Assistant Surgeon to H.E. the Viceroy and Governor-General of India, who had retired from Government service in April 1888, wrote an introduction to the *Sarvajanik Satya Dharma Pustaka* in which he said that Jotirao had shown in his book authoritatively how false religious ideas, idol-worship and the caste system created disharmony and confusion and led to the ruin of the nation. Nobody had seen God in His true form. Nobody therefore could form an image of Him. It was evident that the caste system had resulted in many social and economic disadvantages. It was one of the main causes of hatred, disputes and slavery.

Dr. Gholay further observed that Jotirao had been delivering speeches for the past forty years on religious and practical subjects and had removed the cloak of ignorance from the eyes of the people. Jotirao wrote books and leaflets and booklets; he discussed several subjects in newspapers and devoted all his life to the service of the people. He worked and lived for the people. He taught people to think over religious rites and their origins, and he interpreted to them their correctness or falsehood as the case might be. He refuted idolatry and upheld belief in one God. He believed that people should not be exploited in matters of religion and in the practical world. He explained these matters to the people and had done tremendous good to them. The toil and suffering he had undergone for so many years were bearing fruit. People had realised that there were faked stories and hypocrisy in the *puranas*.

Gholay summarised Jotirao's teaching as follows: "Belief in one God, right conduct, equal rights, abolition of the caste system, equal rights of men and women, and brotherly conduct towards all. Man will not be happy unless his conduct is truthful. Truth is the home of all things. Truth is the home of all religions. Happiness of all kind is the offspring of truth. Truth is the pillar of happiness; the rest is darkness. Truth puts the cunning to consternation. All hypocrites and poseurs lose their peace of mind at the thought of truth. Jotirao prays people not to be a party to falsehood or hypocrisy."

In the *Sarvajanik Satya-Dharma Pustaka* Jotirao further observes: "All religious works are written by men and they do not contain truth from beginning to end. Changes were made by certain obstinate men in these books to suit certain occasions and the requirements of the times. So religions have not become equally helpful to all; and they give rise to divisions and cults full of hatred and envy.

God created all things. He is kind and desires that all should enjoy human rights. If the earth we inhabit is created by God why should the peoples of different countries be torn asunder by enmity and the madness of patriotism, and why should religious bigotry prevail so much? When there are so many rivers in different countries, how can a particular river in a particular country become the most sacred? That most sacred river does not hesitate to carry with its water the droppings of dogs. All men possess the same kind of features and intellect. Nobody is sacred by birth. Everybody has his virtues and vices as a human being.

God is unknowable, unreachable. Not even one direction towards him can be fully explored. The universe is limitless and boundless. Man should not cherish ambition to search for God. Man is insignificant. Man is not sure of his existence. He is weak; his knowledge is limited. Brahma who is supposed to have been born of the navel of an imaginary Vishnu could not have had a glimpse of the Almighty.

God has created flowers and sweet-scented things for the use of man. So it is useless and meaningless to dedicate the flowers to God who is the creator of them. Flowers should be used for garlanding men who support their families by honest labour and liberate the poor from the clutches of selfish persons.

Turning in mind countless times the name of God is not worship of God. The closing of the eyes, the holding of the nose, the burning of incense, the atmosphere of a sanctuary and the muttering of *mantras* is not worship of God. One cannot support his old parents by mere worship of God. Those who take opium and live idly on food given by the people are hypocrites. One should fear God, keep Him always in mind, and work honestly and sincerely. That is the worship of God. Right conduct is the true remembrance of God. To believe in *japs* is wrong. On account of this wrong belief gosawis, bairagis and recluses live idly like parasites on the society.

Offering food to God, is not the proper way of honouring him. Those men of the society who serve the people and by chance become helpless in old age, should be supported, and the orphans and crippled children should be maintained. The man whose conduct does not show discrimination, and who loves and serves all irrespective of caste or creed, be he a Brahmin, or a Red Indian or a Mahar, he should be entertained at dinner.

There is no such thing as heaven. It is no part of the universe. Woman is superior to man. One can repay the gratitude of all persons except the mother. She is the beauty of the home; she is the kind eye that guards all.

Woman is by nature weak. Man is greedy and bold. So he bent her to his will and kept her under his domination very selfishly by preventing her from acquiring worldly knowledge. Polygamy is cruel. Man is the source of greed, hatred and sin.

The vices of a man visit his offsprings and have bad effect upon them. Those who marry more than one wife a time create a hell in their homes and catch vices and diseases. Those who cohabit with women in menstruation get dangerous diseases like leprosy. Marriages of old men with young girls must be condemned. Widow remarriages of young girls are prohibited by Brahmins, but old men are not probihited from marrying in old age and ravaging the youth of girls. So girl widows, persecuted by their male relatives, fall a victim to their lust. Foolish goldsmiths and Kunbis are following the example set by Brahmins in not allowing young widows to remarry. In Vedic times a widow was allowed to cohabit with the brother of the husband and to produce children.

There should not be discrimination between laws for men and women. One law should be applicable to both. A man is allowed to marry three women, but a woman marrying three persons is not tolerated. So a man must not be allowed to marry more than one woman if his first wife is alive. Greedy men have adopted these selfish laws. There should not be one law for the Brahmins and another for the Shudras. British rule has introduced laws before which every man, Brahmin or non-Brahmin, is equal.

III

When a man does not inflict pain, physical or mental, on any creature for his own selfish ends, it becomes his meritorious act. To exploit the poor in the name of religion and to give grand feasts to lazy people is not virtue. To enjoy the company of prostitutes or to attend tea-party, or to feast on drink and mutton and then to observe untouchability in regard to one's co-religionist is no virtue.

To observe the caste system is no religion. The caste system is a fraud. Annihilate the idea that a Brahmin is sacred at all times, at all places. Originally, there was no caste system. The Aryans, the Brahmins, introduced it for their own selfish ends. If a sweeper is to be considered a lowly man then one's mother should be classified a member of that class. The caste system should not be based on occupations either. A Brahmin boy may not be as meritorious as the first Shankaracharya; and a Chamar boy may be as virtuous as the Shankaracharya.

The difference between man and animal is that man can think. Animals are sometimes better than greedy men.

Profession is not religion. One who shaves is a barber by calling, but not by religion. One who washes clothes is a washerman by calling but not by caste or religion. A man is by calling a gardener, but not by caste or religion. To make shoes is a shoemaker's calling and not his religion. To receive bribe is not the religion of a Government servant, but disloyalty. To live on the exploitation of others in the name of religion is no religion, but selfishness and hypocrisy. To cohabit with a prostitute and next day again assume sacredness is no religion but degradation. To live on carcasses is not the religion of the Mahar-Mangs but utter helplessness. To impose taxes on subjects for their protection and convenience is a duty of the Government and is not a religion. Parents bring us up and educate us with boundless affection when we are mere dumb children. It is our duty to look after our parents when in their old age they are helpless and crippled. The bairagis, the gosavis, and all their kind are parasites. To feed them is false religion.

God has provided for mankind; but human beings are not living peacefully as brothers and sisters. People forget their mothers, their brothers and their sisters. They do not behave well with their mothers, sisters, daughters and daughters-in-law. Many, on the contrary, give them bad treatment and charge them with cunning, deny them human rights, and do not lead a truthful life, otherwise there would have been the kingdom of God on earth and mankind would have been happy. If men do not behave with one another lovingly, loyally and piously, fraternity will not be awakened in their mind. Unless fraternity is awakened in men's minds, God's kingdom will not come down upon earth. "Do unto others as you would be done by," is the message of the Great and Good Man.

Of Morality, Jotirao says: "Had Ravan been of a different species of society, he would not have been invited to the competition arena which was held to select a spouse for Sita. The Ramayana is not a true history. It consists of fabricated tales and conveys no moral lessons. Islam teaches fraternity and equality to its followers. Islam has one sacred religious book, the Koran. It can be read by all Muslims. It allows marriages among its adherents, and they share food in company with one another. The man. who keeps in mind the fear of truth and behaves rightly with all men, Muslims, Christians and others, is a moral man." Jotirao has criticised cantos twelve and thirteen of *Dnyaneshwari*. He has also harshly criticised Shri Ram for his conduct towards the wife of Mahi. He means that the conduct of Ram and Krishna did not befit a God.

According to Jotirao, there is no such thing as luck. When people ascribe all sorts of failures in education, business and war, to bad luck or fate, the belief is not justified, it is not true. Either the people concerned were not up to the mark in their studies or preparations, or they had some faults. Nothing is ordained by fate. Everything has its reasons. The Bible is open to all, the Koran is open to all, the Vedas are not open to all. Believers in the Bible and the Koran have no fears. The Vedas are not open to all because believers in them are afraid of the weakness in these scriptures being exposed.

IV

Those who believe that man and woman are born free and they have all rights to enjoyment are followers of Truth. Those who do not worship stars and stones but the God of the Universe are followers of Truth. Those who, instead of dedicating things to God with the false notion of propitiating Him, do not prevent human beings from enjoying things created in the world and who allow others to sing the glory of God, are followers of Truth. Those who do not hurt causelessly any creature in the world are followers of Truth. Those who do not individually or unitedly make aggression on others are followers of Truth. God has given us freedom and religion. Those who do not deprive others of their rights or put others to a loss are followers of Truth.

Those who regard excepting their wives, all other men and women as their brothers and sisters, are followers of Truth. Every man or woman has a God-given right to freedom of expression in writing, speaking and publishing; he or she should not do it in such a way as to deprive others of their rights. Then alone they are followers of Truth. Those who do not condemn others for their political views or religious beliefs and do not harass them are followers of Truth.

Men and women should be appointed to village and Government posts according to their qualifications. Those who ensure that the appointments are given to the proper persons are followers of Truth.

Those men or women who respect their parents and other elders are followers of Truth.

Those who protect the rights of all men and women to property and freedom, and protect them from harassment are followers of Truth. Those who do not take wine and opium, or those who do not help such drunkards are followers of Truth. Those who do not kill beings except bugs, lice, scorpions, serpents, jackals, lions and tigers, and do not help greedy persons and murderers or suicides are followers of Truth.

Those men or women who for selfish ends do not tell lies to ruin others or who do not help liars are followers of Truth. Those who do not steal or help robbers are followers of Truth.

Those who do not set fire to others' houses and articles or keep friendship with such men are followers of Truth.

Those men and women who selfishly revolt against a prince or a king who rule justly, or against a representative appointed by the public, and destroy lakhs of houses are not followers of Truth. Those who help such rebels are not followers of Truth.

Those who do not believe the wicked and boastful men who claim that they have prepared religious books for the welfare of the world and yet do not show them to others, are followers of Truth. Those men and women who neither regard themselves as superior or high-born nor regard selfishly others as inferiors are followers of Truth.

Those teachers who do not show partiality in teaching their pupils on account of casteist prejudices or those who condemn men who do so, are followers of Truth.

Those who are impartial in dispensing justice are followers of Truth. Those who respect the men who cultivate lands and do some artisan's work or respect their helpers are called men of right conduct. Those who appreciate the work of men who work in Chamar localities or respect those who appreciate it are men of right action.

Those who do not exploit poor people either in the name of religion or because of astrological superstitions are men of right conduct. Those who do not exploit the poor by selling them amulets are men of right conduct.

Those who do not entertain men who set the people by ears are men of right conduct. The men who live in a brotherly way with men of different habits and styles of dress, or food, are men of right conduct.

Those who help the men suffering from dangerous disease, or orphans or crippled or respect them who do so are men of right conduct. The religious books which are prepared by great men for the use of the common man contain some truth. If in a family a woman on reading Buddhism follows Buddhism, her husband on reading the Bible follows Christianity and her daughter follows Islam if she has read the Koran, or if the son is a Satya-Shodhak Samajian, they should not hate each other's faith. They should consider themselves as belonging to God's family and as children of one God.

Astrology has nothing to do with the future of a man. The birth of a daughter should be as pleasing to man as the birth of a son. The function of naming the male child should be performed on the 12th day and in case of a female child should be performed on the 13th day. A child should be given milk at the breast of the mother for the first six months if possible. The mother should teach the child gradually.

Marriage should be settled by a girl or a boy in consultation with their elders. The boy and the girl should give proper thought to the matter. They should take a vow just after the marriage. They should give gifts to poor men irrespective of caste or creed.

Those who have lived virtuously and unselfishly die a peaceful death. They have no terrors of anything. While on the deathbed one should call his relatives and friends, advise them to follow the path of truth, and then bid them farewell:

'Oh God! you gave me conscience and reason. I lived a truthful life in the world in obedience to your commands. I am quite confident you will receive me. You will receive my relatives and others also for their having lived a truthful life. Let your kingdom of Truth prevail. Thus one should pray.'

The dead body should be disposed of according to the wish of the deceased, either buried or burnt.

The body of the dead person should be given a scented bath by his relatives. It should be dressed, put on the bier and covered with garlands. The bier should be carried by changing hands. The clothes of the dead person should not be taken off. Then a virtuous man should pray to God. On the thirteenth day, a dinner should be given to those who had come for the funeral, and they should be given flowers. Their children should be given money, if possible even cows for their school-going children. The death anniversary should be performed by giving a dinner to relatives and friends and kinsmen and help should be rendered to poor students.

CHAPTER XIX

Great in Death

The first month of the year 1890 brought a great triumph to Jotirao who was ailing. In the Bombay High Court the Otur case was decided in favour of Balaji Kusaji Patil, and the Brahmin priests with their eminent legal luminaries were defeated. The law supported Jotirao's stand. He could succeed in overthrowing the yoke of the Brahmin priests who regarded the other classes as inferior and yet sought to impose a tax on them in every way, even after death.

When the case came up for hearing in the High Court for the first time, the Brahmin advocate Mahadeo Chimnaji Apte said for the appellants: "The appellants are the hereditary Joshis, and as such are entitled to officiate at the marriage ceremonies at the defendant's house. There was an invasion of their privileges by the person who performed the ceremonies. They were entitled to whatever was paid to the Kunbi priest employed by the defendant."

The advocate Ghanashyam Nilkanth Nadkarni of the respondents said: "The marriages were performed without any prescribed ceremonies, and no priest, as such, was employed. There was no *Ganeshpujan** the initial ceremony of the marriage. There was nothing beyond the placing of garlands round the necks of the bride and the bridegroom. There was no distribution of fees (dakshina); therefore the village *Joshis* (priests) cannot claim any fees. There is a separate ritual of the Shudras of the defendant's caste. That ritual was not performed."

The Chief Justice, Sir Charles Sargent, Kt., sent down the following issue for a finding by the District Court: "What ceremonies were performed on the occasions of the marriages, or either of them and by whom? Parties to be allowed to give fresh evidence. The finding to be returned to this court within two months."

* Invoking the god Ganpati.

The finding came and the judgement was delivered by the Chief Justice, Sir Charles Sargent and Mr. Justice K. T. Telang on January 8, 1890 in favour of Balaji Kusaji Patil. It was now established beyond doubt that the marriages performed in accordance with the simple ceremonies prescribed by the Satya-Shodhak Samaj were valid. No Brahmin priest had any right to officiate at the ceremony, and no fees were to be paid to him. It was a signal victory for the movement of the Satya-Shodhak Samaj.

While Jotirao was struggling to overcome the stroke which he had suffered, his followers were showing great courage in fighting for their rights and contributing to social progress. Sweepers in the service of the Bombay Municipality had gone on strike, first in June 1889 and again in July 1889. The Mahars employed by the Alibag Municipality had bent that Municipality to their will in October 1889. They had struck work as they were ordered to mow the grass in the streets. That Municipality had also turned down the application of the sweepers for an increase in their salary. So both Mahars and sweepers struck work, Their leader was deprived of his job. The Municipality had, however, to surrender, and the leader of the strikers was recalled.

Jotirao's followers made great efforts to give a blow to the custom of tonsuring widows. Jotirao wanted to give a turn to ths tussle that was developing between the barber community and the Brahmins. Month by month reports would appear in the Press that widows were forcibly tonsured. The *Dnyanprakash* denounced this several times as a cruel practice. There were several denouncements in the *Dnyanodaya*.

In October 1880 there was a note in the *Subodha Patrika* on the tonsuring of widows. It was suggested that if they were to be tonsured at all, it should be done either by ladies in the family or by female barbers. A female barber who was shaving widows at Nasik was threatened with excommunication. It was suggested that this woman should be given protection by public men, and she should be taken to Poona and given support in her calling, so that she could earn her bread without any trouble or danger. Brahmins, whenever boycotted by barbers, had done the tonsuring of the widows in the past. Jotirao always said that those who could not save their widowed mothers, sisters and daughters from the cruel custom would never be able to help the cause of social progress.

The problem was now coming to a head. The Poona barbers had announced a boycott of the tonsuring of widows. There was some compromise, but the *Din Bandhu* decided to give battle on the issue. A series of articles appeared in it denouncing the cruel practice, and it appealed to the barbers not to be a party to this cruel practice if they were brave men. It gave vent to Jotirao's burning desire and iron will to stop the cruelty. Taking a clue from those articles, Mama Parmanand, a great political recluse, took up the torch and held it high, so that the pointed attention of all distinguished men of progressive leanings might be attracted to the cruel practice. He wrote an article dated the 24th February 1890 in the *Indian Spectator* of Behramji M. Malbari, the Parsi poet, Indian social reformer, and a selfless editor, who ran the weekly not as a business but as a holy mission.

Parmanand wrote: "Yesterday's issue of the *Din Bandhu* has an admirable article in Marathi, on the barbarous custom of shaving widow heads. It is admirable both on account of the exhortation which the writer addresses to the barbar community, and on account of the unique and valuable idea for which the editor must be given the credit of originality. In describing the wretched condition of the barber of the Bombay Presidency as compared with that of his fellow professionals in Bengal and other parts of India, he attributes all the misfortunes of the barber in his calling, and truly so, to his hard-heartedness, his unmanliness, and unparalleled cruelty in robbing young and helpless widows of their hair, an ornament given by nature and which they value beyond everything else, not only while they are young, but even when they have passed that happy and charming period of human existence."

"He exhorts the barbers," Parmanand continued, "to hold a general meeting of their castemen as they did some years ago, and that, too, so successfully against the Brahmins, and to make it compulsory upon every member of the community to refrain from shaving widows' heads. The idea is, to say the least of it, a good one and well-intentioned, and aims an effectual blow at the cruel custom of shaving widows' heads—a custom which is as unauthorised by that bugbear, or call it scapegoat—which the Hindus call to their aid, which they name the shastras— simple individual thoughts and opinions of uncultured ordinary Brahmins—as encouraged by the ever greedy priest who scruples not what means he employs to put a few rupees in his pocket. The idea, too, if properly worked upon, will do more in suppressing the inhuman custom than what all the endeavours of the present Hindu reformers, who are better known for their writings and lectures than for the courage of their convictions, have hitherto done to achieve."

"It may be added here," Parmanand remarked, "that the writer has perhaps lost sight of the fact that the barber can be made as much amenable to law for disfiguring a widow as her relations, who compel her to have her head shaven against her wish. A number of hand bills distributed in all the important towns will make the editor's aims better known than confining his article to his journal alone. The *Din Bandhu* has done more than any other Marathi journal towards checking the power of the priestly class and rescuing the uneducated masses from the thraldom of Brahminical superstition, and it is probable that most of the journals which are in the hands of the Brahmins will strongly oppose the idea. It is to be hoped, therefore, that every sincere reformer will join in the hope, that your influential journal will give its support to the *Din Bandhu* and its suggestion. Great things often come out of small beginnings."

About a week before Mama Parmanand wrote the above-mentioned letter, "a bonafide advertisement" had appeared in the *Indu Prakash* or *Moonlight*[1]. The advertisement announced: "An earnest sympathiser with the sufferings of young Hindu widows, who are at present subjected to brutal disfigurement by their heads being shaved, offers to defray all legitimate expenses of the criminal prosecution of those who may be concerned in bringing about such brutal acts, before a Magistrate having jurisdiction, under section 352 or any other section or sections of the Indian Penal Code. (1) The prosecution to be in the case of a minor belonging to one of the Brahmin castes, the prosecutor to be anyone in the position of a guardian of the girl victim; but when the accused is the father himself or other person or persons acting as her guardian, than the father-in-law or other persons acting on behalf

1. 24 February 1890

of the family of the deceased husband to undertake such prosecution. (2) The prosecution should be carried through all necessary stages till an authoritative decision is obtained on the question of criminality or otherwise of the act complained of.

This offer will hold good till the end of the year 1890; renewable if circumstances permit. Applications for the fulfilment of the above offer may be made to 'A' care of the Subodha Patrika or of the *Indu Prakash*—15 February 1890."

Upon this Mama Parmanand again wrote a letter on March 11, 1890, to the *Indu Prakash* congratulating the gentleman who had given the above-mentioned advertisement. "It is gratifying to learn," he stated, "that the gentleman who has volunteered to defray the expenses consequent on the persecution of a case of disfigurement of a young widow, and who has been advertising to the effect in some local journals, has extended his offer so far as to include the barber in the criminal procedure. This is, indeed, a good sign of the times and speaks volumes in favour of the reform. This advertisement ought to serve as a warning to the barber, too."

"But what is still more pleasing," Parmanand observed, "is that a Brahmin from Nasik, the seat of orthodoxy, has come forward definitely to perform the purification of a widow without submitting her to the hateful task of the barber. All glory to him! While writing on the subject, he says that the custom of shaving widows originated with the Peshwas. Before their time it was unknown in this part of the country. The all domineering Peshwa in order to impress the people with a sense of superiority of his caste over the down-trodden priesthood of his time, collected at one time about 300 widows and had them forcibly shaved at the Nakzari in Poona. This was done in order to assert his equality with the priests of Talegaon among whom, it appears, the practice prevailed at the time and will go on a long way to show that the hateful custom has not the support of the shastras. Whatever they may be, the opponents of the reform will show their wisdom by withdrawing honourably from the task of opposition while they have yet time to do so.

"The Nasik Brahmin's account ought to convince them that Heaven frowns on such oppression on poor, tender, helpless creatures, who are man's solace while he is alive, and who are paid in return in indescribable misery after his death, and if anything cost the Peshwa his empire, it was this most brutal oppression," Parmanand concluded.

II

The *Bombay Gazette* in its editorial note of March 8, 1890, observed that the editor had received several communications relating to the very practical movement set on foot by reformers of sense and spirit to dissuade barbers from perpetrating the outrage of depriving widows of their hair at the moment of their bereavement. The editor expressed happiness that even the barbers were ashamed of their share in the enforcemenrof the cruel practice, that the practice was not so much rigorous in north India, the widow being required to shave her head only when she visited some shrines of special sanctity. "It would be," concluded the editor, "well if European and native gentlemen who employ barbers for shaving and hair cutting would decline to have anything to do with men who disgrace themselves by cutting off a woman's hair, in the hour of her affliction or subsequently."

While the movement was going on, some orthodox journals angrily said that if barbers refused to shave widows, the Brahmins themselves would apply the razor to the heads of the widows.

A mammoth[2] meeting was held behind Elphinstone High School, Bombay, on April 14, 1890. Over a thousand barbers attended it. Police kept good order. Placards declared that barbers had decided to do away with the barbarous custom of shaving widows. Sadoba Krishnaji, a barber, presided. Touching speeches were made. Their trade had fallen, it was said, because they were performing tonsorial operations on heads of innocent widows and depriving them of their best ornament. They resolved that no barber in future should shave the head of a new widow. The barbers took the hint and abstained from participation in the cruel work. The Marathi orthodox journals hurled their shafts at Gadre and Kelkar who took a prominent part in this meeting of the barbers.

Mama Parmanand again wrote a letter to the Bombay Gazette[3] appealing to the Hindu reformers and their friends to give one pice

2. The *Bombay Gazette*, 17 April 1890.
3. Ibid.

more a week to the barbers who had shown a good deal of boldness and generosity. He further appealed to the reformers and their friends to stop coming to their houses a barber who had shaved a new widow.

The piteous wails of the widows and the agitation for their deliverance reverberated in England, too, which was throbbing with social changes.

By April 1890 some women barbers had come to stay in the basement of 65, Chancery Lane. London. A neat little saloon had then been fitted up and opened for shaving and hair cutting. These women barbers were neatly dressed, trim figured and young. They did their work very skilfully. The proprietor of the saloon got the idea of having women barbers, from San Francisco and Malta, where he had been shaved by women barbers and had found that they handled the job far more delicately than men. Their wrists were more supple.[4]

When the ladies in London heard about the movement of the Bombay barbers, they felt sympathy for the Indian widows and were in agreement with the barbers. The proprietors of the Women Penny Paper therefore decided to send to the barbers of Bombay a letter of thanks, observing: "Our action will show that the women of England are eagerly anxious that the liberty of women in India shall be respected and that everywhere, progress in their emancipation from thraldom shall go hand in hand with the progress in all peaceful arts. The shaving of young widows is an odious and repulsive custom, which deeply degrades those who are subjected to it."[5]

As a result, the following memorandum was sent to the *Bombay Gazette*: "We the readers of the *Women's Penny Paper*, offer our thanks to the barbers of Bombay for the courageous step they have taken in refusing to continue a custom which is odious and degrading to Hindu widows. We believe that no better example than this could be set to the Indian fellow subjects, both men and women, in their own self-respect and in the estimation of other nations."

"Here follows," observed the editor of the *Bombay Gazette* in its issue dated June 17, 1890, "a long list of names which any barber, or

4. The *Bombay Gazette*, 25 April 1890
5. Ibid, 17 June 1890.

other gentlemen interested may inspect on calling at our office." The Bombay barbers also thanked their sympathisers in London.

Commenting on the episode, the *Indian Spectator* in its issue of June 22, 1890, said: "Such expression of fellow-feeling and kindliness were not unexpected of a nation whose struggle for freedom and personal rights are a continual protest against enslaving the human race and they ought to find an echo in the hearts of all true Indians, especially the famale world of this country ought to thank them for their good wishes. On the other hand, those good hearted English ladies would do well to prove the practicality of their benevolent motive by banding themselves together for the continual agitation to remove the social hardships of the widows and to secure to the womanhood of this country those birth rights which are practically denied to them by the despotic lords of creation."

The English progressive group of women was not showing this sort of sympathy with Indian women for the first time. They had helped Rakhmabai, a woman of twenty-two, who refused to stay with her husband even after the decision of the Bombay High Court in 1886 which ordered her to stay with her husband. Her husband was a poor, illiterate, sickly man to whom she had been married before she had arrived at years of discretion. Her husband was bought off by the reformers, and he gave up his claim. Rakhmabai went to England where she was acclaimed in April 1889 as a champion of women's rights. Later, she became an M.D. and served for many years in Gujarat as Chief Medical Officer in some leading hospitals. This lady whose life had been involved in a problem of national consequence died on September 25, 1955, at the age of ninety-one, at her residence near French Bridge in Bombay.

In America there were already some female Magistrates, Barristers, Physicians, and Professors, but in England women had not succeeded so well. In America and in England Dr. Mary Walker and her sister Dr. Elize Walker were honoured.

Jotirao, who had struggled endlessly for over forty years for the betterment of the Indian woman, was pained to see the condition of the Indian widows. This was the last fight he had witnessed during the struggle. The first struggle of the Barber Community with the Brahmins, at the instance of Jotirao came in 1884. But it will not be an exaggeration to say that his heroic struggle and volcanic movement had provoked the lower classes to stand for the vindication of their rights.

How difficult Jotirao's work was can be seen from the under mentioned advertisement which is an indication of the depth and difficulties of the social problems of his day.

"Wanted. An earnest Gujarati speaking preacher whose duty will be to travel through Gujarat and to induce the various castes to give up the practice of premature marriage and to take legally enforceable pledges in this behalf. The Hindu Social Reform Association of Gujarat undertakes to pay his expenses and to provide a fair remuneration. Native of Gujarat preferred—Apply to Mahiputram Rupram, Esq., C.I.E., Ahmedabad." Real reformers and real patriots are born. They are not made; nor can they be hired.

III

During Jotirao's illness, the Rev. Baba Padmanji, a Hindu convert to Christianity, who had helped him many a time in his work and was said to have written an introduction to Jotirao's *Priestcraft Exposed* under the name of B.P., came to inquire after his health. He asked Jotirao whether his mind was at peace and was not worried about the prospective end of his earthly journey. Jotirao said calmly that he had lived a useful and unselfish life; he had fulfilled the mission of his life. He had no dread of anything. His mind was full of tranquillity and was at peace.

As his illness assumed a threatening look, Jotirao became certain that the end of his earthly pilgrimage was approaching. He sent for the workers of the Satya-Shodhak Samaj and calmly advised them to continue to work for the emancipation of the lower classes. When they sobbed, he consoled them by saying that every life has an end, and he was going the way all human beings go. To everything in the world an end was inevitable. He gave them the charge of his wife and son and requested them to look after them. He said he was confident that his wife who had shared in his career for over forty-five years, taking the bitter along with the sweet and developed a calm philosophy, would

7. The Indian Spectator, 16 March 1890.

continue her work, and his son also would devote himself to the cause of the down-trodden.

Colleague after colleague and worker after worker came to have the last glimpse of the venerable man. Lokhande clung to Jotirao's bed; Bhalekar bowed to him. Sasane, Dr. Lad, Ramayya Vyankayya Aiyyavaru and Moro Vithal Walvekar visited him. Walvekar's dying friend was worried about the publication of the book *Sarvajanik Satya-Dharma Pustaka.* Walvekar, a Brahmin, who had formed a lifetime friendship with Jotirao, was moved at the sight of his friend. He promised him that he would publish the book at his own expense and relieved his friend of the anxiety on its account. A great burden was removed off his mind. Jotirao sang in a poem the praise of his friend. "Moro Vithal is a noble man, tolerant endlessly, stayed in Bombay, was the giver of thought of Subodha, father of the household, friend of Jotirao."

Jotirao's friends and admirers were anxious that he should spend the rest of his life in comfort; his family should not be hardup. Mama Parmanand did his best to get some financial help from H.H. the Maharaja of Baroda. He was trying to do it through Ramchandrarao Dhamnaskar. Jotirao in his *Sarvajanik Satya-Dharma Pustaka* said gratefully in a poem that he was helped by three persons, Nageshwargir Buva, Dr. Gholay and Sayajirao Gaikwad. This proposed aid must have been in addition to the other and a sort of provision for his family.

Mama Parmanand, the Bombay political recluse, although himself an ailing man, wrote on July 31, 1890, to Dhamnaskar that he was enclosing a petition of Jotirao for the support of his family and it should be submitted to His Highness. "The bare statement of public objects," observes Parmanand, "to which Jotiba has devoted his life is not calculated to present an impressive picture of the earnest and troublous period through which he passed or the disinterested nature of his labours. But I trust His Highness will appreciate them as they deserve for a Maratha to have educated his wife and attempted through her to instruct the daughters of Brahmins and that too at their headquarters was a venturous task enough. But to have opened schools for Mahars and Mangs and to treat them as members of society in the same quarters was like bearding the lion in his own den."

"Yet Jotiba," Parmanand continued, "did it with the aid of two Brahmin friends one of whom turned a renegade and has died but the other is living and still faithful to him and his views; and it is he who though himself in poor circumstances is printing in his press Jotiba's book at his own cost simply to gratify the last wish of his old friend."

"Jotiba might have," proceeded the saintly personage, "if he had not thus neglected his worldly interests, made money and by this time would have been independent and comfortable. But he chose otherwise and served public interest at the cost of his own. There was another rare virtue which he showed. Young, healthy, handsome-looking and of an agreeable presence, he became an object of unhallowed desire to some women of easy virtue who thrust themselves on him; but like a true hero he cast them aside and remained pure in the presence of so much temptation!"

"His fatherly care," he observed in assessment of his work, "for years of erring high caste widows and generous relief and rescue from the crime of child-murder was also a work of self-sacrificing humanity. His last and greatest public service is connected with what he calls the emancipation of the Maratha mind. To this he devoted his later life and for it he wrote, preached, sang and voted as he preached, and it is to his single exertions, I believe, that the Maratha element in the Deccan and elsewhere shows that consciousness of its wrongs, its desire for amelioration and freedom from implicit submission to the higher castes merely as such which did not exist before!"

"If you recollect," he continued his assessment, "and compare what you heard and saw 25 years ago, with what you do now regarding this matter I think you will agree with me. The creation of such a spirit ought to be welcomed in these days of a general desire for progress; but it is first this part of Jotiba's work which has served to discredit him with the higher classes and led to a forgetfulness of all his previous good offices. This was partly natural, but unluckily Jotiba aggravated it by the use of harsh language. He had some excuse in his higher caste friends and fellow-advocates of reform turning their back on it and also an invidious advice proceeding from a different quarter."

8. Moro Vithal Walvekar.

"A few of his followers too," he opined, "without his excuses or his powers have copied his mistakes and thus thrown dirt on his life's good work. But in questions involving party interests and feelings this kind of thing is unavoidable and most of Jotiba's critics are doing just what he did where they think they are similarly situated. Jotiba's fault then is not quite inexcusable and it cannot be held to nullify all his good work or justify his neglect in his day of suffering indigence and old age when he deserves the gratitude of the public. He has, however, no opulent friends to support him, and he cannot go about begging for aid from the public when in his prostration he is forgotten by it nor indeed would he seek help even in high places where there is no intelligent appreciation of his work, but has appealed to the only quarter where such appreciation exists and this is no longer age of flattery."

"Of course," Parmanand further said: "I cannot and do not wish H.H. to be, much less to appear, a partisan on any side, but he can, while disclaiming any sympathy with misguided or sectarian views or offensive language and simply in recognition of his disinterested and self-sacrificing work, bestow a maintenance for life on Jotiba and his wife; for the woman deserves even more than the man for co-operating with her husband and suffering with him in that work in a manner not yet witnessed in the highest educated of the higher castes. Services like theirs indeed deserve well of the state; but the British Government is foreign and cannot be expected to put their hands to such matters." Parmanand then cited the worthy example set by the first Sir Salarjung who bestowed a monthly pension of Rs. 100 on Dr. Bhau Daji Lad.

And concluding his appeal, Parmanand said: "What is wanted is an allowance say of Rs. 30 per mensem to be begun now and continued during the lifetime of Jotiba and his wife, to be reduced on the death of either and stopped on the decease of survivor and the completion of his son's education. None of the events can now be postponed indefinitely, and so the expenditure will neither be heavy nor continued very long. This then is all that is desired. One word more and I have done.

"Dr. Vishram Gholay who attends free of charge, and being a friend is acquainted with his condition, appeared to have written to

Pestonji on behalf of him. What he wrote and what he asked I do not know, but I am told of this reply being sent, 'H.H. said there are many such applicants and he cannot promise anything just yet. He might do some time hence.' I trust however this will be reconsidered and what is intended to be done would be done at once after what I have said above. I hope it will be seen that there are not many applicants like Jotiba. In fact there is not a second and delay in his case, prostrated as he is, might frustrate intended kindness."

Again in the third week of August 1890, Parmanand reminded Dhamnaskar of Jotirao's case and said that the prayer could be granted on the simple ground of the man's self-sacrificing work of many years and his existing needs which were real. Compliance with the prayer would not be interpreted as a concession to any class because the applicant was a Maratha. "But otherwise," he said, "Baroda, which has lavished its money, the fruit of the *ryots'* toil on all sorts of Brahmins, good, bad and indifferent, may well spare some of it, on a deserving non-Brahmin and one of the producing class." Guru, guide and friend of K. T. Telang and M. G. Ranade, N. M. alias Mama Parmanand thus gave in a judicious, perspicuous style and in historical perspective the assessment of Jotirao's life and mission.

IV

On Thursday, November 27, 1890, Jotirao's health showed signs of an approaching end. At five in the evening he called the members of his family to his bed-side. He advised them one by one to conduct their duties righteously and unselfishly. He moved his hand over their faces. He called his wife and bade her farewell. She stood looking at him sadly and serenely. Then he asked his son to burn incense and say prayers to God. He himself began his prayer and entreated God to receive him without any further delay. He was fully conscious. His face was serene. The expression was happy. His mind was at peace. At night he gradually closed his eyes with prayers on his lips. Such a peaceful happy death comes rarely to great men. It is a very important thing in the lives of eminent men how they face the death. At twenty minutes past two A.M. Jotirao's tired heart ceased to beat. The stomach cramps that had caused him physical pain vanished. The sobs of the persons around his deathbed faltered into silence. A deep silence fell.

The news spread like wild fire. At dawn poor men and women ran with their children to Jotirao's house to have a glimpse of their Mahatma. They all grieved at the death of their great and good man. Almost all of his colleagues had come to Poona on the previous night. Jotirao's followers in the neighbouring villages ran to Poona. In the morning vast crowds gathered near the house. The body of the Mahatma was kept at dawn in the front part of the house in a chair. Hundreds of poor men had the last glimpse of him. Their saviour was gone. The sword that was being brandished around their lives was broken. The incarnation of social justice, love and social equality was disappearing from view. He was their sire, seer and saviour. Their grief was unspeakable, terrible.

On the morning of November 28, at ten, his body was given a scented bath. His clean usual dress was put on. Hundreds of garlands were put on the bier. The near relatives and his colleagues lifted the bier, and the vast crowd comprising of all communities followed sorrowfully. Some women also joined the funeral procession. The streets were alive on both sides with sympathetic whispers and hot tears. It took two hours for the funeral procession to reach the cremation grounds. Jotirao had expressed his desire in his will that his body should be buried. It seems that his colleagues did not know about it.

The leaders put the body on the pier. Jotiba's son Yashwant said prayers. Then Bhau Kondaji Patil, Jotirao's trusted colleague, made a stirring speech. He said very sorrowfully: "The great man who devoted his life to the mission of the emancipation of us all Shudras and Atishudras, who wrote, spoke and struggled and spent his life in winning us human rights, has departed this world as is the ultimate way of everyone in this world. But his fame is everlasting. Because of our ignorance, we are unable to assess the worth and greatness of this man; but when in future truth-seekers will study his life, they they would realise his greatness and their hearts would be filled with gratitude. Let us keep gratefully his mission ever green in our memory."

Then Jotirao's adopted son Yashwant lit the pier and Jotirao's earthly remains were reduced to ashes on Friday, the 28th November

1890. A Mahatma emerged from it. The people were silently witnessing the melting of their great leader into the soul of the universe. Then the crowd dispersed, whispering that it went to whom it belonged.[9] The good-natured Brahmins exclaimed: "Blessed be the name of Jotirao!"

On the third day people in their hundreds gathered at the Mahatma's house. The tomtom-beaters, the drummers, the band-players, the native gymnasts, all crowed at the Mahatma's house. They took a palanquin. They went in procession to the cremation ground with bands, tom-toms and drums blaring and gymnasts performing before them. Observing great sanctity, and chanting long prayers in chorus, they put the holy ashes in an urn. The sacred urn was placed in the palanquin and the procession returned with resounding thunders of jai to Mahatma Jotirao Phooley. Then again, amidst prayers and in a dignified atmosphere, the ashes were lowered into the pit[10] which had been already marked for the purpose when the Mahatma was alive and the Samadhi was closed amidst deep emotions. They then returned home, praying God to make them worthy of Jotirao's noble life.

The *Subodha Patrika* edited by his friend Moro Vithal Walvekar lamented Jotirao's death. The Din Bandhu, the mouthpiece of the Satya Shodhak Samaj, was loud in its sorrow. The *Indu Prakash*[11] said that it was sorry to hear about the sad death of Joti Govindrao Phooley. It paid him a tribute for his untiring industry and his intellect. But his intellect, it observed, was obsessed by the mad idea that the Brahmins had for their selfish ends kept the other castes in the abysmal depth of ignorance, and their backwardness was the result of Brahmin designs. That was why he hated the Brahmins and he was hypnotised by the idea.

One of the contemporaries, the *Indu Prakash* proceeded, had said that he was responsible for the bitterness that existed between the Brahmins and non-Brahmins. But the *Indu Prakash* differed from that view. In its opinion the rulers' policy of divide and rule had no mean part in it. Phooley might have been the expression of it. Whatever might be the result of his policy, his life was a good example of how

9. The *Dnyanodaya*, 18 December 1890.
10. The *Dnyanodaya*, 12 December 1890.
11. 29 December 1890.

a man should labour untiringly for the work he undertook. A critic's house should be nearby. The Brahmins also were put to a great loss by his death. If men of other castes struggled without prejudices as vigorously for the uplift of the people as did Jotirao for his own people, much good would be achieved.

The *Daily Telegraph* and *Deccan Herald*,[12] Poona, said in its obituary: "We regret to announce the death of Jotirao Govindrao Phule Mali the champion of the Maratha community which occurred at his house in Vetal Peit yesterday morning." The publisher of this daily English newspaper was a Parsi named Dadabhoy Sorabjee.

The *Dnyanodaya*[13] said that Jotirao devoted his life to the service of his country. In doing that he did not care either for the opposition of Government or for that of the people. Men of such sincerity and resolute will would be rarely found in his day. It appreciated Jotirao's untiring and splendid work which he had done for the uplift of women and the lower classes. It was sorry that such a man should have failed to come to the fold of Christ!

V. K. Oak, editor of the *Balbodh*,[14] in a brief obituary said that Jotirao Govindrao Phooley died in last November. He was the defender of non-Brahmins. He used to criticise bad-natured Brahmins. No tribute could be more eloquent and just than this one, paid by a Brahmin contemporary of Jotirao. Volumes could not have said more.

12. 29 November 1890.
13. 18 December 1890.
14. January 1891.

CHAPTER XX

Passing of an Era

NOBLE FRIEND that he was, Mama Parmanand did not give up his attempt to persuade the Maharaja of Baroda to give some relief to the devoted wife and adopted son of Jotirao. He himself had sent once again some financial help to Jotirao and after his death Parmanand again wrote to Ramchandra Dhamnaskar that an attempt would be made to collect another small sum for the use of Jotirao's family. He insited that his letters in the matter should be shown to the Maharaja of Baroda in the strictest confidence.

At last, on Jotirao's death, his wife Savitribai and son Yashwant were helped by the Maharaja of Baroda. In February 1892 he sent a cheque through Ramchandrarao Dhamnaskar for Rs. 1,000 to Mama Parmanand out of which Savitribai received Rs. 50 every three months according to the arrangement. The money was deposited in February 1892 with S. Narayan and Co. at 5 per cent interest. Jotirao's friend Tukaram Tatya Padval was a partner in this company.

A few days later the Maharaja expressed his wish to Ramchandrarao Dhamnaskar that he wanted to make some grant-in-aid for a memorial to perpetuate Jotirao's memory. Ramchandrarao Dhamnaskar wrote to Mama Parmanand asking him whether he could start a fund with that aim in view and formulate a scheme for the erection of a memorial to Jotirao. Mama Parmanand had been confined to bed for over ten years, and so, it seems, he could not give effect to the suggestion made by the Maharaja of Baroda. Parmanand died on September 13, 1893. In the obituary Lokhande wrote in the *Din Bandhu*, he observed "Parmanand earnestly appealed to us to erect a memorial to Jotirao, but since all amongst us have become Jotiraos and assumed his pose, nobody could pay attention to it."

Jotirao's son passed his Matriculation examination in 1893 and, obtaining a medical diploma, he took service with the Army.

Unfortunately Savitribai died of plague in 1897 in Poona, and it seems that about eight years later Yashwant also died.

Jotirao was the first Indian leader to start a movement for the removal of the social and economic ills of the lower classes who were starved, stunted and suffering untold privations. He gave vent to their age-long rage and grief. His movement aimed at establishing social equality and securing social justice. He struggled for the dignity of human personality and human rights, as he considered all Indians equal. His movement was thus a part of the social revolution that had been started all over India. Jotirao started with the education of the lower classes, for it was his belief that life could not be lived satisfactorily without the means to live a full life, and he believed that education was one of the chief means for opening the gateway to a full and satisfying life.

In doing so Jotirao whipped the conservatism of the privileged classes who opposed the education of the lower classes, and also their inertia which was the result of their age-long ignorance. A great man is he who scourges society of its ills. Jotirao had to break down the formidable mountain of opposition of the Brahmin class to the education and liberty of the lower classes. It was, therefore, inevitable that he should come into clash with the Brahmins who constituted the privileged class.

Every social, religious or political movement is started by a fanatical man of faith. The leader of a social movement is always a man of one idea, and this often makes him intensely intolerant. The weapons he ruthlessly wields are in accordance with the exigency and the size of the impediments he meets with in his way. Jotirao was the first Indian leader to start a movement for the uplift and welfare of the lower classes, to use the weapon of boycott, to teach the peasants to fight for the removal of their grievances, and to preach to the labourers to voice their grievances. Indeed the labour movement in India, as already noted, was itself an off-shoot of Jotirao's Satya-Shodhak Samaj.

Jotirao put his combative genius into his work. He sublimated his vitality to remould a stagnant society and devoted his talents to preaching radical reforms in the character and pattern of the people. His movement disturbed the stagnation in Maharashtra. The intensity of his sentiment lasted over forty years. It is not strength, say Nietzche, but the duration of sentiments that makes great men. In Jotirao's case the duration was unusually long, and the sentiments were so undivided, so incorruptible, so impeccable!

For the achievement of his goal Jotirao sacrificed all honour, all happiness, all positions that would have come to him if he had given up the struggle which aimed at reconstructing the social order. In those days the British Government bestowed titles on men of importance. But no Government title had its wings broad enough to cover the personality of Jotirao. He had opposed the Poona Municipality spending money on the welcome of a British Governor-General, and also the setting up of a Municipal Market even though it was named after a British Governor.

Although Jotirao had helped the social reformers, he had no much sympathy for them, for they thought like radicals and acted like social Tories. When men give up doing what is right they give up their aims for compromise. So did the social reformers.

Makers of a new world or a new society are always out of step with society. Men of dominant will, they overstep ancient laws and customs. The ignorant always live in slavery; ordinary men live in submission; but a man of mission breaks all bonds. Jotirao broke the bondage of Indian woman and enabled her to make herself free. He broke the bonds of mental slavery that were tied to the neck of the lower classes by scriptures and priestcraft. He broke the fetters of the untouchables which they had borne for ages. It heralded a new dawn for them. It was he who raised a hue and cry against their exploiters and tried to impress upon the nation that if the farmer was happy and contented, the whole nation would be happy and contented. Jotirao was thus the face of liberty in revolt.

The present benefactors of women and the historians of their movements have systematically drawn a veil over Jotirao's name, so it is difficult for them to know their foremost liberator. Neither do Indian women show due reverence to the memory of Savitribai Phooley, who left her father-in-law's house, followed her husband like a chaste and dutiful Savitri, suffered untold hardships with her husband, endured showers of abuse because she became a teacher and taught girls. There is hardly any parallel example in the nineteenth century which can be compared to Savitribai's noble life devoted to the cause of the uplift of the Indian women.

The veil was, however, lifted by Acharya P. K. Atre. An eminent educationist, a leading playwright, a fiery editor and a gold-medalist director, he produced a brilliant picture depicting the life of Mahatma Jotirao Phooley. When Acharya Atre started the picture, in his inaugural speech Dr. B. R. Ambedkar said: "Atre's picture will revive the memory of Jotirao Phooley who was one of the greatest of our social reformers."

His name was Joti, which meant a flame. It showed the right path of equality, humanism and reason to the nation. His surname was Phooley, a florist. He struggled for over forty years to weed out the garden of the nation, so that the flower plants might blossom with scented flowers to adorn humanity. The garden,is growing, but it is not yet in its bloom. His florism, however, has nothing to do with Communism. Humanism flows from his florism. For his garden is not without odour and scent just as true music is not without melody.

II

Jotirao was one to whom the law of life was duty. He possessed tremendous energy of will which is the soul of every great character; and his energetic character was governed by a noble spirit. He was a theist, a moralist, a rationalist. Strong in heart and rich in spirit, he was the archetypal man of character who represents conscience in every age.

"Him I call a Mahatma," said Swami Vivekanand, "whose heart bleeds for the poor, otherwise he is a Duratma (wicked man). So hold every man a traitor who while educated at their expense pays not the least heed to them." Few leaders who have started a movement for the uplift and welfare of the lower classes are more entitled to the title of Mahatma than Jotirao, the peasant philosopher. Saint Tukaram sang in a poem: "He who calls his own those that are afflicted and sorrow stricken, is a saint and in him God resides." So was Jotiran a saint to the backbone. It is no wonder a great man like Dr. Ambedkar, Father of the Indian Constitution, leader and liberator of the suppressed people, called Mahatma Jotirao Phooley his master and placed him in line with Buddha and Kabir.

Yet Jotirao Phooley did not become proud or insufferable, as he truly possessed two more qualities of a Great Man. He possessed gratitude and purity of character. For ingratitude and impurity of character on the part of the leaders make them unbearable. Intolerant Jotirao indeed was; so is any selfless leader who leads a movement. His courage was the reflection of his soul and such moral courage springs from belief in the right. He had something in him of William Wilberforce, his crusading zeal, and besides which he possessed the force of Martin Luther. Jotirao and Dayanand may be worthily called the Martin Luthers of India.

Jotirao did not rise in revolt against British rule. The revolts that had broken out while he was young were all suppressed. People had no energy to fight a war of liberation. Their social condition and the unrest caused by continual fighting had thoroughly sapped their energy and they were completely prostrated. Besides, Jotirao feared that if India fell again into the hands of Brahmin leaders she would relapse into social reaction and the lower classes would be totally crushed. Knowing well that the British rule would fall some day, he did not wish to fight it, as the benefits he thought it conferred on the lower classes, such as the right to education and employment, peaceful working, modes of travelling and freedom of dress wrre conducive to the welfare and well-being of the lower classes. He felt that they could improve their lot under the British rule.

There was then no political movement worth the name in India. It was beyond the dream of the leaders of that generation. Nor was a revolution possible. To fight a war of inde-pendence great preparations were necessary. So rarely any leader in his day turned to the path of revolution. Jotirao did not allow his colleagues and followers to talk of war against British rule. All he wanted them to do was to secure their social, religious and economic rights. Those who called themselves revolutionaries and fought against the British power as best as they could, had no ideas of social reconstruction and social justice. They were mere revivalists. They merely wanted their raj back.

Damodar Chapekar, for instance, who heroically went to the gallows on April 18, 1898, had a burning hatred for the social reformers of his times. He was an extremely orthodox Hindu.

So were, his brothers. He looked down upon social reformers as Dheds. Writing about a group of native soldiers in his autobiography, Damodar Chapekar said:[1] "I had given up conversation with the Marathas among them as English men have fairly imbued their minds with the idea that the Brahmins were the cause of their ruin. My intelligent readers are doubtless aware of the existence at Poona and Bombay of a large anti-Brahmin Association founded by one Jotiba Phule. The sole aim of this association is to stir up hatred against the Brahmins among all other castes. Its members are moving about delivering lectures to create a feeling of animosity against the Brahmins."

"Their principal organ," Chapekar continues, "is the *Din Bandhu*, a weekly newspaper, published in Bombay. Its columns are usually filled with the abuse of Brahmins. On the death of Jotiba Phule, one Lokhande took up the lead in the matter. This Lokhande, although a perfect numskull, has been honoured with the distinction of a Justice of the Peace by the English for the simple reason that he has undertaken the important task of creating dissensions among his own country men."

In those early days these heroic men wanted to end British rule, so that they might revert to their own system of rule. Their best contribution was the noble sacrifice they made in the cause of political liberation, but they utterly lacked the ability to understand the ills of the lower classes and to read the spirit of the changing times. They proudly clung to cultural roots and traditions and looked to the past for inspiration.

They had nothing to say against the social system which kept them at the top of the ladder, but kept large masses at the bottom of the ladder to rot and deprived them of any chance of growth. The axiom that men who cry the most for liberty are the least to give it to others is true in such cases. Most of these fiery patriots were filled with abstract ideas of patriotism, otherwise they would have given serious thought to the criticism and desperate denunciation of Brahminism made by eminent men such as Acharya P. C. Roy, Deshbandhu C. R. Das and

1. *Source Material for a History of Freedom Movement in India*, Vol. II, p. 987.

Dr. P. Varadrajalu Naidu. Dr. P. Varadrajalu Naidu of Madras once said: "British Imperialism has enslaved our body, while Brahminism has enslaved our soul. British exploitation has drained India of its wealth while Brahminism still dominant in the social and religious sphere has destroyed the spirit of self-respect and yearning for freedom among her masses."[2]

The leaders of the Indian National Congress, Dadabhai Nawroji and, for a certain period, Tilak and Gandhi were demanding Indianisation of the services. Jotirao was not satisfied with the mere Indianisation of the services. He wanted to make the Government administration even by Indians free from corruption, bribery and nepotism. He wanted the Government to take effective actions against those who were corrupt and were hampering the economic welfare of the people. He deplored the failure of the Government in its efforts to keep a check on the administration, and he raised angry protests against hoarders and profiteers of his day.

III

Jotirao gave up his life to the service of the lower classes. His followers worshipped him. But they could not always practise his philosophy worthily. They converted, on the death of their master, the ideology of the Satya-Shodhak Samaj into the political philosophy of a Non Brahmin Party in Maharashtra and detracted from their rational opposition to Brahminism. They developed their Party into a weapon against Brahmins as a class. Yet it was a fact that they gave an impetus to education among the lower classes and created a consciousness of political rights in them, compelling the Brahmins and other higher classes to take into consideration the principle of equality. Jotirao hated Brahminism which bred ideas of inequality and untouchability; but he never hated Brahmins as a class.

The leaders of the movement like Keshavrao Jedhe and Dinkarao Jawalkar who bolstered it up, were possessed with hatred of Brahmins to such an extent that they even appealed to Dr. B. R. Ambedkar to get rid of his Brahmin colleagues who were fighting for the liberation of

2. The *Brahman-Brahmanetar*, 16 October 1926.

the Untouchables. This attitude on the part of the non-Brahmin leaders provoked a serious rebuke from Dr. Ambedkar.

In inaugurating a social or political movement the leaders have to preach hope and create faith in the minds of their followers for their future. In the movement inaugurated by the non-Brahmin leaders, except Chhatrapati Shahu Maharaj of Kolhapur, none raised hopes in their followers. Instead they roused their hatred. They turned the social movement started by Jotirao into a political one and that too devoid of nationalism and drive against foreign rule.[3] They totally lost sight of social equality and disregarded the untouchable classes whom Jotirao regarded as members of the Kshatriya community. On top of it they set up a gadi of Kshatriya Shankaracharya and revived the institution of priestcraft against which Jotirao had fought. Later some of them even opposed in the Bombay Legislative Council, the Temple Entry Bill introduced in favour of the Untouchables and discouraged leaders like Bhai Madhavrao Bagal from propagating the removal of untouchability.[4] It was, however, a fact that Bhaskarrao Jadhav and Karmaveer Bhaurao Patil struggled hard to promote education among the non-Brahmins, and S. K. Bole worked untiringly for the welfare of the lower and labour classes and fought also for removing the social ills.

The leaders of the non-Brahmin movement regarded all who were not Brahmins by birth as belonging to their fold and so their movement embraced the Marwaris, landlords and moneylenders against whom Jotirao had launched an attack. The result was that spirited young leaders like Yashwantrao Chavan and great leaders like Dr. Ambedkar turned away from them, one for their lack of nationalism and the other for their having lost the urge to fight for social equality.

Prabodhankar Keshavrao Thakare, a historian and a stormy petrel in the non-Brahmin movement in Maharashtra, rightly reprimanded the leaders of the movement which went under the flag of Jotirao Phooley as non-Brahmin movement. Thakare said that they had committed a blunder and spoiled the good work of Jotirao Phooley by creating again the *gadi* of Kshatriya Shankaracharya and by including the

3. Keshavrao Jedhe in the *Prasad*, Special Issue of Diwali, 1955.

4. Bagal, Madhavrao, *Jivan Prakash* (Marathi Autobiography), p. 103.

money-lenders and landlords in their movement. Thereafter leaders like Shankarrao More drove it, in utter desperation, to the other extreme. True to their confused thinking, they tried to wed it to Marxist philosophy making a hotchpotch of both. Dr. Ambedkar had therefore to rebuke once again the leaders of the movement. So in his message to the Satya-Shodhak Samaj Conference he observed: "The non-Brahmins have not only disgraced the memory of Jotirao Phooley but also have betrayed shamelessly his philosophy. The mission of the Satya-Shodhak Samaj must reach every corner of India."

The India Jotirao visualised was now taking shape. The old methods of agriculture are being gradually replaced. Compulsory education, with facilities of boarding for the poor students, is being gradually launched in every State. The education of girls is advancing, but the progress is rather slow, the major obstacle being lack of women teachers. The new forms of the breeding of sheep, goats and bullocks which Jotirao envisaged is being realised in India. India is becoming a better land for the peasants and workers. Women are made free from the shackles of their slavery and enjoying a status equal with men.

Jotirao was pre-eminently a patriot of humanity. Like all really great men, he was a universal man. He stood for human rights, justice, peace and prosperity, and not for power. He wanted a religion which recognised social equality. He was not one who could be called a religious personality in the sense that Jesus Christ and Gautam Buddha were. Neither was he God-intoxicated. He did not hanker after the salvation of the soul. Religion is something not to be professed but to be experienced. Jotirao's personality was more ethical and social and rational than religious. His virile and rational attack on the theory of incarnation was quite shocking in those days. He wanted to divest the Hindus of their false belief that God would come to their rescue in times of danger, and from the belief that their fate was pre-destined. He infused self-reliance into them and made them stand for and secure their human rights.

It was his firm belief that all the sacred books like the Bible, the Koran and the Vedas were man-made and not God-made; they did not embody the unalloyed truth from beginning to end. It was Jotirao's movement that saved the lower classes from being denationalised by Christianity and other religions. In his day there was no Muslim problem in Poona or Maharashtra. Jotirao's vision was to create a better man with better understanding, education and ideas of equality and liberty. Political freedom without social equality creates an unstable society. If equality is not established in social and economic spheres by offering opportunities to the poor classes to develop and rise, there will be a threat to freedom and political democracy.

Some educated but blind followers of the Poona school of thought, whose knowledge and sympathy never went beyond Vishnushastri Chiplunkar and Lokamanya Tilak, think that the non-Brahmins need some image to worship and so they have pitted Phooley against Tilak. These very men had opposed the proposal before the Poona Municipality in 1925 for erecting a statue to Jotirao Phooley and they were vehement, bitter and rancorous about it. The struggle between the two parties, Brahmins and non-Brahmins, which was fought in 1925 is known as the battle of statues. Afterwards, statues of Jotirao were erected in Poona and at some important places in Maharashtra.

Jotirao's birth centenary was celebrated all over Maharashtra with gratitude and sincerity it deserved. That is why Yashwantrao Chavan, now India's finance minister, aptly said when he assumed the reins of power as the first Chief Minister of Maharashtra State in May 1960, that Saint Dnyaneshwar, Chhatrapati Shivaji, Mahatma Jotirao Phooley and Lokamanya Tilak were symbols of Maharashtra.[5] Pandit Jawaharlal Nehru, Prime Minister of India, too, while inaugurating the Mahatma Phooley Technical School Building, said, "The days when Mahatma Phooley fought for women's education and the removal of untouchability were such that there was no possibility of help forthcoming from any quarter."[6]

IV

After Jotirao's death Ramayya Vyankayya Aiyyavaru, Bhaskarrao Jadhav, Bhaurao Patil, Keshavrao Jedhe and Dinkarao Jawalkar preached the philosophy of Jotirao by taking a leaf out of their master's

5. Chavan, Yashwantrao, Sahyadriche Ware (Maralhi), p.58
6. Siddharth College of Law Magazine 1963-64.

book and working according to their ability and power. But the work that did good to thousands of poor men and brought about social change could not have been done without the mighty lever and labour used by Shahu Maharaj of Kolhapur. The present non-Brahmin leaders who have risen in Maharashtra in political, social or educational fields have sprung from the labour and liberating work done by Shahu Maharaj who was for a number of years the mainspring of the Satya-Shodhak Samaj. But better achievement would have crowned the efforts of the non-Brahmin leaders had they laid emphasis on their self-respect and self-development instead of their inferiority complex.

Most of the non-Brahmin leaders who eulogise Phooley are not enthusiastic about his casteless ideology which is based on equality, liberty and fraternity. Socially and educationally, the non-Brahmins are yet far behind. In spite of Mahatma Jotirao's gigantic efforts and the impetus given by Sayajirao Gaikwad, Shahu Maharaj, Madhavrao Shinde, Bhaskarrao Jadhav and Bhaurao Patil, they still lack the urge for higher knowledge, superior scholarship, competition and self-improvement. As they are lethargic and afraid to lose what they possess, they are not bold enough to make sacrifice for the achievement of their aims. Because their prestige has not stemmed from sacrifice, struggle and continuity of learning, most of them are either exhausted early or easily dominated by others. So they could not dominate an all India field as did the Bengali non Brahmins by dint of their sacrifice and thirst for knowledge.

Another glaring defect noticed was that except Shahu Maharaj and Bhaurao Patil, no non-Brahmin leader has reached the lower strata of the society which Mahatma Phooley had reached eighty years ago. Karmaveer V. R. Shinde, who devoted his life to the removal of untouchability, was, although a Prarthana Samajist, a great devotee of Jotirao. He alone shared with Jotirao the honour of serving the cause of the Untouchables. Jotirao wrote in a prophetic vein in his last book that when the children of the Shudras and the Atishudras including Bhils and Kolis, whom the Brahmins have condemned as low-caste Untouchables and sub-human beings, take to acquiring true knowledge, they would, in course of time attain it, and then it might happen that a great man would spring from amongst them, would shower flowers on our tombs and declare victory and joy in our names."[7] That was his sincere prophesy, he said.

Jotirao's prophesy came true when Dr. B. R. Ambedkar. a man of great learning, action and courage, fought for the rights of the down-trodden and wrote the Constitution of India. He was the man who arrived to deliver the suppressed classes, as predicted by Jotirao Phooley. When, therefore, after the third reading of the Constitution, the Constituent Assembly of India and the nation showered praise on Dr. Ambedkar, these tributes must have given divine satisfaction to the soul of Mahatma Jotirao Phooley.

The centenary of the Satya-Shodhak Samaj fell on September 24, 1973. A tiny Prarthana Samaj is passing its days virtuously and silently, bereft of any social vitality; the Brahmo Samaj became a term of reproach in the eighties. But the mission of the Satya-Shodhak Samaj has been kept alive by its numerous adherents who are scattered all over Maharashtra. The villagers are not yet free from superstitions. ignorance, prejudices and rituals. The corruption and exploitation against which Jotirao had raised his voice, although the exploiters are not Brahmins now, still reminds Maharashtra of Jotirao and, in the words of Wordsworth, it cries: "Thou shouldst be living at this hour." The centenary was celeberated with enthusiasm in Maharashtra.

Great men of all ages speak in different languages, but their teaching is the same. Each sun brings a new day, so every great man offers a chance to society for improvement.

Jotirao, the peasant philosopher, was the first Indian leader to use the axiom "Truth alone triumphs". He used it on his letter-head. This is very significant. Great sages of India have stressed this message, which is the mainspring of Hindu culture and tradition. So deeply impressed was his personality with the message of truth that Jotirao said in one poem: "Salvation is a humble servant at the door of truth; devotion bows before it." A follower of truth attains salvation. Such was Jotirao's belief in and emphasis on truth. When Mahatma Gandhi

7. Phooley Jotirao. *Sarvajanik Satya-Dharma Pustaka*, pp.123-124.
8. Letter dated 25-5-1885 by Motilal Ghose, to Mama Parmanand, quoted by P. B. Kulkarni in Mama Parmanand and His Times (Marathi), p.503.

was only four years old Jotirao was already preaching the message of truth to the people.

Filled with a heroic ethical purpose, Jotirao's ethico-religious personality stands on a high spiritual plane. By his emphasis on Truth, Equality and Humanism, Mahatma Phooley occupies a place in the pantheon of great thinkers and sages of India. Gautam Buddha adorns the central place in this. Then follow a number of reformers, thinkers and rebels who showed the people of their generation the right path and revolted against the conservatism of the then existing society. When, therefore, our society will attain the goal of social and economic equality and every man will uphold every right of every other man which he himself enjoys, Jotirao's aim will be fulfilled.

Chronology of Important Events

1813	The Charter Act adopted by the Government of India setting Free education
1818	Collapse of the Peshwa rule
1819	First School for Hindu girls started in Calcutta
1820	Bombay Native Education Society established
1821	Establishment of Sanskrit College in Poona open only to Brahmins
1821	Hindu College for Brahmins
1824	Missionaries start Marathi School in Poona
1825	Ramoshis led by Umaji Naik make an unsuccessful attempt against British Rule
1827	Joti born to Govindrao and Chimanabai (11.4. 1827 Date Uncertain)
1828	Bombay Native Education Society sets up schools
1828	Joti's mother dies
1830	Secret attempt by some reformers to educate girls
1832	*Darpan* first Marathi fortnightly edited by Balashastri Jambhekar starts publication
1832	Pratapsingh of Satara installed on Gadi
1833	Slavery abolished in England
1835	Macaulay's 'minute' in favour of western education
1835	Joti goes to school
1836	Village school started
1838	Joti at school, briefly
1834 to 1838	Joti educated in a private school. Marathi education in Pantoji's school
1840	Married to Savitribai, the daughter of Khandoji Nevase Zagade Patil at Naigaon
1840	Board of Education set up
1841 to 1847	Primary education (English) in Missionary School
1841	Joti resumes education in a Mission school
1841	Balashastri Jambhekar starts the first Marathi weekly *Prabhakar*

1843	Sadashiv Ballal Govande teaches at Poona Sanskrit College
1847	Joti completes education in an English School
1847	Study of Thomas Paine's book *Rights of Man*
1848	Humiliation at an upper caste marriage procession
1848	Started school for girls of shudra and atishudra.
1848	Karl Marx publishes *Communist Manifesto*
1848	First women's rights convention in USA
1848	Lokahitwadi starts writing 'Shatapatre' in *Prabhakar*
1849	Left parental home with wife because of oath taken to educate the Shudras
1851	Joti forced to close his school
1851	Started girl's school at Chiplunkar's wada
1852	Major Candy felicitated Jotiba Phooley for his contribution in the field of education.
1854	First cotton mill established in Bombay
1854	Joined a Scottish school as a part-time teacher.
1855	Writes a play *Tritiya Ratna*, perhaps the first play in Marathi
1855	Started a night school
1856	An attempt on Joti's life
1857	The Rising against the British
1858	Took retirement from the Management Board of the school
1860	Supports remarriage of widows
1862	Official village school scheme given up
1863	Slavery abolished in USA and Russia
1863	Establishes a Home to prevent infanticide
1865	Publishes Tukaramtatya Padwal's second edition of *Jatibhed Viveksar*
1867	Prarthana Samaj established
1868	Death of Jotirao's father Govindrao
1868	Throws open his private water tank to the untouchables.
1869	Writes 'Chatrapati Shivaji Raje Bhonsale yancha povada' (1.6. 1869)
1869	Writes *Brahmananche Kasab* Writes *Vidyakhatyatil Brahman Pantoji*

1873	Writes *Gulamgiri*
1873	Establishes 'Satya Shodhak Samaj'. 24 September 1873
1875	Dayanand Saraswati of Arya Samaj visits Poona, taken in grand procession
1877	Writes a tract regarding famine conditions
1877	Report of Pune branch of Satya Shodhak Samaj (20.03.1877)
1880	Writes against issue of new Liquorshop Licenses
1880	Millhands Association founded by Lokhande
1880	Death of Sarvajanik Kaka (Ganesh Vasudeo)
1876 to 1882	Appointed Member (Commissioner) of Pune Muncipality
1882	Made presentation to Hunter Education Commission (19.10. 1882)
1882	Submits report to Hunter Commission
1882	Death of Vishnushastri Chiplunkar
1882	Tilak and Agarkar imprisoned in Kolhapur case. Jotirao lionises them on release
1883	Writes *Shetkarayacha Asud* ('Cultivator's Whipcord')
1885	Jotirao takes lead in restoring samadhi of Shivaji Maharaj on *Raigad Fort*
1885	Published the book *Ishara*
1885	Letter to Maratha Granthakar Sabha (Literary Conference)
1885	'Satsar' starts publication
1885	Junnar Court's decision in favour of villagers' rights (29.03.1885)
1886	Letter to Mama Parmanand
1887	Formulates ritual for Satyashodhak wedding ceremony
1888	Duke of Connaught reception (2.03.1888)
1888	Felicitated by public and was honoured with the title of 'MAHATMA' (11.05. 1888)
1889	Started writing 'Sarvajanik Satya Dharma Pustak' (1.4.1889)
1890	Death of Mahatma Jotirao Phooley (28.11.1890)

Bibliography

Works Cited

Alteker Dr. A. S.	Position of Women in Hindu Civilization
Chokshi R. D.	The Last Phase
Douglas James	A Book of Bombay Report of the Education Commission, 1833
Ghurye G. S.	Caste and Class in India
Hampton H.V.	Biographical Studies in Modern Indian Education
Mazoomdar R.C.	The Life and Teachings of Kestub Chandra Sen
Mehta S.D.	The Cotton Mills in India, 1854-1954
Mitchell	The Recollections of My Early Mis onary
Natrajan S.	A Century of Social Reform in India
Park Mark wood	Front Darr Lobby, The Bombay, 1851, 1852, 1853
Parulekar R. V.	Selections from the Records of the Government of Bombay-Education
Ranade M.G.	The Miscellaneous Writings of the Late Mr. Justice M.G. Ranade Report of the Director of Public Instruction 1861-62
Samerrell D.C.	Modern Briton, 1870-1939 Source Material for a History of Freedom Movement
Vivekanand Swami	The Complete Works of Swami Vivekanand

Journals

Friend of India, 1854

Hindusthan Times Weekly, 1962

Report of the Board of Education, 1850-51,1851-52 1853-54

The Poona Observer, 1852

Oriental Christian Spectator, 1855

Indian Statesman

Education Commission, Bombay

The Times of India, 1960

The Indian Spectator, 1883

The Native Opinion

The Bombay Gazette, 1890

The Social Service Quarterly, 1855

Siddharth College of Law Magazine, 1963-64

Works of Jotirao Phule

1. *Tritiya Ratna: The Third Eye.* A play written in 1855, but first published in the journal *Purogami Satyashodhak* (Marathi), vol. 5, No.2, April-June 1979. Perhaps the first written play in Marathi.
2. *Chhatraapti Shivaji Raje Bhosale yancha Pavada.* Life of Shivaji in Political Metre. This work was published in Bombay in June 1869.
3. *Brahmanache Kasab:* Priestcraft Exposed. First published in Bombay in 1869.
4. *Vidyakhatyatil Brahman Pantoji:* Our Brahmin-ridden Policy-Educational System. This ballad was published in the journals *Vividhadnyan Vistar and Satyadipika* (both Marathi) in July and June 1869 respectively. Discovered by Dr. Rosalind O'Hanlon and published in Purogami Satyashodhak in March 1984. The comments that accompany the ballad in the *Vividhdnyan Vistar* suggest that the ballad was one of a larger collection written at the same time.

5. *Gulatnagiri:* Slavery (in this civilized British Government under the cloak of Brahmanism). This work was published in Poona in 1873.
6. Memorial *Addressed to the Education Commission.* A long statement to the Hunter Commission on Education in India in 1882. This was not published independently during Phooley's lifetime.
7. *Shetkaryancha Asud:* The Cultivator's Whip-Cord. This was made up of a collection of Phooley's speeches delivered to Satyashodhak Samaj in 1882-3. He put these together to send to the Earl of Dufferein. This manuscript is preserved in the National Library of Kolkata. Parts of this were published in *Dinbandhu.* This was edited by Dhananjay Keer and S.G. Malshe.
8. *Satsar.* The Essence of Truth. Issues one and two, published in Pune in 1885. This was meant to be a regular series, but was discontinued after the second issue.
9. *Asprushyachee Kaifyat: 'The Tale of the Untouchables'.* This work was completed in 1885, but was not published during Phooley's lifetime. The manuscript is in Shivaji University Library, Kolhapur. The editor of *Mahatma Phooley Samagra Vangmay* have doubts about the authorship of this work.
10. *SatyashodhakSamajoktaMangalashtakasahaSarvaPujavidhi:* AlltheRites,Ceremonies,andVersesusedbytheSatyashodhak Samaj. This small book was published in Bombay in 1887.
11. *Sarvajanik Satya Dharma Pustak:* A book of true religion. Completed in 1889, it was published in 1891 a year after a death of Jotirao Phooley.

Note: Some small pieces published in contemporary newspapers and some letters written by Jotirao Phooley are published in *Mahatma Phooley Samagra Vangmay* (4th edition 1991) ed. By Dhananjay Keer and S.G. Malshe and revised by Y.D. Phadke for Maharashtra Rajya Sahitya ani Sanskriti Mandal, Mumbai.

G.P Deshpande has brought out an English translations of some of Phooley's writings our different translaters under the title *Selected Writings of Jotirao Phule*, published by Left World, New Delhi. His work *The World of ideas: Phule, Vonoba, Savarkar* was published in 2009 by Tulika Books.

Among important books on Phooley published after the publication of Keer's biography is *Caste, Conflict and Ideology: Mahatma Jotirao Phule and low caste protest in nineteenth-century western India* by Rosalind O'Hanlon and published by Cambridge University Press in 1985.

Gail Omvedt has several books on the movement started by Phooley among these Dalit Visions and Understanding Caste from Buddha to Ambedkar and Beyond. M.S. Gore's Non-Brahmin Movement in Maharashtra explores among other things Phooel's movements.

Index